Media Concentration and Democracy

Why Ownership Matters

Objections to concentrated ownership of mass media are widespread. Often, however, critics merely point to the fact of huge and growing media conglomerates without explaining precisely why this is bad. This book fills the gap in the critique of concentration. Firmly rooting its argument in democratic and economic theory, the book argues that a more democratic distribution of communicative power within the public sphere and a structure that provides safeguards against abuse of media power provide two of three primary arguments for ownership dispersal. It also shows that dispersal is likely to result in more owners who will reasonably pursue socially valuable journalistic or creative objectives rather than a socially dysfunctional focus on the "bottom line." The middle chapters answer those, including the current Federal Communication Commission, who favor "deregulation" and who argue that existing or foreseeable ownership concentration is not a problem. The final chapter evaluates the constitutionality and desirability of various policy responses to concentration, including strict limits on media mergers.

C. Edwin Baker is the Nicholas F. Gallicchio Professor of Law at the University of Pennsylvania Law School and has been on the faculty at Penn since 1981. He has also taught at NYU, Chicago, Cornell, Texas, Oregon, and Toledo law schools and at Harvard's Kennedy School of Government, and he was a staff attorney for the ACLU. He is the author of three earlier books: *Media, Markets, and Democracy* (2002), which won the 2002 McGannon Communications Policy Research Award; *Advertising and a Democratic Press* (1994); and *Human Liberty and Freedom of Speech* (1989). He has written more than fifty academic articles about free speech, equality, property, law and economics, jurisprudence, and the mass media, in addition to occasional popular commentary.

Politics and relations among individuals in societies across the world are being transformed by new technologies for targeting individuals and sophisticated methods for shaping personalized messages. The new technologies challenge boundaries of many kinds – among news, information, entertainment, and advertising; among media, with the arrival of the World Wide Web; and even among nations. *Communication, Society and Politics* probes the political and social impacts of these new communication systems in national, comparative, and global perspective.

Titles in the series:

C. Edwin Baker, *Media, Markets, and Democracy*
W. Lance Bennett and Robert M. Entman, eds., *Mediated Politics: Communication in the Future of Democracy*
Bruce Bimber, *Information and American Democracy: Technology in the Evolution of Political Power*
Murray Edelman, *The Politics of Misinformation*
Frank Esser and Barbara Pfetsch, eds., *Comparing Political Communication: Theories, Cases, and Challenges*

Continued after the index

Media Concentration and Democracy

WHY OWNERSHIP MATTERS

C. Edwin Baker

University of Pennsylvania Law School

CAMBRIDGE
UNIVERSITY PRESS

CAMBRIDGE UNIVERSITY PRESS
Cambridge, New York, Melbourne, Madrid, Cape Town, Singapore, São Paulo

Cambridge University Press
32 Avenue of the Americas, New York, NY 10013-2473, USA

www.cambridge.org
Information on this title: www.cambridge.org/9780521868327

First published 2007

Printed in the United States of America

A catalog record for this publication is available from the British Library.

Library of Congress Cataloging in Publication Data

Baker, C. Edwin.
Media concentration and democracy : why ownership matters / C. Edwin Baker.
p.   cm. – (Communication, society, and politics)
Includes bibliographical references and index.
ISBN 0-521-86832-7 (hardback) – ISBN 0-521-68788-8 (pbk.)
1. Mass media – Ownership – United States.   2. Freedom of the press –
United States.   I. Title.   II. Series.
P96.E252U6257   2007
302.230973 – dc22   2006013920

ISBN-13   978-0-521-86832-7 hardback
ISBN-10   0-521-86832-7 hardback

ISBN-13   978-0-521-68788-1 paperback
ISBN-10   0-521-68788-8 paperback

for Char
with many smiles

Contents

Preface

In 1989, having published my basic views on the First Amendment in *Human Liberty and Freedom of Speech* (1989), it seemed time to move to a different, even if related, topic. In that first book, I describe a view that sees the First Amendment prohibitions against abridgment of freedom of speech and freedom of the press as embodying different concerns. Freedom of speech seems fundamentally to be about respect for individual liberty, a value of autonomy that a government committed to being able to justify its legal order must respect. On the other hand, the press is essentially an institution or, as Justice Potter Stewart put it, is the only business explicitly protected by the First Amendment. Constitutional protection of the press seems necessarily related to instrumental values. In particular, as commentators beginning in the eighteenth century have recognized, the reason to protect the press from government abridgment lies in its contribution to democracy or, more broadly, to a free society. It provides a source of information and vision independent of government.

I had already argued almost ten years earlier[1] that press freedom and its capacity to serve its democratic role could be threatened from two directions: from abuse of government power or from private power and the dynamics of the market. Though my earlier work had emphasized the need for strong constitutional protection from government threats, I now turned to the other side of the equation and considered how the press needs government protection from private forces that could otherwise undermine its performance. At first I assumed the danger of private power lay primarily in media owners' potential abuse of power over the press – over the entities' freedom and performance. I discovered, however, that a different threat may be greater and, in any event, provided an easier target: the threat to press performance and to distortion of its content resulting from the press's dependence on advertising support. Thus,

I put the issue of ownership on hold until after I published *Advertising and a Democratic Press* (1994). Then I discovered that I could not sensibly identify problems with ownership until I considered what appeared to be a more fundamental problem: distortions created by the market. I also could not do so until I considered what light a commitment to democracy provided on the question of the type of press that a society needs. These issues led me into an investigation of media economics and democratic theory, which I published as *Media, Markets, and Democracy* (2002).

Finally, ownership was the aspect of private power left to be considered. At this point, Fritz Kubler invited me to present a description of American views on ownership at a conference to be held in Germany in September 2001. I wrote a paper for that conference. But a week before I was to leave, I felt the need to participate in political efforts to oppose what I feared would be an American military response to the criminal acts of September 11, so I stayed in New York. Fritz presented my paper in my absence. That paper,[2] and a subsequent much modified law review article based on it,[3] became the foundation of this book.

A number of people have contributed greatly to this book, by reading portions of the manuscript and giving comments or by providing sounding boards for discussion, references, inspiration, or, in some cases, all of the above. Two people, Fritz Kubler and Michael Madow, fit in that final category and to them I give special thanks. I especially appreciate the great support and critical comments that I received from the series editor, Robert Entman. Donald Conklin and Gabrielle Levin provided excellent assistance. I also need to thank Ann Bartow, Yochai Benkler, Mark Cooper, Harry First, Eleanor Fox, Charlotte Gross, Carlin Meyer, Rudolph Peritz, Margaret Jane Radin, Christopher Yoo, and two anonymous readers from Cambridge University Press. The book would have many more errors and would have been much shallower without their insights – and, I am sure, would have been much better if I had been capable of incorporating more of their wisdom. I also need to thank the Grey Dog and Patisserie Claude for providing good coffee and an appealing place to do much of the work on the book.

Finally, I have benefited from comments when presenting portions of the argument in various venues: Conference: Penn Film and Media Pioneers (Philadelphia, 2005); Penn Law School Faculty Retreat (Philadelphia, 2005); Conference: Not from Concentrate, Media Regulation at the Turn of the Millennium, University of Michigan Law School (Ann Arbor, 2005); Testimony: Media Ownership and the Third

Circuit, Senate Commerce Committee (Washington, D.C., 2004); American Sociological Association Annual Conference (San Francisco, 2004); Faculty Workshop, Penn State Law School (Carlisle, 2004); Conference on Federal Regulation and the Cultural Landscape, Vanderbilt Law School (Nashville, 2004); interview on Odyssey, WBEZ (2003); New America Foundation's Breakfast Senate Briefing (Senate Office Building, Washington, D.C., 2003); and the New York City Bar Committee on Communications and Media Law (New York, 2003).

Introduction

On June 2, 2003, the Republican-dominated Federal Communications Commission took a predictable step in its seemingly unstoppable movement toward media deregulation. It announced a major relaxation of its already relaxed rules restricting media concentration.[1] The communications sector, the FCC found, is rife with competition. Ownership concentration presents little threat. More surprisingly, reducing restrictions on media mergers produced a storm of protest, from both the left and right, involving more vocalized public opposition than any FCC action ever. The FCC basically ignored nearly two million people of all political persuasions who registered their opposition.[2] William Safire argued that "concentration of [media] power . . . should be anathema to conservatives."[3] Safire credited much of the effectiveness of "the growing grass roots" movement "against giantism" in the media to "right-wing outfits," although he also noted the role of progressives including Bill Moyers.[4] Opposition was not without at least temporary effect. Congress partially reversed the FCC action.[5] Then the Third Circuit Court of Appeals found most of the remainder unjustified, sending the relaxed rules back to the FCC for reconsideration.[6]

The primary causal explanation for the FCC's ill-starred action may lie in the power and economic self-interest of major media companies. Political causal explanation, however, is not my subject. Policies require justifications. This book defends the merits of restricting ownership concentration. It then evaluates the intellectual and policy arguments offered for the FCC's hardening view that media concentration is now not a real problem and that ownership restrictions can thwart the public interest. And the book presents, as clearly as I can, an explanation for why these arguments are wrong – for why media ownership concentration is objectionable.

The journalist and press critic A. J. Liebling long ago opined: "Freedom of the press belongs to those who own one."[7] Liebling's cynical quip makes ownership central. This book explores his view, considering among other things whether ownership is in fact central, and concluding that it is. As the twentieth century progressed, virtually all Western democracies saw growing media concentration as a threat to press freedom and to democracy. Most democracies adopted policies designed to support press diversity, whether through competition laws (both antitrust- and media-specific) or subsidy arrangements (often specifically targeted to support weaker media competing with the dominant players).[8]

Fear of media concentration and the goal of more robust diversity have been strong themes in the United States too, although actual legal responses have been somewhat different and often weaker than in Europe. Here, policies embodying these values probably originated with the beginnings of the American Republic. In the eighteenth and nineteenth centuries, postal subsidies supported, as intended, a growing number of newspapers.[9] Governmental policies promoting a diverse media environment continued. Over a hundred years ago, New York law required local governments to place their ads equally in at least two local papers of different parties, thereby subsidizing competition and diversity.[10] As early as 1938 and reaching a policy-justifying peak in the 1970s, the FCC found that the public interest required severe restrictions on ownership concentration in broadcast stations and required outlawing most local cross-ownership of different types of media entities. In 1945, the Supreme Court explained that application of the antitrust laws to newspapers served the goals of the First Amendment.[11] In 1949, Representative Emanuel Celler, Democrat of New York and a co-sponsor of crucial antitrust law amendments, asserted that these amendments could and should be interpreted generally to preclude the merger of a community's only two newspapers.[12] In 1970, Congress adopted the Newspaper Preservation Act[13] in an effort to keep independent, competing editorial voices alive even though the resulting Joint Operating Agreement maintained editorial competition only by sacrificing commercial competition between the two newspapers.

The most important, semi-official, policy-oriented study of the mass media in U.S. history, the Hutchins Commission Report of 1947, saw the problem of media concentration – as it described it, the "decreased proportion of the people who can express their opinions and ideas through the press" – as one of three factors threatening freedom of the press.[14] (This problem of concentration, the commission said, combined with the other two problems: that these owners did not provide adequately for the needs of society and that they sometimes engaged in practices that society condemns.) The Hutchins Commission, however, accepted the reality that modern economic forces drive inexorably toward media concentration.[15] Most American cities already in 1947 faced daily newspaper monopolies. In 1910, some 689 American cities or towns had competing daily newspapers. By 1940, despite many more newspaper readers and many more towns and cities, the number of places with competing dailies had fallen to 181 – a decline that has continued steadily. In 2002, only fourteen cities had separately owned and operated daily papers.[16] One interpretation of the Hutchins Commission's central recommendations, which emphasized the need for a "socially responsible press,"[17] is that it aimed to make the best of a bad situation, namely, the existence of media concentration.

Today's media critics continue to sound the alarm. But often they argue as if simply pointing to the overwhelming facts of concentration – the list of media outlets owned by major firms or the size of the latest mergers – can end the discussion. Mark Crispin Miller presented a center-fold diagram of media ownership that he seemed to think graphically made the argument against media concentration.[18] Ben Bagdikian, the most readable critic of media concentration, a Pulitzer Prize-winning journalist and dean emeritus of Berkeley's graduate school of journalism, is more analytic in his objections to concentration. Still, Bagdikian is most cited either for his purely descriptive 1983 claim in the original edition of his book, *The Media Monopoly*, that the majority of the media in the United States were owned by fifty companies,[19] or his subsequent assertions that the situation is worsening, with the 2004 edition reporting that five multinational conglomerates provide the majority of what Americans see, hear, and read.[20]

Critics of concentration rightly view the media as a huge, nondemocratically organized force that has major power over politics, public discourse, and culture. Unsurprisingly, media ownership concentration receives great attention. In Europe, pressure for governmental responses came mostly from left and centrist political parties, trade unions, journalists' associations, and consumer groups, though often a political consensus of the left and right existed on the issue.[21] Many in America, too, especially on the left and center but many conservatives as well, see media concentration as a problem and believe that dispersed ownership is crucial for democracy.[22] However, as the recent FCC attempt to relax

3

limits on media concentration implies, the step in the argument that jumps from the press's vital democratic role to solid objections to existing levels of media concentration has not gone unchallenged. Not only profit-hungry corporations but serious scholars, FCC commissioners, and some courts have found existing restrictions on media concentration much stricter than need be. Much of the public seems instinctively to believe the opposite, but often they provide no or weak explanations for their view. To fill this gap, chapter 1 presents a statement of the primary reasons that the popular view is right: concentration is a problem and the legal order should respond. The next three chapters evaluate the quite serious objections to the argument of chapter 1. Finally, chapter 5 analyzes possible policy responses to media concentration.

ONE

Democracy at the Crossroads: Why Ownership Matters

A uthoritarian regimes regularly try to censor or control the mass media's provision of vision and information. The health of democracies, in contrast, depends on having a free press. Edmund Burke reportedly observed that "there were Three Estates in Parliament; but, in the Reporters' Gallery yonder, there sat a Fourth Estate more important far than they all."[1] Among many others, Supreme Court Justice Potter Stewart saw the democratic role of this Fourth Estate as central to the rationale for constitutional protection of the press.[2] Of course, much more must be said about the idea of democracy before fully understanding its implications for the ideal of a free press. Questions include: What is the best conception of democracy? How do alternative conceptions of democracy suggest different ideals – and different constitutional interpretations – of "press freedom"? Even the notion of "fourth estate" requires unpacking. (I often use this term and the idea of the press's watchdog role interchangeably, but more precisely the watchdog role consists in being a "check" against abuse by government, while the fourth estate role may include that plus a more active involvement in governing and in influencing which political possibilities prevail.) Though these questions require investigation,[3] the initial point is simple: *democratic* concerns should be central in formulating legal policy relating to the press. Legal rules that inevitably structure the press as an institution should embody, to a substantial degree, democratic values or ideals.

Consequently, this chapter emphasizes the democratic role of the press as the chapter considers three major reasons to favor the widest possible dispersal of media ownership. It then discusses four additional, more pragmatic points. To begin, the single most fundamental reason to resist concentration of media ownership derives directly from dominant visions of democracy.

THE THREE MAIN REASONS FOR OPPOSING
OWNERSHIP CONCENTRATION

1. A MORE DEMOCRATIC DISTRIBUTION OF COMMUNICATIVE POWER

Rationales for and interpretations of democracy vary. Some theories of democracy, especially pluralist and elitist theories, are in major ways empirical: they predict that democratic governments (maybe of a certain type) will lead to better results for society than available alternatives.[4] Normative theories of democracy, however, typically share the premise of people's equal right to participate in collective self-determination. The egalitarian premise, as well as the autonomy or "self-determination" premise, is crucial. This normative view values democracy as an end, not merely a means, because it embodies these values of equality and autonomy. Thus, democracy is widely understood as respecting the view that each person equally should have a say, at least a formally equal right to have a say, in choosing at least its officials and, ultimately, its laws and policies and maybe its culture.

The one-person/one-vote institutional principle interprets the politically egalitarian normative value, and in this country is widely (and constitutionally) seen as fundamental to the idea of a self-governing people.[5] Of course, a one-person/one-vote principle for an electoral districting rule turns out not to provide actual equal political power, but that was not its point. Rather, a normative conception of democracy requires that the structure itself embody or at least be consistent with respect for citizens' equal claim to be recognized as part of the self-determination process. Despite this fundamental egalitarian structural distributive principle, the actual distribution of political power depends on people's political preferences as they act within the structure. Many factors, including the boundaries of voting districts as drawn normally by state legislatures, unequal wealth as produced by people's (hopefully) legal practices within a fair legal order – even if limited by the most stringent campaign finance reform legislation – and each person's individual political perspective inevitably affect her effective influence on elections. Thus, actual power does not and could not meet an egalitarian standard. Still, the rationale for formal equality of voice in elections, manifest in the one-person/one-vote principle, both is basic to democracy and applies to the broader arena of voice in a democratic public sphere. Two later arguments for opposing media concentration – that dispersion creates democratic or political safeguards and gets media into the hands of owners more likely to favor quality over profits – have a more pragmatic logic. This first claim, however, is that this more constitutive egalitarian principle is a central, possibly the most fundamental, reason to oppose media concentration. Still, more argument for and, in the end, important caveats to this normative claim are necessary. The complexities of the idea of equality in respect to the relatively simple institution of an electorate are multiplied when policy attempts to translate this egalitarian commitment into a guide for the more complex structure of the public sphere generally – the communication order – and of media ownership in particular.

More must be – and will be – said about the notion of democracy implicit in the above claim. Still, the basic claim bears repeating. The same egalitarian value that is embodied in people's equal right to be self-governing and that requires "one-person/one-unit-of-formal-political-power" applied to the ballot box also applies to the public sphere. The public sphere influences how people choose to exercise their vote. Equally important, through the creation of public opinion,[6] the public sphere should and often does influence how elected and appointed public officials actually exercise their formal decision-making power. In any large society, the mass media constitute probably the most crucial institutional structure of the public sphere. To be self-governing, people require the capacity to form public opinion and then to have that public opinion influence and ultimately control public "will formation" – that is, government laws and policies.[7] For these purposes, a country requires various institutional structures. The media, like elections, constitute a crucial sluice between public opinion formation and state "will formation." The mass media, like elections, serve to mediate between the public and the government. For this reason, a country is democratic only to the extent that the media, as well as elections, are structurally egalitarian and politically salient.

The best institutional interpretation of this democratic vision of the public sphere is, I suggest, an egalitarian distribution of control, most obviously meaning ownership, of the mass media. The basic standard for democracy would then be a very wide and fair dispersal of power and ubiquitous opportunities to present preferences, views, visions. This is a *democratic distribution principle* for communicative power – a claim that democracy implies as wide as practical a dispersal of power within public discourse. As applied to media ownership, this principle can be plausibly interpreted structurally as requiring, possibly among other things, a maximum dispersal of media ownership. An older Federal Communications

Commission adopted this view when it stated that "a proper objective is the maximum diversity of ownership"[8] or "maximum diffusion of control of the media of mass communications,"[9] a view echoed by the Supreme Court when it emphasized the relation between the First Amendment and "diverse and antagonistic sources."[10]

The democratic distribution principle is an end in itself, not a means predicted to lead empirically to some desirable result. It structurally embodies a "pure process" value.[11] The distributional principle partially constitutes a normatively defensible conception of democracy. Normative appeal, not empirical evidence, provides its justification. Nevertheless, this principle needs further explication and, it turns out, some significant modification from this initial elaboration of maximum ownership dispersal. Two issues, two caveats, stand out, the first relating to the interpretation of democracy that the current elaboration seems to embody and the second involving a refinement given the nature of mass media as compared with individual speech.

Chapter 4 discusses in more detail different normative theories of democracy and their relation to theories of the First Amendment.[12] The most appealing theory I label "complex democracy." A democratic political order involves, *in part*, a struggle among different groups, each with its own projects and interests, its own needs, and its own conception of a desirable social world. In relation to this struggle, democracy aims at a fair bargain or fair settlement among these different groups or interests. Fairness here refers roughly to an egalitarian weighting of different people's interests and visions and an egalitarian opportunity to formulate these visions. Achieving this "pluralist" or "liberal" notion of fairness is the primary value embodied in the democratic distribution principle described above. Each group needs its fair share of the media to participate in political (or cultural) struggle.

Democracy, however, also purports to be about recognizing and pursuing a republican or Rousseauian "common good." To find or formulate, whenever possible, such a "good of the whole" requires an *inclusive* discourse involving the whole society. How such a discourse could exist is not entirely clear. As an approximation, media that reach and appeal to all elements of the public and that fairly include the voice of all could embody this "republican" vision. Such media are consistent with, and may be most likely to exist under, largely monopolistic conditions. Elihu Katz described television performing that inclusive discourse role in Israel at a time when (and because) it was a public monopoly.[13] Though disagreeing with Katz on many points,[14] British scholar James Curran proposes that providing this inclusive discourse should be the democratic remit of the BBC. Obviously, this vision of a single inclusive discourse is in at least potential tension with the democratic distribution ownership principle. From this republican perspective, not only is widest possible dispersal of ownership not needed, but it could undermine this common discourse by segmenting audiences.

Complex democracy asserts that both egalitarian dispersal and an inclusive common discourse are real requirements of democracy, and that both are absolutely fundamental despite the tension between them. In practice, acceptance of both requirements means that neither premise determines all issues but also that neither should be abandoned. The democratic distribution principle is always an adequate reason, without more, to oppose any move toward concentration and to favor a maximum dispersal of media ownership or control. Nevertheless, other reasons, especially the simultaneous existence of the other democratic discursive requirement – to have a common discourse – can always justify compromise with this principle.

I leave consideration of appropriate compromises mostly to chapter 5. Still, note the possibility of different policies according primary weight to each principle. Inclusive public discourse might thrive best within media not compromised by inherently partial interests of private owners but that instead operate under rules of fair public discourse. This consideration is possibly the reason Katz and Curran both identified public broadcasting as the ideal location for performing this inclusionary role.[15] This institutional structure leaves open the possibility of requiring maximum possible dispersal of media power as the goal for *privately* owned media. Or, contrarily, maybe some private media could succeed at growing into this common discourse role, a view imperfectly suggested by the casual description of the *New York Times* as the "paper of record" in this country. Arguably, the legal order should allow any media entity to seek to play this role, a view that provides an objection to any government policy limiting the reach of an individual media entity.

Note, however, the difference between media "entity" or outlet – that is, a specific content provider – and a media "firm," which may include many media entities. The inclusive discourse value has no logical, certainly no necessary, relation to a single firm owning multiple "media voices." Under this understanding, while there might be no objection to immensely large media entities arising – a newspaper or network reaching as large a portion of the public as possible – this inclusive discourse value is not inconsistent with a policy, informed by the democratic distribution principle, of preventing any media firm from owning more than one media entity or outlet, more than one media voice. The wisest adjustments between these two democratic principles require inevitably contested and properly contextual judgments. Rather than further pursue here the possibility of compromise between or adjustments to the reach of these two democratic principles, this chapter asserts only the fundamental nature and explores the implications of the democratic distribution principle. That is, I want to emphasize the point made above: the democratic distribution principle is always a proper, whether or not a conclusive, reason to oppose concentration and favor media ownership dispersal.

This leads to the second caveat. *Mass* media involve a move from the individual, which was the fundamental unit in voting, to a concern with aggregates. (In this sense, it might have some analogies with the outcome of voting in a proportional representation system.) The original analogy to the vote suggests an individualistic interpretation of the ideal distribution of power within the public sphere. Each person equally gets one voice. Even in voting, realities make the notion of one-person/one-vote more an egalitarian slogan (or a formal implication of equality of respect) than a grant of equality of voting power. The departure from individualist equality is even more overt in the public sphere. An egalitarian distribution of actual communicative power is inconsistent with the very idea of a "*mass* media," which almost inevitably contemplates a limited number of entities, a limited number of speakers, communicating to many.

The technical possibility that each person could own a limited "mass media," with which she communicates occasionally to a large group, may motivate some policy initiatives related to the Internet or unlicensed wireless communications, but such communications could hardly duplicate the roles and functions that are now generally attributed to the mass media. Complete equality of actual communicative power is not only not possible, but it is probably not appropriate even as a goal.[16] Even in a purely oral community unaided by technology and without mass media, doing without opinion leaders – people, maybe elders, who because of skill, desire, and respect from others specialize in communication about issues of public moment – is hardly desirable or required by any appealing conception of democracy. Hopefully, people want to receive and assimilate informed and thoughtful communications. Having information "specialists" or opinion leaders can serve individuals and their society well. Moreover, people vary greatly in the extent that they desire to make – or are talented at making – discursive or informational contributions to the public sphere. In a democracy, the epistemological hope is that those speakers with better arguments will prevail over those without – and this hope presumably requires that these better arguments ultimately gather larger audiences. Still, fairness and democratic epistemological presumptions also require that all people can experience inclusion. Good arguments can come from any part of society. Useful challenges usually come from the margins.[17] The inclusionary goal suggests that all groups should have a real share and no one group or individual should have too inordinate a share of media power. Although the democratic distributive goal may have multiple strands, it must include the notion that members of all groups can experience themselves as being served and represented by mass media that are in some sense "their own." Their media should not only give voice to their concerns but also provide them room for the internal discussions and questioning they need for formulating their own views. Ownership should be distributed in a manner that results in no one feeling that discourses of groups with which she identifies are neglected or subordinated. This goal is typically furthered by maximum dispersal of ownership and, to this extent, provides a reason for dispersal. Nevertheless, as the discussion of a democratic argument for a "common discourse" illustrates, "a reason" does not mean a necessarily "prevailing argument."

The move from each *individual's* formal right to an *equal* vote to a principle of dispersal of media power that at best merely provides voice to all *groups* merits further comment. Once the focus is on mass media, on one-to-many communications, the individual claim cannot be to equal individual power but only to having her interests, questions, and difficulties, which as to public issues will usually overlap with those of others, be a fair part of the process. Individuals are part of many fluid, changing groups, many without recognized borders or even methods for an individual to be included or excluded as a "member." When "group" is used as a bureaucratic operating concept, definition – which groups with which definitional boundaries should be included – presents grave difficulties. Bureaucratic definitions are sometimes needed for pragmatic purposes – in terms of media ownership, perhaps primarily for remedial purposes, such as when a grouping that has salience to individuals can be seen as systematically significantly marginalized.[18] This pragmatic approach might justify special attention to ownership by local people, racial or ethnic groups, organized partisan groups, or income groups. Though this point receives some attention in chapter 5, it is not central to concern with groups in the current discussion. Those definitional problems can be largely sidestepped here. The democratic goal of inclusiveness is achieved when people experience their views or values or people with whom they identify as having significant media voice and when they do not find a few owners or groups dominating the media realm. As a justification for maximum dispersal of ownership, this democratic value does not require government policy makers to sort people (or even to have individuals sort themselves) into their "appropriate" groups. Rather, the policy is based on an expectation that ownership dispersal will contribute to the desired result. Specifically, dispersal is more likely than more concentrated ownership to lead to more diversity of ownership that is more likely to generate this experience of inclusion. Although maximum dispersal does not guarantee that result, its probable contribution to both the reality and experience of broad inclusion provides a strong, I suggest possibly the single most important, reason to favor such dispersal.

This democratic distribution principle is, I believe, accepted in at least an inchoate and unarticulated form by large portions of the public; it is also a value that once largely motivated FCC policies. Certainly, the reign of media conglomerates, however profitable and however appealing many people find their products, does not seem to be popular. An unprecedented number – nearly two million people – took the trouble to register objections to the FCC's 2003 proposal to relax its arcane rules on media concentration.[19] Given polls that report that people pay little attention to any but a few major public issues, usually ones centered on the presidency and Congress, it is remarkable that soon after the FCC announcement, the Pew Research Center found that the portion of the public reporting that they had heard of the FCC decision to relax media ownership restrictions was 48 percent. For democratic policy, arguably private opinion should count more the more it is informed. Interestingly, on this issue, the more people reported that they had heard of the issue, the more they opposed relaxation. Among those who heard "a lot" about the FCC plan, 70 percent thought its likely impact on the country would be negative, while 6 percent thought it would be positive. Among those who had heard "a little," the view that its impact would be negative dominated, 57 percent to 8 percent.[20] Curiously, even among those who reported they had heard nothing about the issue, 40 percent thought the impact of the FCC's plan would be negative, as compared with 12 percent who thought it would be positive.[21]

Arcane changes in general antitrust policies "never" raise such public outcries. The people who registered their opposition to the FCC plan were unlikely to have been motivated by hopes that less concentrated media would offer slightly better products or slightly lower prices. The issue clearly raised civic values more than consumer concerns. Many people responded to organizing efforts of both politically conservative and politically liberal groups – conservative groups such as the National Rifle Association, the Conservative Communications Center, and Christian fundamentalists, plus more liberal groups such as Common Cause (which reported the biggest membership mobilization on any issue in decades) and the National Organization of Women.[22] Whether or not clearly articulated, I suspect that the primary motivation of these millions from widely disparate groups was related to civic values, such as an at least inchoate sense of this *democratic distributive value* combined with *democratic safeguard* values considered below.

Thus, the claim is that despite other principles that might require compromise or justify adjustment, this democratic distributive value, without any need for complicated empirical investigations or controversial economic analyses, provides an entirely proper reason to oppose *any* particular media merger or to favor *any* policy designed to increase the number or diversity of separate owners of media entities. This is the normative claim that the Supreme Court repeatedly accepted when it upheld the FCC's restrictions on mergers without asking for any empirical evidence to justify the restriction.[23] The important caveat, also recognized by the Court, is that countervailing considerations can contextually provide a basis to override this normative reason for dispersal. Still, this value premise goes a long way toward justifying the early FCC's strict local and national limits on broadcast licenses and its other rules restricting cross-media ownership. Contrarily, only by being completely blind to this democratic distributive value have some recent scholars and some lower court judges been able to opine that many of these limits – especially, national limits on ownership of broadcast stations and cable systems or possible limits on chain ownership of newspapers – are virtually inexplicable and sometimes constitutionally unacceptable.[24] Geographically dispersed media entities, they rightly observe, do not compete against each other for audiences. These entities simply do not operate in the same (geographic) product market. Hence, from the narrow perspective of providing commodities to a public, combined ownership of these entities can hardly create objectionable anticompetitive effects. Antitrust law offers no objections. (Though in the extreme case of a very few owners fully dominating the national market, these judges and scholars do recognize that these entities might be able to exercise monopsony power over content suppliers.)

The FCC, in contrast, long explicitly aimed to disperse ownership (and control) nationally as well as locally of the organs of public opinion. The antitrust view has been that national chains create no anticompetitive *economic* power. A merger of a station operating in Vermont with one in California does, however, increase the owner's power over opinion within the broader national public sphere. Objections to *this* concentration of power and the aim to have more, potentially antagonistic, sources of information is surely the primary concern embodied in the national ownership restrictions, which long prohibited a single entity from owning more than seven AM, seven FM, and seven television stations[25] – a far cry from rules that now permit Clear Channel to expand beyond the over 1200 radio stations it currently owns. Concern with power in the broader, national public sphere was also behind the "chain broadcasting rules," which formerly prohibited contracts that would give networks power over programming on their local affiliates and that were overtly designed to maintain the independence of each separate broadcaster.[26] And it is essentially this distributive value that the Supreme Court approved when it held that strict limits on media cross-ownership were appropriate to prevent an "undue concentration of economic power" in the communications realm.[27] The economic power was "undue" neither because it created antitrust problems nor because of the communications firm's general economic heft – the size of even the largest media entities pales beside the legally permitted size of oil companies and banks, much less Wal-Mart.[28] Rather, the economic power is "undue" because it should not exist within the public sphere. Dispersal of media power, like dispersal of voting power, is simply an egalitarian attribute of a system claiming to be democratic.

Observe the way this democratic distributive value interprets diversity, a value commonly invoked in media policy. Diversity can refer to different attributes: medium, format, content, viewpoint, and source, just to begin the list. Commentators do not always use these terms in the same way, and nothing rides on the orthodoxy of my usage. My primary point is to observe the variation and to emphasize that diversity of one sort need not imply diversity of another. For example, the "same"[29] news obviously can be presented in different *media*, that is, in broadcast or in print and in subcategories of these – television or radio, newspapers or magazines. In a single medium, different formats are possible – Jon Stewart of the *The Daily Show* might present the "same" facts as Brian Williams on *NBC Nightly News* but use a notably different *format*. *Content*, protected by copyright law, within a medium is infinitely variable. It can be more or less diverse between media entities of the same medium that have the same format – shorter or longer playlists of country music in radio, for example. Here, mere greater choice is often said to serve the consumer well – although in reality, the commentator always is concerned with sometimes unarticulated but always value-based, not merely empirical, criteria of the content differences she counts as salient. In contrast, the more political impulse that lies behind a policy emphasis on diversity often emphasizes the centrality of *viewpoint* diversity – the public should not hear only Democrats or environmentalists.

The shorter country music playlist that includes the Dixie Chicks or various progressive country musicians could be more diverse than the station with the longer list. Commonly, commentators (wrongly) believe that the ultimate concern must be content and viewpoint diversity – with other differences being merely instrumental to this goal, merely means to this end. This belief, I suggest, reflects a commodity-oriented perspective that often dominates among economic and antitrust theorists. Content, including varying viewpoints, is what they see consumers receiving and valuing. From this perspective, the positive contribution of ownership dispersal – or, more generally, varying sorts of *source* diversity – must depend on the empirical prediction that this dispersal provides audiences with greater choice among (desired) content and viewpoints.

Whether ownership dispersal actually leads to such content or viewpoint diversity turns out to be a complex empirical and contextual matter. In many circumstances diverse owners will produce more diverse content. No theorist of whom I am aware believes, however, that this is always true. Economists predict and empiricists (purportedly[30]) find the opposite in some contexts.[31] This complexity destabilizes the argument for ownership dispersal as long as policy makers adopt this commodity perspective in understanding the ultimately significant type of diversity. In contrast, from the perspective of the democratic distributive value, *source* diversity – effectively ownership dispersal – is directly, substantively central. As the FCC once argued in rejecting cross-ownership of a local newspaper and broadcast station, "it is unrealistic to expect *true* diversity from . . . [the combination]. The divergency of their viewpoints cannot be expected to be *the same* as if they were antagonistically run."[32]

Content diversity sometimes pales in significance, missing the point about why democracy requires diversity. When people *freely* agree, they achieve a republican ideal, and democracy does not require viewpoint diversity. Democracy does require, however, that people in general, and especially differing groups, get to debate their views internally among themselves, receive information relevant to their interests and views, rally support for their group, and finally present their views to the world at large. When this democratic process leads to content or viewpoint diversity, this diversity is valued precisely because of the process that produces it. But when this process does not lead to content or viewpoint diversity, democracy does not require it. An egalitarian political order relates to the distribution of expressive power, the activity of communicating, just as an egalitarian economic order relates to the distribution of commodities. Democracy does not, however, require that speakers provide or listeners choose a maximum (or any particular, high level of) diversity in commodity content. On the other hand, an absence of content or viewpoint diversity that reflects independent but congruent judgments of many different people – judgments of many different owners with ultimate power to determine content – differs fundamentally from the same absence imposed by a few powerful actors. The latter is democratically objectionable. That is, source diversity is most importantly a *process* value, not a *commodity* value. Again, the key goal, the key value, served by ownership dispersal is to directly embody a fairer, more democratic allocation of communicative power.

2. DEMOCRATIC SAFEGUARDS

The widest practical dispersal of media ownership also provides two safeguards of inestimable value. In any local, state, or national community, concentrated media ownership creates the possibility of an individual decision maker exercising enormous, unequal and hence undemocratic, largely unchecked, potentially irresponsible power. History exhibits countless instances of abuse of concentrated communicative power in this and other countries at either local or national levels. Historical stories, however, are not crucial here. Even if this power were seldom if ever exercised, the democratic safeguard value amounts to an assertion that *no democracy should risk the danger*. The Constitution delineates three separate branches, the system of "separation of powers." The separation is, in part, a structural means to reduce the risk of abuses of power in government. So too should a country structure the fourth estate. The widest possible dispersal of media power reduces the risk of the abuse of communicative power in choosing or controlling the government.[33] Again, ownership dispersal serves a basically constitutional *process* role independent of any commodity that the media produces and distributes on a day-to-day basis.

This safeguard reflects a particular vision of the democratic public realm. A minimalist conception of democracy – for example, a "ratification democracy" that merely counted votes and assured victory to the person or party getting the highest total – might require only that people have a formal chance to accept or reject particular holders of political power. Democracy is simply equated with majority rule. This conception, for instance, apparently conforms to the view offered by some legal theorists and popular commentators who view judicial reliance on the Constitution to invalidate acts of Congress as undemocratic because the invalidation is purportedly countermajoritarian. Such a limited conception of democracy would be consistent with people repeatedly and unreflectively electing rulers, call them demagogues, who disproportionately control the communications system.

The United States, born under a constitution, has never accepted that minimalist form of democracy. Moreover, the normative element of any "participatory democracy" theory (as well as typical theories of constitutional democracy) requires that both public opinion and election results reflect processes that *fairly* allow competing groups to put forth visions and evaluate other's visions. Of course, different participatory theories unpack the crucial notion of "fairly" differently – a point noted implicitly in connection with the caveat discussed above in relation to a republican inclusive common discourse and revisited in chapter 4. Nevertheless, the democratic safeguards discussed here serve *all* participatory democratic theories. All are threatened by the possibility that the media overwhelmingly communicate views – and, as a result, favor policies – of a narrow, unrepresentative group or even a single person. Any form of participatory democracy needs media that provide serious presentation, and then professional scrutiny, of alternative offerings.

Both the distributive value (even if interpreted differently from what is described above) and the structural risk-prevention value are fundamental to participatory democracy. They are twin impulses behind, for example, campaign finance reform. Put aside difficult questions of whether campaign finance reform can be effective and fair and whether it is a constitutionally permissible regulation of speech (I have argued that it can be).[34] Clearly, the underlying normative impulses behind campaign finance reform, like those behind mandating media dispersal, are to prevent one person or small group from being able to use the power of wealth to dominate the (electoral) public sphere and to provide a more egalitarian distribution of opportunities to participate.

The need for dispersal of power based on media ownership may be even more basic than the need for campaign finance reform. Imagine doing without one or the other. Even without campaign finance reform, adequately dispersed media power within a potentially robust public sphere still allows an independent and potentially engaged media to scrutinize the wealthy candidate who vastly outspends her opponent. The situation is more dire, the potential for blockage more complete, without dispersal of control of the news media. As a gate keeper, a media owner can thwart even rich candidates. Of course, even then, as events in the former Soviet bloc countries, including their mass demonstrations (that, despite our First Amendment, would be illegal in many American cities[35]), suggest, popular resistance is sometimes but – as the suppression of pro-democracy demonstrators at Tiananmen Square also reminds us – not always effective at achieving change opposed by those who control the mass media.

Dispersal of ownership structurally prevents what might be called the "Berlusconi" effect. (Despite virtually no connection with organized political parties, Silvio Berlusconi, apparently Italy's richest individual, formed his own party, Forza Italia, and used massive media power – his Mediaset controls about 45 percent of national television along with important print media – to catapult himself into the Prime Minister spot in 1994 and then again in 2001, heading Italy's longest lasting government since World War II.[36]) More partisan media than we have at present in this country might contribute greatly to democratic participation by energizing different publics and encouraging a sense that participation matters.[37] A beneficial rather than a perverse contribution of such partisanship is, however, plausible only against a background of a relatively fair distribution of media power. The absence of this background condition, combined with a fear that media concentration could not be avoided, may have been what lead the Hutchins Commission in 1947 to advocate a social responsibility conception of journalism.[38] Media partisanship combined with media concentration can lead to authoritarian results. Certainly, abstract economic or social theory provides no basis to predict whether, when, or how often those who own or control American (or global[39]) media conglomerates will use their power in a partisan fashion to dominate the public sphere. Whatever bad consequences resulted from Hearst's yellow journalism[40] or will result from either Murdoch's commercial or his political agenda,[41] an undemocratic distribution of communicative power presents real dangers. German democracy certainly did not benefit from Alfred Hugenberg's ability to use his (Germany's first) media conglomerate to substantially aid Hitler's rise to power.[42] This danger is a simple matter of logic. It provides the reason that dispersal of media ownership, like separation of powers, is a key structural safeguard for democracy.

A CAUTIONARY ASIDE: APPROPRIATE USES AND MISCONCEIVED DEMANDS FOR EMPIRICAL EVIDENCE. The value of knowledge about the world and how it works cannot be overstated. I put aside my theoretical belief that our "factual" knowledge is always embedded in ways of life that reflect values or commitments such that there is no purely "objective" or value-neutral knowledge. At a more mundane level that relies on everyday distinctions between facts and values, both the relevance of evidence and the relevant *type* of evidence for any policy inquiry depends entirely on the issue(s) raised. In this book I regularly offer evidence that I believe to be relevant to testing the truth or falsity of various theoretical predictions. But above I have several times claimed that empirical evidence is irrelevant. At those points my claim is that the inquiry raises solely a value, not a factual, question. When the question is about what to value or what a particular value requires – for example, whether to value a fair democratic process or whether a fair democratic process requires that all can identify some significant media entities as "theirs" – empirical evidence is not seriously at issue. Evidence is only marginally more at issue when the question is whether dispersal of media ownership provides part of the best interpretation of these democratic values. Certainly, neither a Ph.D nor an expensive study is needed to determine whether media mergers increase or decrease media ownership dispersal. In this aside, I only offer several cautions about occasional irrelevance or misuse of empirical evidence. First, though, I note how this became such a legal issue.

Recently in the media context, some courts and some policy makers routinely ask for empirical evidence to support government policies. In *Turner Broadcasting v. FCC*,[43] a cable company challenged a law that required cable systems at a local station's request to carry the station without charge, thereby benefiting TV stations.[44] A primary rationale for the law was apparently Congress's conclusion that noncarriage (or being forced to pay for carriage) would damage the economic foundations of many local TV stations to an extent detrimental to the public. Absent mandated free carriage, some stations would predictably fail and others would lose sufficient revenue that the quality of their programming would decline. Over Justice Stevens's protest – he would have upheld the law without further inquiry – the Court sent the case back to lower courts to determine whether there was adequate evidence to support this rationale. After three years, millions of dollars spent for studies and litigation, and extensive attention by lower court judges, the final result was to reach the basically reasoned (rather than evidenced) conclusion that Stevens saw as already justified.[45]

The primary negative fallout of the Court's remand in *Turner* was not, however, the wasted millions. Its request for more evidence emboldened some lower courts to strike down sensible media laws and regulations for lack of the empirical support that some individual judges wrongly believed relevant to constitutional legitimacy.[46] This misguided search for empirical evidence, purportedly required by *Turner*, also clouded the FCC's recent approach to revising its media ownership rules.[47] Various value conclusions (e.g., does greater dispersal of media ownership embody an appropriate conception of democracy?) and normative evaluations of possibilities (e.g., despite whatever has occurred in the past, does greater dispersal provide a meaningful safeguard against demagogic power in the public sphere, and how valuable is this safeguard?) should have been adequately determinative. Often positivist statistical evidence is simply irrelevant to the basic policy issues concerning media concentration.

Of course, the opposite is sometimes the case. Empirical information in various forms, including ethnographic and historical reports and sociological observation as well as statistical information, is sometimes relevant. Fear of demagoguery does relate not merely to values, but also to probabilities, which is an empirical matter. But care must be given as to what evidence is needed. Here, I want to offer six cautions about the use of positivist social science research.

(1) BE CLEAR ABOUT THE ISSUE THAT IS RELEVANT. Too often researchers start trying to provide "relevant" evidence without being clear about what issue is contested. For example, after hearing that the appealing notion of "diversity" is important, some researchers immediately begin looking for evidence of whether ownership dispersal *produces* content diversity, though often floundering on the issue of determining the relevant type of *content* diversity. However, if diversity is not the central issue or if the most significant diversity value refers to separate and independent *sources*, these empirical inquiries are irrelevant, at least irrelevant to the policy inquiry. That is, some issues are centrally a matter of values. When this is the case, the relevance of factual information is limited. For example, when the Supreme Court established that the Fourteenth Amendment required one-person/one-vote, it did rely on the existence

of malapportioned districts to show there was a problem, but the basic issues, the basic controversies, were normative, not factual. Are malformed districts consistent with the equality of respect that the Constitution demands be given to all people? Likewise, the claim that democratic values require maximum feasible dispersal of media ownership does not raise factual questions – or, at least, not the factual questions for which those looking to find content diversity provide evidence. The claim must be evalutated on the basis of a preferred conception of democracy. If the claim is right, the primary empirical issue is whether greater dispersal is possible using acceptable means.

Other issues, the *risk* of dangerous abuse of media power, for example, can be both empirical and evaluative (how significant is the risk?). Here, however, the nature of the issue affects the type of information that is relevant. Social science research that purports to be relevant for media ownership issues often takes the form of statistical analyses of content produced by different ownership structures. In the late 1980s and early 1990s, evaluations of the relative merits of independent versus chain ownership of newspapers sampled content on random days, over a six-month period or so, of a set of papers representing each ownership form.[48] Somewhat similar analyses have recently sought to find diversity in broadcast content. Such an approach in looking for improperly demagogic use of media power is simply inapt for multiple reasons, one of which I mention here. A danger that dispersal is designed to prevent is the possibility of a rare but overwhelmingly bad result. Rare but extraordinarily significant events are simply not likely to be seen effectively using available statistical treatments. For example, a six-month sampling of nuclear reactors built with two different designs that finds that each design has the same statistical likelihood of a catastrophic nuclear meltdown – in this case, no likelihood, as none were observed during this six months – hardly provides reason not to worry about whether one or the other design is more dangerous and to make decisions based on the study of the two designs. In the media context, anecdotal tales of seriously objectionable past abuses by media moguls could be much more informative, subject to the real possibility that changed context means that the danger is now more or less real. This last caveat about context means that even (counterfactually) an absence of historically or existing "bad" results from media moguls' political demagoguery would prove little about either the current danger or the evaluative significance of the risk. Rather, a discursive account of structural opportunities for abuse, perhaps supplemented with a psychological (or even abstract economic) assessment of why owners might take up these opportunities, probably provides better "evidence" than any statistical inquiry.

Finally, as in the last two examples, the relevant claim often takes a noncommodity or process form. Although not intrinsic to economic analyses and statistical positivist treatments of the media, their analyses usually focus on what the audience receives – on "commodities." Such analyses simply do not address the key issues.[49] The democratic safeguard value does not take a typical commodity form. People do not self-consciously purchase or consume it in a market. Rather, it serves as a background condition that reduces risks within the political order. People who do not consume the media "freely" benefit. Despite its potentially huge significance, this safeguard escapes identification and consideration by most market-oriented economic efficiency analyses. In economic terms, the benefit to nonpurchasers is a positive externality.

Analogously, consider the danger of catastrophic nuclear accidents mentioned above. The social science point was that statistical studies of the frequency of Hiroshima-level accidents will not be informative despite real reasons to be concerned with the risk, reasons that justify safety-oriented policies and practices. Here, the economic point would be that even given that energy consumers, as well as everyone else, value nuclear safety, the market simply does not bring their valuation, and certainly not the value to nonpurchasers, to bear on energy producers.

The same market failure occurs in respect to the safety potentially achieved, if it is, by ownership dispersal. When Justice Potter Stewart called the press a "fourth estate," he was making a structural or process, not a commodity, claim. The primary manner people can show that they personally value safeguards provided either by nuclear safety or by media ownership dispersal is not through their market purchases but through their political expression, such as their opposition to the recent FCC attempted relaxation of media ownership rules or demands for a vigilant nuclear regulatory commission or a legal prohibition on nuclear power plants. The general point is that when the issue is about noncommodity matters – about process, distribution, or noncommodified activities – the relevant form of empirical information will not be a sampling of content.

(2) VALUE-LADEN "FACTS" ARE OFTEN MOST RELEVANT TO INTELLIGENT POLICY CHOICE. Even if sensitive media *observers* can identify and describe bad empirical consequences of ownership concentration, many positivist statistical analysts will miss them, partly because they ubiquitously attempt to rely on purportedly[50] "objective," value-neutral

criteria. In the 1980s and 1990s, to determine whether chain owner-ship of newspapers harms society, researchers considered statistically whether this ownership form had good or bad effects on graphics, story length, color pictures, size of news-hole, or the portion of news that was hard news. Not only do these statistical investigations miss the issues emphasized so far in this chapter, how chain ownership affects the demo-cratic distribution of communicative power or provision of democratic safeguards,[51] they hardly examine the most important *content* criteria. Although not irrelevant, these "objective" factors divert attention from a more significant, but more contested content issue: the quality of the papers' contribution to the public sphere. None of these typical positivist criteria would, for example, identify the comparative merit of having a pre–Civil War newspaper that merely had good graphics to one that took an abolitionist position and provided information helpful to antislavery causes.[52] Surely, the effect of ownership structure on whether a news-papers would play this abolitionist role – or whether TV stations today will undertake the modern-day equivalent – is more significant but more difficult to determine. Focus on whether an ownership form increases the likelihood of more professional graphics is a distraction. The trouble is, it may be easy to say what should have counted as meaningful content a hundred and fifty years ago, but no consensus exists regarding today's content. Still, putting aside the more important issue because of lack of consensus on how to evaluate (or find) evidence and instead looking at objectively measurable data does not make the study scientific. Instead, it amounts to misleading the discussion into debates about matters that matter little, making intelligent choice impossible. This impulse of many social scientists to be value-neutral is equivalent to the ostrich sticking its head in the sand.

(3) AVAILABILITY OF EVIDENCE SHOULD NOT DETERMINE THE CONTENT OF INVESTIGATIONS. Related to the above is the danger that a researcher will allow the availability of particular objective data to determine the issue she investigates. As noted above, the finding related to this issue can confuse the policy matter. Much of the statistical work on the effect of newspaper chain ownership in newspapers published in *Journalism Quarterly* and similar journals during the late 1980s and early 1990s arguably fits this description.[53] If a researcher shows that X is better than Y in relation to the comparatively insignificant factor B, the danger is that the more significant quality A will be ignored because it is value-laden or because the evidence cannot be easily developed. Determining whether X or Y predictably contributes more to A, even if the determination

implicates disputed, unscientific judgments, is the more relevant issue for scholars to investigate and discuss, and finally is more likely the proper basis of intelligent policy decisions. Certainly, if the concern is with performance of the watchdog function, better graphics or layout and maybe even longer stories or larger news holes (possibly filled with press releases) is not central.

(4) HISTORICAL CHANGE AND HISTORICAL CONTEXT CAN BE CRUCIAL. Though this has not been a major issue in the recent ownership debates, evidence from one historical period or context can be of dubious value in another. One possibility is that the relevance of past data is undermined by the Internet, a hypothesis evaluated (and rejected) in chapter 3. Likewise, data – and policy recommendations – may not be appropriately the same for different countries or, more generally, under different historical conditions. For example, autocratic governments are often found to produce bad social outcomes. It might be thought that in a comparative evaluation of whether government ownership of broadcasting or structural intervention in the realm of newspaper markets produces good social outcomes, the level of autocracy should be held constant. In fact, though, the issue is more complex. The democratic prediction should be that government involvement will produce beneficial results in democratic countries and bad results in autocratic countries, so increased ownership would be hypothesized to have opposite effects on social outcomes depending on whether the level of autocracy is high or low. To test this hypothesis, holding autocracy constant, as one prominent study did,[54] would simply wipe out the relevance of any correlation between levels of government ownership and good or bad outcomes. As this example illustrates, any empirical evidence must be read in relation to both the precise policy aim and hypotheses about the factual context. Failure in either respect can cause evidence to be misleading. Government ownership of broadcasting simply cannot be expected to produce the same results or even the same direction of results in Britain or Germany as in (at the time of this writing) Belarus, Singapore, or China.

(5) INTERPRETING THE MEANING OF EMPIRICAL EVIDENCE. The high number of peer-reviewed studies that overtly misinterpret their own data is disappointing.[55] Sometimes the errors involve simple logic or statistical meaning, but in others information really presents interpretive difficulties. For example, if the concern is performance of the watchdog role, what empirical information about good performance should be sought? A count of exposés produced by media with different ownership structures? Not necessarily. First, a relative absence of significant

exposés could reflect either a very effective newspaper having deterred most public and private abuses, leaving few to expose, or an awful paper not discovering or reporting obvious problems that occur under its nose. Second, regular reports of minor misuses or objectionable nonuses of official (or corporate) power *may* have less significance than a willingness to put resources into uncovering and dwelling on abuses of greater significance in a manner that makes the reporting salient for reform. (Consider whether the better criteria to rank qualitatively different TV news or current events programs is the number or the significance of exposés presented.) Third, a numerical count provides no evidence whatsoever on whether a few, potentially the most serious, abuses were ignored, and whether this was due to conflicts of interest created by the existing ownership – abuses that would have been easily discovered and exposed by a different paper that would exist under different ownership rules.

(6) THE RELEVANCE OF STATISTICAL SIGNIFICANCE. Even respected scholars sometimes mistake a null finding for a negative conclusion.[56] Imagine an evaluation of twenty studies designed to determine whether chain ownership is detrimental. (Put aside the contested nature of "detrimental.") Assume that four found statistically relevant evidence that chain ownership was detrimental in relation to the specific factor these studies examined, while sixteen studies, looking at other factors, found no statistically relevant evidence of an ownership effect. Is the proper conclusion "not detrimental," sixteen to four, and thus, overall, chain ownership seems not to be bad? No. The evidence is not even equivocal. Sixteen studies investigated factors that turned out not to provide relevant information (at a statistically relevant level). *All the actual statistically relevant evidence* bearing on the issue points to bad effects of chain ownership. This is not a half-full/half-empty story. Rather, the right interpretation of the data is more like in response to the question: "did I leave the keys in the kitchen?" If I do not find them in the first nine places in the kitchen that I look – places such as in the freezer or dishwasher – but do find them in the tenth, on the kitchen table, the interpretation should not be that 90 percent of the evidence is the keys are not there but rather that the *only* relevant search, the one of the kitchen table, showed that the keys were, indeed, in the kitchen.

Interpretation of the meaning of data also must properly evaluate the notion of "statistical significance." Social science is rightly cautious about making empirical claims concerning either causes or even relationships without a high degree of confidence in the data – statistical significance. It is different with a policy maker. Often she must make decisions under conditions of great uncertainty. If she reasonably concludes that the decision should be based on a judgment of whether X is true, and if the *only* information or basis for belief is a particular study, she acts irresponsibly if she does not follow the direction the evidence points even though the support for that conclusion is not close to being statistically significant.

These six cautions should not be read as a basis for rejecting the relevance of empirical evidence. They only counsel caution, particularly care about identifying the claim or aim for which empirical evidence may or may not be relevant. For example, the third major reason offered below to oppose media concentration does involve empirical claims. I primarily offer theoretical bases to expect that these claims are true. However, some relevant empirical data exist. To the extent they do, that data can greatly support or undermine my claims.

ADDITIONAL, EMPIRICALLY PREDICTED, DEMOCRATIC SAFEGUARDS. The first safeguard aims at avoiding demagogic-related risks of concentration. Dispersal also affirmatively promotes safety in two other ways. Almost definitionally, dispersal increases the number of ultimate decision makers who have power to commit journalistic resources. Absent reason to conclude otherwise, the most reasonable prediction is that the larger number of owners increases the number who will use some of these resources in exposing government or corporate failures or in identifying other societal problems. This increased number will also increase the perspectives brought to bear on issues. (Moreover, the third rationale for dispersal, discussed below, will give reasons to expect that, as compared with larger media conglomerates, owners of nonconglomerate media entities will choose to devote a higher proportion of their resources to this effort.) Thirty-five years ago, a more democratically sensitive FCC made this point explicitly. It recognized that safety lies in diversity of *sources*, whatever the contribution this source diversity makes to everyday content diversity:

> A proper objective is the maximum diversity of ownership. . . . We are of the view that 60 different licensees are more desirable than 50, and even that 51 are more desirable than 50. . . . It might be the 51st licensee that would become the communication channel for a solution to a severe social crisis.[57]

As the FCC saw the matter, the only empirical issue concerning an ownership rule is whether it results in more independent media owners. Under this view, media mergers are presumptively objectionable.

Dispersal also promotes safety in an additional structural fashion. Those who most need to be watched, those with political or economic power, will predictably wish to co-opt the media. Co-optation is likely to be easier, the fewer media entities that the relevant elite needs to control. A few entities can be threatened or bribed, befriended or purchased. More difficult is controlling a larger numbers of *influential* media. ("Influential" is important. Major benefits that Internet blogs purportedly provide include opening the communications realm to anyone able to make an exposé.[58] Examples of blogs doing so in a manner that has attracted wider attention exist. But history gives reason for caution. In the past, the alternative press often reported abuses only to have the mainstream media, the larger public, and the political order largely ignore the reports. Mere exposure in a theoretically accessible public media often accomplishes little. The reality to which people in power must respond sometimes seems to exist only due to stories being given adequate prominence by media entities recognized as significant and trustworthy by both the public and those in power. The societal salience of content may be firmly rooted in place and context.[59] A key empirical issue, needing more investigation for purposes of understanding democratic practice, involves the lines of dispersion of stories among media at different levels, patterns that may vary with the type of story involved.)

This safety in numbers is an iteration of a more general principle. The structure increases safety, the more the structure makes corrupting the watchdogs difficult. Safety thus also increases if different influential media entities vary in their financial bases and organizational structures and thus vary in their points of vulnerability. Observing that during Prime Minister Thatcher's reign, the government was subject to "more sustained, critical scrutiny [by public broadcasters] than [by] the predominantly right-wing national press," James Curran concluded from this and other examples that "[s]tate-linked watchdogs can bark, while private watchdogs sleep."[60] Generalizing any entity may be especially vulnerable to some but not to other forms of structural-based or intentional corruption of its capacity or inclination to expose abuse or raise societal problems. The same is true for different structural organizations of media entities. Any specific vulnerability typically will not exist to the same degree within differently organized portions of the media, especially those with different financial bases, each of which will have its own vulnerabilities. Like diversity of private owners, this structural diversity – organizational or financial – strengthens the overall system.

Analogous to the safeguard against co-option provided by dispersal of ownership is a possible advantage of general (national) financing of public broadcasting combined with guaranteeing each public broadcast station independent authority to make its own policies and program decisions. Corrupting the centralized system's editorial integrity would be worse than corrupting that of an individual station. Moreover, authority in individual stations creates more ultimate decision makers who can choose to be crusading. The additional point here, however, is that a centralized system's editorial integrity can also be more vulnerable in particular ways to corruption of its independence. It would constantly need to evaluate the risk of governmental retaliation, for example, a decline in funding, for its editorial choices. In contrast, as long as public broadcasting as a category has relatively strong support in public opinion, a funding system in which government budget reductions apply to all public broadcasters would be a blunt, politically expensive, and easily opposed method for reining in individual crusading stations. A targeted attempt to cut off only an individual offending station for its critical exposé would be so overtly censorious that it would typically generate strong and probably efficacious public criticism or judicial invalidation. In public choice language, the crusading station effectively externalizes most of the political "costs" of its "offending" action on the other public broadcasters. The larger group can use its larger reservoir of public support to defeat the government's attempt at retaliation. That is, the general logic of ownership dispersal in creating a strong and democratic communications realm applies broadly.

In sum, a key rationale for ownership dispersal (as well as ownership diversity) lies in the three safeguards it offers. Dispersal reduces the risk of undemocratic dominance of the public sphere – the Berlusconi effect. It increases the likelihood of having decision makers who will decide to devote resources to important watchdog roles. And it reduces the likelihood of effective corruption of media that perform the watchdog role.

3. Quality and the Bottom Line

Possibly the most significant economic problem involving the mass media is massive and systemic failures of media markets. Ownership dispersal predictably reduces this problem. It must be emphasized, however, that dispersal is not a complete fix. This major problem justifies an array of additional policy responses, a few of which are noted in chapter 5 and the Postscript. The main point is quite simple and can be understood without following the specifics of the more complex explanation given below. The two-part point is, first, that relentless pursuit of profits and constant focus on the bottom-line restrict investment in creating the news and other cultural media content that people want and citizens need. Second, this bottom line orientation tends to be most extreme among larger conglomerates, especially publicly traded ones. Many readers will find both parts of this claim intuitively acceptable. To understand the claim fully, however, requires additional elaboration. Three economic considerations, which I describe here only briefly,[61] combine to explain the first claim. The second empirical claim finds support in sociologically and structurally based predictions.

(1) MARKET FAILURES. Media markets fail to give people the media content for which they would pay, at least the media content for which they would pay in an imagined market in which all the costs and benefits of media products could be brought to bear or captured by the producer and, thus, are reflected in its production decisions. And media markets fail to give people the media content for which they would pay if people had a fair amount of resources with which to pay. The failures occur in at least three qualitatively different ways, and these failures combine to set up an argument for dispersal.

When producers charge more than the cost, too little of a product is produced (demand is artificially reduced), and when they charge less than the cost, too much is produced (demand is artificially increased) in relation to the social optimum. This first failure relates to externalities, both positive and negative, which cause a deviation of actual selling price from appropriate selling price. For example, many *nonreaders* of a newspaper benefit by a paper's high-quality investigative journalism that exposes corruption, hopefully leading to correction and better government. This benefit to nonreaders, however, does not generate revenue for the paper that would give it an incentive to provide this journalism. Even less does the paper known for its deep, hard-hitting investigative journalism receive revenue for possibly the greatest benefit that its watchdog operation provides: deterrence of governmental or corporate corruption due to fear of exposure. Here, the paper's journalistic commitments provide benefits without ever producing a story to sell. Or to pick another example, many people benefit if election results and governmental decisions reflect a public opinion that is based on accurate factual views and well-considered policy arguments – and suffer from elections and policies based on misinformation and ill-considered views. If this relatively uncontroversial claim is true, even though people often disagree about which media content is accurate, relevant, and well considered, they should agree on the proposition that they benefit from higher quality journalism. Moreover, the point here is that they benefit even if they themselves do not consume it and are hurt by the ubiquity of the opposite.

The problem is that the market does not (fully) bring the value or disvalue of these effects, positive and negative, to bear on the media entity's journalistic or creative expenditure decisions. A paper or station receives little bottom-line revenue for benefits it provides to nonreaders or nonviewers – benefits for which people in the aggregate would probably pay plenty. Theoretically, this high valuation could be measured by the value people would honestly place on correcting or preventing the exposed corruption or on having better informed fellow voters. A hint of the extent of this valuation is indicated by society's willingness to use expensive police, judicial, and citizen resources in enforcing its laws. The paper, however, will provide less of this quality journalism than it would if the market worked to bring this high valuation to bear on the media entity's decisions. Of course, media entities do "cash in" to some extent on their reputation for quality journalism. Still, they cannot expect to translate their reputation into enough audience purchases to equal the full value that their commitment to investigative reporting can produce. This discrepancy follows simply because their revenue does not include compensation for benefits to nonpurchasers. The aggregate value to nonreaders or viewers can be even greater than the value the journalism provides to its actual audience. Thus, a newspaper or station will always have inadequate profit-based incentive to produce the good journalism that actually would produce net value for society. Transaction costs (and free rider problems) prevent translation of this real value to individuals (that is, the public) into payments to the media. People get less quality journalism, and the market-oriented firm produces less quality journalism, than people's preferences justify. (Corresponding points apply to negative externalities, which include the media's roles in inducing antisocial or misguided behavior, ranging from violence to stupid voting, that affect nonreaders or nonviewers.)

Second, a central premise of a market economy is that (some) goods should be distributed on the basis of willingness and ability to pay. But all democracies also identify some goods and opportunities (though not always the same goods or opportunities[62]) that they attempt to distribute more equally than simple reliance on the market can achieve. Wide normative consensus exists that some goods – the vote, basic education, freedom from restraints on basic liberties, some cultural and environmental goods, and, somewhat more controversially, at least basic food, medical care, shelter, or police protection – should be distributed on a basis that responds more to people's desires or "needs" than to their wealth. Most people, however, probably accept the idea that entertainment goods do not normally fall into this category, though the economics of *public goods* (consider parks and some other entertainment facilities) can still justify more egalitarian distribution of some forms of entertainment. Most media products combine edification and entertainment qualities, though usually their emphasis varies. Some media products function primarily as typical entertainment goods. Presumably, these should be distributed roughly on the basis of willingness and ability to pay. But other media products have a more educational, electorally relevant, or significant cultural content. Arguably, these should be distributed on a more egalitarian basis. From this perspective, the market normally will not adequately produce and distribute the educational, political, and cultural media products responsive to real preferences or needs of some portions of the population, especially of the poor but sometimes also of other demographic minorities or groups not valued by advertisers. In response, proper responsiveness to people's preferences requires subsidies that sometimes are provided, though seldom adequately. However, other responses are possible, and one is central here. Owners who are able (and many technically are) could choose to be more responsive to creating and distributing these valued goods than they would be if they follow only market incentives.

Third, successful media entities typically have unusually high *operating profits*. Two specific features of communications as economic goods contribute to this result. The first is that normally each commercial media product has a relatively high first copy cost: the cost of producing the movie, the cost of investigating, writing, editing, and laying out a print story or shooting a video news story, or the cost of producing and broadcasting a program so that even one person can receive it. Additional print or digital copies or additional broadcast audience members require a comparatively low to nonexistent expenditure. The resulting declining average cost is a feature of natural monopoly products. The second feature is that each media story and each "brand" (e.g., newspaper or TV series) is technically a legally created monopoly. Copyright law, for instance, prohibits others from producing identical content even though potentially substitutable content is sometimes ubiquitous. Trademark or unfair competition law does the same for brands. These two features make this area best understood economically under a combination of monopolistic competition and public goods theory.[63] Each product is a monopoly that often can be most profitably priced above not only its marginal cost (often close to zero) but also its average cost, thereby producing monopoly-level profits.[64]

Whether or not this economic explanation of high profitability is complete, the empirical evidence makes the relevant policy point. On an operating basis, most daily newspapers and broadcast stations are exceptionally profitable. In 2000 the average profits as a percentage of revenues of network affiliate TV stations was over 30 percent and for the comparatively few independent stations over 42 percent.[65] These numbers compare very favorably with 6.8 percent profits for the 500 largest industrial corporations.[66] Although clearly most profitable were stations in the largest markets (46%), even stations in the two smallest market categories, the 151- to 175-sized markets and the 176th and smaller markets, were 13.2 percent and 17.5 percent, respectively.[67] And if cash flow as percentage of net revenue (which may be a better measure, given that this calculation eliminates nonoperating reductions to profitability, including the large debt that many owners generated by purchasing the station) is examined, all market size categories had percentages greater than 30 percent.[68] Twenty years earlier, the numbers were similar: for example, 29 percent for affiliates, compared with 4.5 percent for the top 500 industrial corporations.[69] Moreover, cash flow margins of the average station in fifteen of the sixteen market size categories, including the largest and smallest, increased between 1990 and 2000.[70] The FCC found more variable levels of profitability in the radio industry. For the period between 1995 and 2002, probably due to high interest costs reflecting expensive license purchases, the FCC found the net profit margin for the typical radio firm examined in most time periods to be less than that for the average S&P 500 corporation. On the other hand, the arguably more relevant measure of underlying profitability, earnings before interest and taxes (EBIT), varied greatly by quarter but were most often higher than those for the typical S&P 500 firms and were higher than the S&P average during the most recent quarter examined.[71] Newspapers, however, are overwhelmingly profitable. In 1998, the seventeen publicly traded newspapers averaged profit margins of 19 percent, while the operating cash flow, or EBITDA (earnings before interest, taxes, depreciation, and amortization), of the thirteen companies reporting one or the other figure was 27 percent.[72] Of course, newspapers currently have (as they seemingly always have) a sense of being under siege, losing circulation in their paper editions (although that may be largely due to the presence of their online editions, which they are still trying to figure out how to turn into revenue, and does not apply to papers willing to put added resources into their journalism) and losing advertising, especially in the lucrative category of classifieds, so it might be asked whether this data from 1998 are still applicable. Maybe these threats to economic viability portend a bleak future (as has been being said for decades), but the *New York Times* reported in 2006 that "the newspaper industry had average profit margins last year of more than 19%, double that of the Fortune 500" – which, assuming the *Times* meant the same thing by "profit margins" as Cranberg did in 1998, is basically the same, even a little higher than in 1998.[73]

(2) OWNER RESPONSES. Extraordinary profitability combined with huge market failures, particularly failure to spend sufficiently on quality journalism and creativity, opens up a valuable opportunity. Media entities frequently have the capacity to benefit the public substantially by eschewing an emphasis on the bottom line. The ideal would be for media entities to accept less than their abnormally high operating profits and to spend more on producing and widely distributing content that produces high externalities. The structural goals of legal policy ought to include getting ownership more into the hands of categories of people *most likely* to do so, most likely to focus on providing this "quality" content. For example, such owners of newspapers might disdain maximum exploitation of their monopoly product by keeping newsstand or subscription prices comparatively low, thereby increasing socially valuable availability and circulation. As long as newspaper reading is a major factor determining political participation[74] and also affects, one suspects, the quality of participation, William Blankenburg suggests that the decision over price is a major form of editorial policy. He argues that the choice to maximize profits by raising prices not only "suppresses information" but fails to treat the "expelled subscribers" as "citizens."[75]

In eschewing profit maximization, media owners could also choose to "spend" potential monopoly profits on "quality" content that benefits the public beyond the extent that the expenditures produced compensating revenue gains. The policy justification for this practice is, in economic terms, that better journalism typically produces more "positive externalities." An already profitable paper or other media entity can often make even more by cutting the newsroom budget. Those owners (or editors) who reject or reverse this choice better serve the public interest. Society benefits by owners' social responsibility, by owners' willingness to emphasize journalistic or creative quality. Of course, "social responsibility" is too uncertain a criterion to be legally enforceable, and in any event, any attempt at enforcement would be inconsistent with the press freedom on which democratic societies depend.[76] Legislators act properly, however, when they consider whether particular structural rules make it more likely that the resulting owners will not be unduly bottom-line–focused.

The policy question is whether it is possible to identify any legally specifiable categories of people who will predictably avoid a monomaniacal focus on the bottom line. Stories within the profession clearly attest to both very good and very bad owners populating every ownership category. Still, both socio-psychological predictions and structural considerations offer some guidance. One prediction is that both high- and mid-level executives of most large, especially publicly traded, media companies regularly measure their own success and are rewarded largely based on the profits their enterprise produces.[77] Such people are especially likely to focus on the bottom line.[78] A (small) empirical study found nonowner managers to favor profits over other goals more than owner managers, which the author interpreted to "support the notion that local newspaper owners may be in the business to achieve other goals besides maximizing profits."[79] Heads (or owners), especially local owners, of smaller, individual, or family-based entities, are likely to identify more often with the quality of their firm's journalistic efforts and the paper or station's service to their communities.[80] The possibility of praise and respect from fellow journalists and members of their community can reinforce this inclination.

These predictions and observations justify journalists' anguish at MBAs or other nonjournalistic professionals running media corporations.[81] The general belief both within the profession and among outside commentators, usually supported by ad hoc observations, is that companies dominated by journalists more often use potential profits to produce good journalism – their professional commitments leading to lower profits but better content that has positive externalities. (Sometimes supporters of this choice attempt to justify it as providing for greater long-term profitability. Though possibly true, it may more often be a mere rationalization of their preferences.) C. K. McClatchy, a respected editor and chair of a newspaper chain, reported that his greatest fear is that newspapers will be run by nonmedia conglomerates such as Mobil. He argued that "good newspapers are almost always run by good newspaper people; they are almost never run by good bankers or good accountants."[82] In conversation in 1992, Warren Phillips, former editor-in-chief of the *Wall Street Journal* and CEO of Dow Jones, made a similar point. Phillips emphasized the importance that Dow Jones had long placed on having their publisher and CEO come from the journalism rather than the business side of the company[83] – though deviation finally occurred in 2006.[84]

Corporate mergers often create direct *structural* pressures that exacerbate the undesirable emphasis on profit maximization. Economists who are inclined (wrongly) to equate profits with efficiency also typically extol markets for allocating resources to their "highest and best use" by getting owners to pursue profits. In the sale of business entities, this happy outcome might be achieved because the person or entity best able and most willing to capitalize on the purchased entity's potential profits is thereby able to make the highest buyout bid. But this bid locks that purchaser into needing to maximize operating profits in order to cover the cost of the debt created by the purchase (or, if the buyer self-finances, the buyer is locked into profit maximization in order to make the purchase decision appear as a wise use of the corporate assets). In contrast, the original or long-term owner is not under this structural pressure. She can normally use some potential operating income to provide better quality products – hire more journalists, provide more hard news, do more investigations. Of course, from a profit-maximizing perspective, the perspective of capital, her "socially responsible" journalistic expenditures will appear to be "inefficient" – a wasteful use of resources. But from the perspective of society as a whole, given inclusion of "positive externalities," these expenditures more often are actually "efficient" at giving the public what it wants.

Empirical evidence concerning these economic predictions is limited and messy. Still, the available evidence provides support. In the largest ever study of local television in the United States, the Project for Excellence in Journalism (PEJ), a research institute affiliated with Columbia University Graduate School of Journalism, recently made striking findings. It ranked a huge sampling of TV news programs into five grades, from best (A) to worst (F), and divided stations into four groups depending on whether the station was owned by one of the ten largest TV station owners, the next fifteen largest owners, mid-sized ownership groups, or those that owned only one to three stations. PEJ found the news programs of the smallest owners (one to three stations) to be 30 percent A (high-quality), compared with 12 percent A for the largest owners. Likewise, the smallest owners had only 17 percent D or F (low-quality), compared with 23 percent for the largest owners. The largest owners had 57 percent of their programs rated in the three worst categories, compared with 35 percent for the smallest owners. Looking at all four groups, as ownership size increased, news quality generally declined.[85]

Studies typically find newspaper quality relates positively to staff size, in particular, the number of journalists employed.[86] A recent study of mid-sized dailies found that ownership by publicly traded companies highly correlated both with significantly fewer full-time and full-time–equivalent newsroom employees (i.e., including part-time journalists) and with higher profit margins.[87] It also found that the reduction in newsroom employees more than doubled for those publicly traded papers or chains whose profit margins were greater than the average profit margins for privately owned papers. The causal explanation is not known with certainty. Still, the most obvious plot line is: publicly traded companies fire journalists, degrade quality, and increase profits. Similar assumptions are reasonable for predicting a reverse relationship between the quality or local responsiveness of radio stations and the stations' employment of announcers and disc jockeys. A recent statistical analysis found here too that increased concentration results in lower employment.[88]

The goal should be to have media entities controlled by people most interested in using a media entities' income to produce high-quality content. Such content typically has positive externalities. Given the goal, economic and sociological theory as well as available empirical data offer varying degrees of support for each of the following policy orientations: favor maximally dispersed, deconcentrated ownership; disfavor ownership by nonmedia conglomerates; disfavor ownership by media conglomerates; and disfavor newspaper or broadcast station ownership by publicly traded newspaper chains or station groups.[89]

The logic of this analysis also suggests the merits of ownership (or at least control) by the professionals who staff the media entity. Their professional identity is most likely to be tied to providing quality journalism. Similar logic supports favoring local ownership. Such owners are more likely to experience social and other self-identification incentives that favor quality over profits. (This advantage is not unalloyed. They also may be more likely to refrain from negative treatment of friends or allies, while an outsider might be more hard hitting and impartial based on strategic or profit calculations.) Of course, these insights are not new. They explain, for example, the former FCC policy of favoring both local ownership and integration of ownership and control via the now abandoned comparative licensing process.[90] Finally, large corporate ownership's deleterious focus on profits not only provides a rationale for nonprofit *public* media entities, such as public broadcasting, but also suggests the merit of media ownership by nonprofit *private* entities, such as foundations.

Empirical support may be available for at least some of these conclusions. Gilbert Cranberg describes how the *St. Petersburg Times* and *New London Day*, two papers owned by charitable organizations, devote much more of their resources to journalism, generating better quality at less price to the reader, thereby obtaining more circulation. This devotion to content and public service may explain why the *St. Petersburg Times* not only became the largest circulation paper in Florida but also generated a 44 percent penetration rate in high black population areas, which compares very favorably with more typical paper's penetration percentages in the teens in black areas.[91]

ADDITIONAL STRUCTURAL CONSIDERATIONS

These three goals – democratic distribution of ownership, democratic safeguards, and ownership focused more on quality and less on the bottom line – provide the central argument for dispersal of media ownership. Three additional though related ways in which concentrated ownership creates problems or dangers merit separate attention. I label these points 4 to 6.

4. VULNERABILITY TO OUTSIDE PRESSURE

Conglomerate ownership can make a media entity more vulnerable to co-opting or censorial outside pressures. The danger is that governmental or powerful private groups may be able and willing to use economic leverage over one portion of a conglomerate to induce its media "division" to mute critical reporting. The more separate businesses in which the conglomerate engages, the more potentially vulnerable pressure points it will have. This structural vulnerability of media content to such pressure provides a good reason for a law to bar media owners from bidding on public contracts – as Greece attempted in 2005 until the European Community unwisely prevented it.[92] Hopes of obtaining a government contract could lead a media entity to stay its journalistic hand to avoid offending the government. Of course, the rationale is double-edged. A prohibition also helps to prevent the conglomerate from using its media

37

ownership to intimidate the government into improperly awarding it the contract, which may have been the main fear in Greece. The public loses either way – because of both the conglomerate's journalistic vulnerability to pressure or its use of journalistic power purely to further its nonmedia economic interests. Both scenarios blunt the media's watchdog role. The ownership form that Greece wisely wanted to restrict allows the conglomerate to pursue its economic interests while sacrificing the integrity of its media operations.

Even pure media conglomerates are subject to this vulnerability. Media companies commonly sell their media product – purportedly representing the press's independent journalistic or creative judgments – to the audience while selling the audience to advertisers. This might not be true for a few media forms, but today product placements are increasingly swamping movies and may even be making inroads into books. The combination of reliance on audience and advertisers creates vulnerability to content-corrupting pressures from the latter, a continuing problem I explored at length in an earlier book.[93] Being a media conglomerate, however, exacerbates this problem. An outside entity or group, whether a government licensor or corporate advertiser, is often able to impose pressure on one element of the media conglomerate in order to get a desired response from, or to punish, another part. President Nixon, wanting to retaliate against the *Washington Post* for breaking the Watergate story, famously planned difficulties for the Post's renewals of its broadcast licenses.[94] The greatest danger is that mere vulnerability will influence, often unconsciously, initial journalistic decisions – a form of self-censorship. If independent of conglomerate endeavors, book publishing is relatively immune from advertiser pressure. Books normally carry little advertising. Nevertheless, a book publishing subsidiary of Readers' Digest Association canceled publication of a book critical of the advertising industry after advertisers used their ability to apply pressure to *Reader's Digest*, the magazine.[95] Similarly, DuPont's threat to withdraw magazine advertising apparently convinced the book club of Time, Inc.'s subsidiary, Fortune, to drop distribution of a book critical of DuPont.[96]

In 1995, at the last minute, CBS pulled a *60 Minutes* segment in which Jeffrey Wigand, a former high-level tobacco company scientist, was to report on tobacco company executives' knowingly false congressional testimony. CBS's purported ground for pulling the show was that CBS lawyers, especially its general counsel, Ellen Kaden, worried that the broadcast might lead to billions of dollars' liability if Wigand's former employer, Brown & Williamson, sued CBS for tortuously causing Wigand to breach his confidentiality agreement or sued Wigand, whom CBS had agreed to indemnify. But consider the context. Loews and its major owner, Laurence Tisch, was about to complete a profitable sale of CBS to Westinghouse. Many observed that the danger of a huge lawsuit by B&W could interfere with the completion of this sale or the sales price. Moreover, Andrew Tisch, Laurence Tisch's son, was president of Lorillard, another tobacco company and a subsidiary of Loews. He was another person whom the *60 Minutes* segment would suggest had committed perjury before Congress, so the segment potentially could help send the son of CBS's main owner to jail.[97] Lorriard was also in the process of buying a number of tobacco brands from B&W. Lawrence Grossman, in possibly the most detailed report on the incident, apparently believed Tisch's statement that he knew nothing of the incident until after the decision to cancel the program had been made.[98] Grossman also objected to the *New York Times's* outraged editorial, which noted that Ellen Kaden, Loew's inside legal counsel and apparently the key decision maker, stood to gain millions on the sale.[99] Still, the general critical, often indignant view of CBS's decision seems warranted. In some cases, after noting that the feared lawsuit had virtually no chance of actually succeeding and after emphasizing the media's need to stand up to threats of such suits, commentators drew the obvious inference "that investigative journalism on US TV is falling prey to the interests of the megacorporations" and tied this observation specifically to effects of the "merger mania."[100] Whatever the actual reasons for pulling the segment, these conglomerate connections hardly hold promise for the lean watchdog press that democracy needs.

Another illustration had a happier ending. Upset pharmaceutical companies apparently threatened retaliation when the *New York Times* began publishing a series of exposés concerning prescription medicines. At first it might seem that the *Times* would not be vulnerable. At the time, drug companies seldom advertised in the newspaper. Nevertheless, the *Times's* parent company owned several medical magazines that were heavily dependent on drug advertising, and the drug companies threatened to withdraw advertising from these. Legitimate journalism prevailed. The *Times* published – and then sold the medical magazines![101] But the scenario as a whole surely illustrates the danger created by conglomerate ownership.

5. INTERNAL DISTORTIONS

The flip side of conglomerates' vulnerability to outside pressure is their internal incentives to distort independent news or creative judgments. An overt illustration might be editor-in-chief Jason McManus's requirement that "Time, Inc. managing editors...sign...'not at any time [to] denigrate, ridicule or intentionally criticize the Company or any of its subsidiaries or affiliates, or any of their respective products.'"[102] The more the company owns, the less its editors can criticize. Many situations can fit in either this internal distortion or the prior category, as the *60 Minutes* tobacco story makes clear. In any event, often conglomerate entities engaged in both media and nonmedia businesses have journalistic opportunities and economic incentives to mold media content to serve the firm's overall corporate interests. They can choose media content as leverage to get outsiders to make purchasing or political decisions that benefit other divisions of the conglomerate. This opportunity amounts to a not very subtle conflict of interest. The potential for this journalistically corrupting use, as well as its potential economic value, increases as the range of the firm's economic activities increase. Not only can journalistic decisions be modified to promote the firm's overall business decisions, it can also use its reporting as a carrot or stick to get outsiders to make purchasing, advertising, or political responses that benefit the conglomerate's various economic activities. Conglomerate ownership automatically, structurally moves the firm away from an ideal of where its economic incentives align with the media's proper mandate to serve its public audience. André Schiffrin reported that during Murdoch's effort to get licenses for an airline he hoped to start, Murdoch found it sensible to promise Jimmy Carter the support of his *New York Post*.[103] After additional examples, Schiffrin concluded: "To Murdoch, the use of publishing to achieve other ends was simply business as usual."[104]

Economic incentives are not bad per se. Economic incentives reinforce strong professional demands to encourage a media business to maintain the integrity of its content. The media entity benefits at least from audiences' *belief* that its editorial decisions are professional, uncorrupted by undisclosed and self-interested economic interests. This economic incentive supports newspapers' ubiquitous self-portrayal of establishing a sturdy wall of separation of "church" and "state," that is, between journalism and the business or advertising side of its operations. Of course, this separation can and does break down. Inevitably, incentives to please advertisers sometimes outweigh professional commitments and the economic incentive to provide uncorrupted journalism. The breakdown will occur more often if the corruption of content can avoid being too obvious. Many editors of local news media report routinely avoiding investigations in areas where the story could be embarrassing to the enterprise's outside interests – often having to do with convention or sports facility development, land use, or other local issues. Editors occasionally admit pressures to consciously design content to promote the conglomerate's other (media or nonmedia) products or to benefit the conglomerate's overall political interests. Even greater is the danger that incentives to color journalistic judgments operate unconsciously, becoming ingrained "self-censorship" or "business as usual" that requires no specific directives that might stimulate guilty consciences or be identified by those who object as the "smoking gun." Thus, unsurprisingly, *overt* molding of editorial content would predictably be seldom observed even if market-induced distortion is a structurally based constant.

The point is not to demonize people like Murdoch or conglomerates like Loews. Rather, the point is that conglomerate ownership structurally creates economic vulnerability to outside pressure and creates internal incentives to trade journalistic integrity for the conglomerate's other economic interests. Desirable responses can take two forms: journalistic resistance and (partial) structural removal of the incentives for distortion. The first certainly occurs. Individuals often take heroic professional stands, and some firms excel at nurturing highly professional cultures. Still, one wonders why society should tolerate structures that unnecessarily sacrifice the careers of courageous journalists to this economic logic. Advantages of an inevitably partial structural solution should be obvious. The most direct response is to reduce the structural incentives for corruption. Conglomerate ownership inevitably increases these incentives, already endemic due to the pressure to coddle advertisers. Whether or not the distortions related to advertising can be eliminated or reduced,[105] laws could prohibit ownership of media enterprises by nonmedia corporations just as ownership of cable systems by telephone companies was once prohibited because of the perverse incentives that ownership structure created. These conflicts of interest would be reduced by laws that prohibit, just as antitrust laws and FCC rules restrict, to a limited extent, mergers of independent media enterprises.

6. Inefficient Synergies

The third reason considered above to avoid ownership concentration involved the desirability of owners not being too focused on the bottom line. The claim was two-fold: first, that profit maximization undermines the journalism and content creation that produce social benefits, that is, "positive externalities," and, second, that ownership dispersal favors owners more likely to have a preferable journalistic focus. A closely related structural consideration provides another reason to oppose concentration. Namely, mergers are often undesirable because they often *create* new profitable opportunities to eliminate socially desirable expenditures. In fact, the hope of creating these unfortunate opportunities for profit is a major reason why firms seek to merge.

Corporate management regularly justifies media mergers to stockholders (and governmental regulators) with loud claims about profitable and efficiency-serving "synergies." As it turns out, many media enterprises that merged during the 1990s have since found profitable synergies difficult to achieve. Some firms are now slimming down, selling or spinning off media outlets in following the new watchword, "focus."[106] Still, many mergers in both news and entertainment media undoubtedly create new opportunities for cost savings or profitable production. In the entertainment media, the hope is that the merged company can benefit by selling the same highly promoted, fictional character or aspects of the copyrighted story in various media. It can use the same material in a theater-released movie, a TV show, a book, a magazine excerpt, or a CD based on the movie soundtrack. Especially in relation to child-oriented media, it can also use the original content in branded subsidiary products or computer game characters.

By clever placements, the conglomerate can also cross-promote its various products. Its broadcast news division or its popular magazine can do stories about its movie studio's release of the "outstanding" new movie or TV series. They can offer in-depth reports about the program's star character, about its Academy Award potential, or other related matters of equally "great public concern." Among various other examples, James Hamilton found that during November 1999, ABC's popular quiz show, *Who Wants to Be a Millionaire*, "was mentioned in 80.2% of the local news programs on ABC affiliates." This compared with "zero mentions on NBC network affiliates."[107] Though *Greed*, Fox's knock-off of the ABC program, may have been less popular, Fox affiliates that month proceeded to mention it on over a third of their news programs. Meanwhile, the "serious" news teams on CBS and NBC affiliates found themselves able to ignore *Greed* completely.[108]

Also problematic on economic grounds is chain ownership, that is, ownership of the same type of media entity in different geographical markets. Although use of syndicated materials has been a media constant, chain-owned media entities inevitably experience intensified economic pressure to duplicate the use of some inputs, including content, which reduces their need for so many journalists. Nationally centralized music playlists may not only profitably replace local decisions on music but also replace expensive local news programs on radio.[109] After Knight-Ridder's *Miami Herald* broke the story of a sexual affair involving presidential candidate Gary Hart, Knight-Ridder papers gave the story greater play than did those non–Knight-Ridder papers that did not use the Knight-Ridder's wire [$p < .05$], while non–Knight-Ridder papers that did use the wire scored roughly halfway in between.[110] Possibly even more dangerous, however, are synergies created by a joint ownership of a local broadcast station and newspaper, a combination generally barred by the FCC cross-ownership rules that the FCC sought to eliminate in 2003.[111] Here, the most obvious synergy is to share reporters, thereby reducing outlays on local affairs reporting and eliminating the "wasted" expense of doing reporting twice from scratch, a point further discussed below.

Business enterprises – and some economists[112] – seem instinctively to interpret any profitable cost saving as an efficiency. This is simply wrong, certainly wrong from the perspective of social welfare or the normal economic meaning of efficiency. A divergence between "profitable" and "in the public interest" can occur in the context of media mergers for multiple reasons, two of which will be noted here. First, profitable cost saving here will often result from reducing expenditures that previously provided significant positive externalities. Second, the merger will also often allow the firm to create profitable market-dominating media goods that sometimes provide less value to the public (even as measured by the unduly narrow economic criterion of "willingness and ability to pay in a market") than would the media goods they drive out of existence.

The first reason is easily illustrated. Consider a merger that allows the new entity to more profitably provide (and sell) news with fewer journalists. If, as is predictable, the work of the average journalist produces positive externalities, the layoffs both increase profits and reduce these positive externalities. If the second effect is greater than the first, which is predictable but is an unexplored empirical issue, the "profitable" lay-offs are inefficient from a societal perspective. The objection can be made more specific. Reconsider the earlier discussion of democratic safeguards. Benefits from investigative journalism's exposure or deterrence of official or corporate malfeasance go equally to people who are and are not the paper's readers or purchasers. Nonpayment by nonreaders means that there are inadequate (monetary) incentives for this reporting, leading the market to under-supply it. A problem with mergers exists if a "synergy" from the merger, for instance, of a newspaper and local television station, enables the merged firm to get by with only the amount of investigative journalism previously provided by one firm, an amount now shared between two entities. In fact, it may be worse. Competition between independent newspapers in their county of origin has been shown to correlate with greater commitment of newsroom resources and, even more strongly, with more full-time and full-time–equivalent newsroom employees.[113] If, similarly, competition between the newspaper and the television station previously provided a major incentive for both to engage in investigative journalism, the merger may allow the new company to largely abandon the effort. If so, the new company would provide fewer investigative journalism resources than either pre-merger entity provided before by itself. The result would be a hugely profitable cost saving, a synergistic "efficiency," but also a potentially huge loss to the public (as well as a loss to the journalists who are laid off).

Failure to see these profitable synergies as "bad" is understandable for economists who are employed by (or have otherwise adopted the economic perspective of) businesses. From their employers' perspective, the synergies are not bad; they are profitable. The failure is also common among unaffiliated advocates of deregulation. For these advocates, the apparent explanation is either ideology or stupidity. True, some economists identify efficiency only with value measured by quantifiable market behavior.[114] Proper economic accounts, however, must take into account costs and benefits not imposed on or captured by the firm – positive or negative externalities. Otherwise, the account breaks any purported connection between economic efficiency, on the one hand, and social welfare or what people want, on the other.

In the FCC's attempt, put on hold by the federal courts,[115] to eliminate its prior rule banning cross-ownership of a newspaper and local broadcaster, the FCC relied on an empirical study that it interpreted to show empirically that local cross-ownership generally has not an undesirable but, on the contrary, a positive effect on news quality.[116] Before examining this study, consider what one should expect to find in examining the quality of news provided by cross-owned entities. To maximally realize synergies in its news-gathering and news-processing expertise, a newspaper would predictably choose to own the local broadcaster that (at least after the merger) specialized most in news. Specifically, the newspaper would predictably buy or create a station that provides better than average, probably the best, news coverage in the locale because this type of station provides the paper with the greatest opportunity for synergies. Often the newspaper could have the station with the best news merely by sharing its existing journalistic staff with the station (while keeping, if the station is TV rather than radio, a few of the station's video people). Certainly, the merged entity could provide stellar broadcast news without the station making near the journalistic expenditures that would be required for a station unconnected to a paper – the broadcaster would merely rely on the paper's efforts. Thus, the prediction should be that the merged entity could achieve significant cost savings while offering the best broadcast news in the area.

Not surprisingly, the FCC empirical study bears out this expectation.[117] TV stations owned by a local newspaper were statistically much more likely to provide high-quality news programming than the average station in the locale. But what does this fact show? That the cross-ownership benefits the public? That does not follow! To evaluate this combination fully requires considering two other matters.

First, did newspaper ownership "cause" better broadcast news, or did it merely reduce the cost of creating the best news while controlling the local station that provides it, thereby increasing profits? The best empirical evidence would probably come from examining whether cross-owned stations provide better quality news than does the best broadcaster in equivalent cities or markets. If not, without increasing in any way the quality of available local news, cross-ownership will have merely had from one to three objectionable consequences. It will have concentrated control over probably the two dominant local news providers – a dangerous concentration of communicative power. It is also likely to have reduced total expenditures on journalists, thereby potentially seriously reducing social welfare by reducing positive externalities. And, finally, it will have reduced economic competition between these two "local news" producers, possibly allowing both to get away with supplying even lower quality than before, thereby further increasing profits. Unfortunately, no study cited by the FCC provided *any* reason not to expect these three bad consequences.

Second, the FCC's empirical study purported to look at consequences of cross-ownership only for broadcasters.[118] Much more socially significant may be cross-ownership's effects on newspapers. Even if people report that television is their major news source, factual news that they actually know may come more from newspapers. Putting aside knowledge that people only think they have, newspapers are probably the most significant source of politically relevant news or current information that people can correctly repeat, that is, can report when asked.[119] As well as knowledge, studies also show that reliance on newspapers is very strongly associated with political participation, while these studies did not find statistical relevance in the correlation of reliance on television and participation, although some found indications of negative effects.[120] Salient, politically relevant information that a person actually remembers often comes from reading a paper even if the person reports that he or she gets news from television. A newspaper can also be a person's media source of information even if it is not read. For example, "news" knowledge often comes from conversations, and the factually informative or politically relevant information in conversations is likely to have originated in the paper. In addition, a person's news knowledge ultimately comes from the paper when, as is often the case, the broadcasters she watches themselves received their substantive news (as opposed to pictures and live reports of accidents, fires, shootings, or snow) from newspapers or news sources, such as the Associated Press. And if papers are the most important news source, surely the *most* relevant issue in relation to cross-ownership is cross-ownership's consequences for newspaper journalists' and their papers' performance. Even if I overstate the comparative significance of newspapers, the impact of cross-ownership on the newspaper is still very important. Again, this issue is completely ignored by the studies relied on by the FCC.

Maybe the FCC and the studies ignored the impact of cross-ownership on newspapers for an understandable (although not a good) reason. Specifically, the evidence of this impact is scarce. Still, some ethnographic empirical investigations suggest what one could easily predict.[121] Cross-media mergers commonly lead to journalists contributing to both news media. Their greater workload has apparent – certainly self-experienced – negative effects on their journalistic efforts. That is, "cost saving" of cross-ownership may be real. But that these cost savings are "efficiencies" seems doubtful. They are not if these savings, for instance, firing or not hiring journalists, impose even greater costs on the public in the form of lower-quality newspaper journalism. And they may not be "efficient" or desirable for an additional reason discussed in the next paragraph.

The merged companies often extend the domain of dominant media products. Market success means, of course, that purchasers (audience and advertisers) collectively value a product in excess of its direct production cost. Thus, the merged firms' new (or newly expanded) successfully synergistic products undoubtedly provide value to society. That is, they "undoubtedly" provide value *unless* this content disproportionately produces bad consequences not taken into account by purchasers – by increased dominance of content that stimulates violence, racism, insensitivity, incorrect factual knowledge, or misguided opinions, as well as damage to highly valued process values, namely, democratic distribution of communicative power and democratic safeguards.

The new "synergistic" product can reduce net social value in a third way. Its success can cause the failure of even more valuable media products.[122] (This possibility was also explained as one of three economic facts supporting point 3, above.) It can provoke a slight downward shift in the demand for alternative media products. If these producers cannot adequately price-discriminate, products that have low or zero copy costs (i.e., declining average cost curves) often are unprofitable even though their creation and distribution would produce more value than they cost. This downward shift in demand can cause the commercial failure of valued, previously profitable, media products. Sometimes, these failed media products would even produce more value, more surplus, than the competitively prevailing product. In that case, the synergistic product, though valued at more than it costs, causes the failure of products that would have produced even more surplus value. The merger is profitable but inefficient – it causes a social welfare loss by impeding people's receipt of media products they value more than the products that they receive.

Whether the societal gains generated by new synergistic products are greater than the societal losses caused by the resulting commercial failures is an empirical question. Abstract analysis offers no generally applicable clear predictions.[123] As a general matter, a "net loss" is more likely when the new product's demand curve is flatter (producing less consumer surplus) than that of the media products that it competitively eliminates. In turn, flatter demand curves are most likely for larger-audience products, precisely the merged firm's hoped-for synergistic "blockbusters." Another important economic feature is that products more able to price-discriminate (e.g., by selling the product in multiple "windows") can change consumer surplus into producer surplus and thereby be successful even when producing minimal total surplus. Again, the merger-based synergies often involve increasing the available selling windows or the firm's capacity to exploit them. That is, these two scenarios, flatter demand and more price discrimination, describe contexts where the dominating product often produces comparatively little consumer or even total surplus. Thus, this third problem with mergers is that often their profitability is predicated precisely on their increasing opportunities for effective price discrimination or for creating "blockbuster" best-selling products and otherwise extending the reach of their combined products. These enterprise hopes should translate into public interest worries. The danger here is that mergers will damage consumer welfare by eliminating more valued, often more relevantly diverse, media alternatives as well as by causing new negative externalities created by its content and by the loss of democratic process values.

7. A PRAGMATIC ASIDE

The ideal legislative or regulatory media policy is contestable for diverse reasons. Fundamentally, competing policy visions will reflect competing ideals of democracy and the value placed on them. It will also reflect empirical issues where the empirical effects are often uncertain (but where the empirical costs of mergers that the firm is able to externalize onto the public are typically ignored by advocates of deregulation). Certainly, policy should reflect experience and policy choices should change as circumstances – economic, political, and technological – change.

These trite observations lead to a final reason to presumptively disfavor media concentration. Entrenched groups have momentum advantages over undeveloped alternatives, thereby impeding needed change. Beneficiaries of existing policy will typically be more effective lobbyists for protecting their benefits than those who have yet to be benefited – who may not currently exist as a coherent group or be conscious of possible gains. Institutional inertia often makes it hard to undo entrenched organizational power. Moreover, potential enterprise "profit" will also often be more effective than potential realization of broad "public interests" (of roughly similar magnitudes) at overcoming inertia. Analytically, this advantage reflects standard public choice considerations. First, the profit recipients will be fewer in number than the large numbers of the public benefited by the better policy and, thus, have fewer organizational difficulties in creating lobbying power. Second, baseline and wealth effects favor either existing or profit-producing policies over yet to be adopted policies that reflect more process-valued changes.[124]

A change that achieves actually valuable and "profitable" concentration is likely to be much easier, due to the beneficiaries' awareness of the benefits, than undoing existing, profitable, but socially damaging concentration. That is, undesirable concentration is likely to be much harder to change than socially insufficient concentration – which is one reason that many countries have a general policy of pre-merger review by government.

This general problem is intensified in the media context. The media's unique influence over politically salient public opinion can make political resistance to dominant media's interests more difficult than resistance to the lobbying power of other economic monoliths.[125] The existence of a few, too powerful media owners with overlapping interests increases this problem and diminishes the likelihood that subsequent debates and decisions, especially in Congress but also at the FCC, will reflect true, informed, and thoughtful evaluations of the public interest by members of Congress or FCC professionals and commissioners. Concentration increases the likelihood that the economic interests of huge media conglomerates will largely control the policy debates and legal outcomes relating to media policy. In contrast, dispersed media owners not only are more likely to have greater organizational difficulties but also are more likely to disagree among themselves about ideal media policy.[126] The point is not to rule out the possibility that change in either direction – toward less or toward more concentration – might be desirable. But since a mistake in the direction of being too concentrated will be harder to undo than a mistake in the direction of being too dispersed, the burden of argument and the presumption of undesirability should be placed on those favoring policies that permit concentration.

8. Countervailing Benefits?

This section merely flags an issue; it makes no claim to being comprehensive. A complete policy analysis would also consider all possible benefits of media concentration. Here, I consider only two important, often suggested benefits: purportedly better provision for consumers and purportedly better service to democracy. That is, deregulation proponents often suggest that mergers will produce great consumer benefits. Usually the claim relates to efficiencies that allow either cheaper prices or more consumer choice. Often separately stated, although still describable as an efficiency, mergers may be said to be better able to advance and to exploit technology. Deregulatory proponents also sometimes suggest that larger, stronger media entities are better able to take on government, thereby better serving the press's watchdog role. These claims are all ultimately empirical even if not subject to easy empirical measurement. I cannot here demonstrate that they should be dismissed. Still, I offer some reasons for doubt. If I am wrong and these benefits are real, then the inquiry properly considers whether their significance is more or less than the "costs" emphasized in this chapter – and my unproven view is that they will almost always be less.

As noted earlier,[127] impressionistic observations from the 1990s suggest that despite lavish claims made at the time of mergers, subsequent experience showed that many mega-mergers produced disappointing results even from the corporate, or at least from the stockholder, point of view. For example, Robert Pittman, COO of AOL Time Warner and beginning two years before the merger of Time Warner, was possibly the major pitchman for the merger's synergistic advantages. But he resigned under pressure in 2002 after the company failed to find the promised synergies and its stock price had collapsed.[128] In retrospect, an observer might be excused for wondering whether ego aggrandizement or other personal and financial interests of corporate leadership, not consumer benefits or even corporate financial benefits, are a major driving force behind many media mergers. But suppose that a merger does make real economic sense for the corporate entities involved, that is, they will be profitable. What does that imply?

The issue has been discussed above. A central problem is knowing where to find evidence to evaluate the assertion that mergers produce net social benefits. At first, a person schooled in economics might think that the answer is easy. As a rule of thumb, profitability relates directly to efficiency at producing (or distributing) goods or services valued by the public. Therefore, observers often take increased profitability as evidence that society benefits. But this parallel can be dead wrong, especially in the media context. As shown above, cost saving and profitability can systematically diverge from efficiency and social welfare. This possible divergence means that media mergers can disserve consumer welfare even as they increase profits. It cautions that claims of efficiency and consumer benefits made by potential merger participants, who have interests in profits at stake, if not simply being disingenuous, may amount to rationalizations of narrow self-interest. To be persuasive, merger advocates should offer empirical (or theoretical) evidence other than reference to potential profits or stock price increases. Providing this evidence is made more difficult by the difficulty of valuing or weighing any benefits. In a luncheon seminar during the 1992 academic year at the Harvard University's Joan Shorenstein Center, Nick Nicholas, Jr., former head of Time, Inc., and subsequently co-CEO of Time Warner until being fired in early 1991,[129] continued to defend Time's merger with Warner Brothers as benefiting the public. Central among his claims was that, without the merger, most of the public would not have the 500 cable channels that the merged company would provide widely by 1995. You might try to think back to whether you had 500 cable channels in 1995 (or in 2000 or 2005). The number more recently has gone up quickly – as of June 2004, some 388 national nonbroadcast Channels exist. Still, at the time, my main puzzlement was why I would want this 500 as opposed to improved quality in those already available, quality that Nicholas was not promising and that spreading audiences over more channels could make more difficult to finance.

Except when legally limited, mergers occur when corporate heads, or at least the head and board of the "purchasing" company, believe the merger will be profitable – or otherwise beneficial to their status or wealth. Their beliefs often prove wrong. But given the systematic reasons not to equate profitability with benefits to the public, an observer would be wise to be wary of the claim that even a profitable merger produces *any* consumer benefits, much less sufficient benefits to outweigh its citizen or democratic costs. So where should one look?

Claims made on behalf of media conglomerates are not limited to normal consumer benefits. Some commentators claim that these media monoliths are better able than smaller independent media entities to stand up to outside pressures and better able to finance expensive investigative reporting or litigation to gain access to records or protect press independence. Again, these empirical claims are difficult to assess. Larger firms *probably* have greater capacity, but capacity is not the same as action. Relying on their own experience as owner/editors of their small Kentucky weekly newspaper, Pat and Tom Gish used dramatic examples to give strong support to their central claim: the possibility of a paper such as theirs doing effective advocacy and exposé journalism depends on not being owned by a newspaper chain.[130] Though they risked, and experienced, their news office being torched and widespread advertiser retaliation in response to their openness and honesty in exposing political practices and social problems, they and their paper prospered. During their now more than forty years of owning the *Mountain Eagle*, they practiced a type of journalism they believed in while increasing the paper's circulation three-fold and at the same time raising its cover price by a multiple of fifteen, from a nickel to seventy-five cents. The public evidently valued their paper. Their experience illustrates a comment of Eric Sevareid, one of the last generation's great TV news commentators. Sevareid concluded that "the bigger the information media, the less courage and freedom of expression they allow. Bigness means weakness. . . . Courage in the realm of ideas goes in inverse ratio to the size of the establishment."[131] He may have gotten it right.

Some explanations of Sevareid's conclusion are plausible. The likelihood of a media entity's standing up to economic and other pressures may have as much to do with journalistic decision makers' courage and commitment to the integrity of their journalism as with the firm's financial resources. This is essentially the story of I. F. Stone, the midcentury hero of journalism who almost single-handedly produced his "weekly" with minimal financial resources, mostly through close reading of documents rather than by relying on self-serving informational tidbits provided by those in power.[132]

Even if this courage and commitment were distributed equally among heads of small and large media news entities, its presence would be more common if there were simply more heads – that is, if there were more dispersal of ownership.[133] Moreover, sociological and psychological factors suggest the distribution of courage and commitment will not be random. Even if larger organizations can potentially provide professional advantages to a journalist, courageous and committed journalists may more often, as compared with other media professionals, choose to lead smaller journalistic enterprises rather than to learn the corporate skills and develop the aptitude necessary to rise to the top in media conglomerates. If so, they will disproportionately populate the leadership of smaller entities. On the other hand, exposés (or creativity) cut against the grain and often generate more risk than financial benefit. The earlier story of 60 Minutes's initial scrapping of the Wigand interview illustrates the point. Risky exposés or innovative experiments may threaten corporate editors' or journalists' security or advancement within the institution. And the larger the corporate entity, the more they will have to lose in taking these risks.[134] In any event, assertions of *any* democratic benefits of concentrated media require affirmative argument. If my admittedly speculative empirical hypotheses in this paragraph are right, their general absence provides additional reason to disfavor media concentration.

Corporate executives at the time of mergers often promise, and advocates of deregulation often claim, that countervailing benefits outweigh any reasons for ownership dispersal. The promises of the first are seldom borne out. The claims of the second are seldom justified by careful evidence or argument. Most important, any minor gains to media consumers would not diminish, would not affect, the central and arguably overriding reasons to oppose concentration: a more democratic distribution of communicative power within the public sphere and safe-guards to the democratic system. This chapter has argued that funda-mental democratic and significant structural economic reasons exist to oppose media concentration and media mergers and to favor the widest practical dispersal of media ownership.

Nevertheless, in recent years, those opposing ownership restrictions have often taken a different tack. Their strategy has been to claim that there is no real empirical evidence of problems of concentration to which restrictive ownership rules need respond. Or, at least, there is no problem not adequately handled by general antitrust laws. It is to these claims the next two chapters turn.

TWO

Not a Real Problem: Many Owners, Many Sources

B en Bagdikian is probably the most quoted, certainly one of the most acute, commentators on media ownership. In the first 1983 edition of his book, *The Media Monopoly*, he reported that "fifty corporations own most of the output of daily newspapers and most of the sales and audiences in magazines, broadcasting, books and movies."[1] Bagdikian asserted that this concentration is dangerous for democracy – that we would be much better off if there were a different owner for each of the country's 25,000 media outlets.[2] In the 2004 edition, he reported something even worse for our society and for democracy: "Five global-dimension firms . . . own *most* of the newspapers, magazines, book publishers, motion picture studios and radio and television stations in the United States."[3]

Bagdikian's claims have not gone unchallenged. Benjamin Compaine, a respected economist and lead author of the most definitive book on media ownership in America,[4] is possibly the most prominent scholarly critic of the view that existing concentration in the mass media is – or that likely future concentration will be – objectionable.[5] Compaine challenges both Bagdikian's factual and evaluative claims.[6] According to Compaine, the top five media companies collect 27.55 percent of the revenue in the media industry. Contrary to Bagdikian's claim, even the top fourteen together collect less than half.[7] As for Bagdikian's claim about the *increasing* extent of concentration, Compaine observes that in his 1982 book, he listed 62 companies "as being a leading firm in one or more media industries," while in the 2000 edition he lists 90 companies.[8] Looking at a specific segment of the industry – book publishing – and using antitrust standards, Compaine found "a very competitive industry well below even the low boundary of oligopoly."[9] More important, Compaine argues that "looked at as a single industry [an approach that he seems to favor], there can be little disagreement that there is more competition than ever among media players."[10]

I will not try to resolve this factual dispute. Bagdikian may well have been too loose in his dramatization. Still, neither he nor other media reformers are likely to be comforted by the "facts" even as reported by Compaine. Moreover, Compaine cannot be cleared of a charge of looseness. Robert McChesney had written about media concentration, "There are fewer and larger companies controlling more and more." Compaine responded, "What are the empirical facts?" – and after saying he had reported the facts in his book, simply asserted that McChesney "is wrong."[11] So, look at Compaine's book. On the two dates for which he provides data, his calculations show the fifty largest media companies in 1997 are bigger and control more (though not a lot more) of the industry than in 1986.[12] Similarly, according to Compaine's method of calculating, the largest firm had a 5.61 percent share of the communications business in 1986. In 1997, the largest had a 9.22 percent share. The four largest had a 18.79 percent share in 1989 and a 24.13 percent share in 1997.[13] That is, despite Compaine's rhetorical claim, his data shows that McChesney was right! I know of no evidence that the mergers since 1997 have reversed the trend toward increased concentration.[14]

More important than number counting is Compaine's challenge to Bagdikian's evaluative assertions. Compaine basically claims that concentration is not a policy problem requiring fixing. His answer to the question of who owns the media is: "thousands of large and small firms and organizations . . . controlled, directly and indirectly, by hundreds of thousands of stockholders, as well as by public opinion."[15] Compaine's argument appears to be: (1) Using the Chicago School economic approach to antitrust, the media, especially as properly viewed as a whole, is not concentrated. (2) The Chicago School economic approach to antitrust law provides a desirable surrogate for any important social and political standards. (3) Thus, this economic antitrust analysis provides an appropriate *measure* of concentration. (4) Implicit in this argument is the view that existing antitrust law provides an appropriate *remedy* for any potential problems of media concentration. (5) Finally, because of the Internet, whatever concentrated media power that existed previously "is breaking up."[16] (I defer until chapter 3 consideration of this fifth point.) These claims lead to Compaine's conclusion that objectionable concentration does not exist, especially as properly evaluated in respect to the media as a whole.

The three Republican FCC commissioners in their 2003 decision to substantially relax media ownership restrictions adopted largely the same reasoning that permeates Compaine's analysis.[17] However, the FCC added to Compaine's analysis a new conceptual device, the Diversity Index (DI), to measure concentration in local news markets. Although this device has subsequently been severely critiqued by the Third Circuit,[18] as an attempt to formalize Compaine's still influential view of concentration, both the DI's rationale and its problems are worth examining.

This chapter describes and critiques the first four points in Compaine's argument and then does the same for the FCC's Diversity Index. The reasons to favor dispersal of media ownership elaborated in chapter 1 turn out to provide insight into the weaknesses of both Compaine's and the FCC's conclusions.

COMPAINE'S ANALYSIS AND THE CHICAGO SCHOOL APPROACH TO ANTITRUST

Whether objectionable concentration exists, Compaine asserts, depends on answers to at least two questions: what constitutes the relevant market and what level of concentration is too much. Facts alone answer neither question. Rather, answers depend largely on the reason for the question – the reason for a concern with media ownership concentration.

Compaine distinguishes two different frameworks for identifying when concentration is too great: a *"conventional antitrust standard"* and a *"sociopolitical standard"* concerned with the needs of a flourishing democracy and free society.[19] Compaine agrees that a society might wisely consider the second to be more fundamental but observes that it provides no clear or accepted criteria for measuring concentration. But he suggests that "presumably . . . it is the sociopolitical standard that the [conventional] antitrust standard is intended to promote."[20] Compaine, however, does not explain why this would be true. To prevent an entity from amassing sufficient economic power to raise prices inefficiently is certainly a legitimate goal by itself but it has no *necessary* correspondence to avoiding an objectionable distribution of influence (power) over public opinion.[21]

Compaine relatedly distinguishes two approaches to antitrust: the currently dominant Chicago School approach and a multivalued approach. The Chicago School approach emphasizes economic efficiency and market power over price. In contrast, Compaine suggests, the "multivalued" approach assumes that antitrust law should directly include (all?) relevant sociopolitical concerns. Nevertheless, he defends relying on the currently dominant Chicago School approach on four grounds: it has the advantage that its "criteria tend to be relatively identifiable, quantified and validated, ... are less likely to run into First Amendment barriers, ... *are [in many ways] reasonable surrogates for socio-political criteria,...*, [and] may be less susceptible to 'the law of unintended consequences.'"[22] If this series of contentions is right, the conventional antitrust focus should be acceptable. Compaine's argument about when concentration is objectionable falters, of course, if this Chicago approach predictably and significantly diverges from securing the proper sociopolitical goals – in particular, if it diverges from the needs of democracy and a free society for ownership dispersal discussed in chapter 1. (Chapter 4 argues that his claim about First Amendment barriers also fails and that First Amendment *values* strongly support more stringent limits on ownership.)

Concentration is objectionable according to the Chicago School when it gives firms power to raise prices to noncompetitive levels. This power leads to (inefficiently) restricted production as well as transfers of wealth from consumers to the firm.[23] The Justice Department's merger guidelines explain that antitrust law's merger restrictions have as a dominant, arguably exclusive, aim "that mergers should not be permitted to create or enhance market power or to facilitate its exercise" in order to prevent "a transfer of wealth from buyers to sellers or a misallocation of resources."[24] The merger guidelines are defined and calibrated to identify any merger that would increase the merged firm's power over prices in any market. Although this approach cannot be applied mechanically, it provides a clear conceptual criterion for identifying objectionable concentration. The criterion of "power over price" provides theoretical answers to both of Compaine's questions. It theoretically determines both boundaries for the relevant markets and the concentration level that is too great. A relevant market is a combination of any category of products and a category of potential consumers, usually those within a particular geographic area, for which a single monopoly firm, if it existed, could raise prices and restrict production in order to make monopoly profits. Cross-elasticity of demand between items increases the items that must be considered within the produce market. A firm might be the only one to produce X, but consumers may be just as happy to substitute Y, which many other firms offer. If so, then the relevant market would not be for Xs, but for Xs and Ys (assuming that some other product, Z, should not also be included because it is substitutable for Xs or Ys). The first firm would have no power to raise the price of X.

From this "power over price" perspective, factors in addition to market share can affect whether concentration is excessive. For example, an absence of barriers of entry can sometimes moot any objection. Even a single monopolistic firm might have no power to raise prices if doing so would quickly draw new competitors. (Of course, in some circumstances, for example, if the monopolist is also the low-cost producer, monopoly prices might not draw competitors if the monopolist can realistically threaten to drop prices below the new competitors' costs and drive them out. The notion of lack of entry barriers thus requires greater explication.) Despite this need for refinement, antitrust regulators have developed the Herfindahl-Hirschman Index (HHI) as a rule of thumb for identifying excessive concentration. The index measures concentration by squaring each firm's percentage market share (expressed as a whole number) and then adding the squares. The procedure creates possible results ranging from 10,000 to just above zero. Thus, two firms each controlling 50 percent would generate an HHI of 5,000 (2×50^2) and ten firms each controlling 10 percent would generate a score of 1,000 (10×10^2). But if one of the ten firms had an 82 percent share and the other nine each had a 2 percent share, the HHI would be 6,760 ($82^2 + 9 \times 2^2$). The squaring emphasizes economists' view that increases in market share generate more than a linear increase in market power. The Justice Department guidelines view a score of under 1,000 as normally indicating an unconcentrated market, while a score of more than 1,800 suggests high concentration that often raises antitrust concerns (depending, as noted, on other factors, such as the presence or absence of barriers of entry). This HHI becomes a standard against which Compaine often makes his comparisons and, as discussed below, is a concept abused by the FCC in its development of the Diversity Index (DI).

Although not entirely consistent in this, Compaine's policy discussions mostly treat the relevant market as the *media as a whole.*[25] After arguing that "focusing on trends in a specific market segment is a distraction" and that "the product market distinctions have become essentially meaningless," he immediately proceeds to examine the media industry as a whole, including content producers, content delivery companies, content packagers, and retailers.[26] Compaine describes commentators, such as Bagdikian, as emphasizing a socio-economic-political concept for defining concentration, which he then interprets as emphasizing "diversity of voices." Since all the different media are voices in the marketplace of ideas, Compaine asserts that to be consistent, these commentators, too, should "support the broader mass communications industry . . . as the proper designation of the market."[27]

Obviously, the broader the market, the less likely that objectionable concentration will be found. A broader market will normally mean more firms, each individually possessing a smaller share of the total market. Thus, Compaine's broader characterization of the market supports his conclusion that there is no problem of media concentration. Compaine agrees that, if "[l]ooked at in small, industry-specific pieces, there is indisputably consolidation in some media segments," but, he argues, if considered as "a single industry, there can be little disagreement that there is more competition than ever."[28] (Actually, his own data suggest otherwise,[29] although not to an extent likely to be particularly relevant.)

Moreover, only his holistic conception of the relevant market can explain Compaine's lengthy and careful attention to the HHI index for the media industry as a whole, which he calculates as 268. This number shows, he says, that the media industry is "one of the most competitive major industries in U.S. commerce."[30] Given the premise that the media should be examined as a whole, Compaine is basically right – at least from his economic antitrust perspective. An HHI of 268 represents a very unconcentrated communications order. Attention to *this* HHI number, however, would be merely obscurantist except for his apparent belief that the media industry as a whole is an appropriate unit of analysis and that economic antitrust criteria measure the relevant concern.

Compaine thus purports to show that there are a plethora of media owners. There are three problems with this claim, which the next three sections below explore, respectively. First, even from a narrow, efficiency-oriented, Chicago School antitrust perspective, the media as a whole is clearly not the relevant market. In this regard, Compaine bases his argument on misapplication of traditional antitrust notions. Second, the economic criteria are not "reasonable surrogates for socio-political criteria." Rather, such socio-political antitrust criteria suggest that undesirable degrees of concentration exist. Third, even the "socio-political criteria," as given content in the manner proposed by most antitrust commentators who reject the undue narrowness of the Chicago School's purely economic model, are still too narrow to capture the more fundamental objections to media concentration discussed in chapter 1. That is, even more thoughtful, encompassing antitrust analyses focus on "commodities" in a manner inadequate to the noncommodified values actually at stake. An adequate response to these noncommodified values requires either a much more radically reformulated antitrust law or, more likely, media-specific restrictions on concentration.

MEDIA AS A WHOLE IS NOT THE RELEVANT MARKET

From a perspective that emphasizes power to set a noncompetitive price, market definition is crucial. From this perspective, the media as a whole is simply not the right market. What is? For the antitrust analyst, the issue involves price elasticity between products. Consider an analogy. If General Motors and a failing Ford merged and DaimlerChrysler closed a money-losing American Chrysler division (though which is failing may have now reversed), the market for what were once called "American cars" would be extremely concentrated (depending, of course, on the definition of "American cars"), the market for "cars" would be much less so, the market for transportation vehicles even less, while the market for "consumer goods," of which cars are only one item, remains extremely unconcentrated. The relevant comparison depends on whether many people find goods in the larger market reasonable substitutes for GM-Ford cars. If a slight increase in the price of GM-Ford cars results in enough people switching from buying cars to buying movie tickets, cosmetics, dishwashers, or ice cream, the last characterization could be right. But that is implausible! Almost surely the relevant category is cars. If the price of the GM car goes up, people are more likely to buy a Honda, but the price increase is unlikely to cause many to switch to buying a speed boat, jet, or locomotive or to taking public transportation. Of course, these claims are my empirical guesses – they might be wrong.

For present purposes, the antitrust question is what is the relevant market category in the media realm. Any reflection shows that the media business as a whole is an incoherent characterization. Compaine himself remarked that whether or not supplied by the same firm, content creation and content delivery are very different products. They are not interchangeable. Including both as media enterprises in the attempt to show lack of concentration, for example, in calculating an industry HHI, is clearly misguided – though this is what Compaine does and does repeatedly.[31] It is like claiming that a single car manufacturing company does not have a monopoly because there are numerous steel companies or car dealerships that contribute to consumers getting cars. Compaine properly notes that the media involve "discrete types of activities," which he describes as substance or content, process or delivery, and format or display.[32] Competition in one does not show that another is competitive. An aside on this point may make it clearer.

Imagine that media delivery is much more expensive than content creation and that there are ten equally sized "media" firms, with nine providing delivery and only one (due to entry barriers, monopoly power reflecting first copy costs, or other reasons) creating content. With each firm having about 10 percent of the total media revenue, the HHI would be 1,000 (10×10^2) – basically unconcentrated. But one company controlling all media content bespeaks monopoly. It certainly represents a threat to democracy even if *potential* entrants cause this monopolist to have no power over price. Problematic concentration likewise exists in the reverse situation – if there are many creators but only one (unregulated) distributor. For antitrust purposes, the two services – content creation and content delivery – should not (and would not) be included as part of the same market.

Not only is the distinction between content creation and content delivery important for antitrust law, but concentration in either is important for other policy concerns as well. Given typically high capital costs of delivery systems, Bruce Owen once argued that First Amendment–rooted interests in diversity are usually best furthered by keeping delivery services separate from content creation and content sale and by subjecting the first to common carrier regulation.[33] Owen hoped that separation of delivery from content creation combined with common carriage would reduce economic barriers to entry into the crucial content realm. Common carrier obligations would help to prevent the carrier from using its power to exercise control over content creators' communicative opportunities. Of course, government regulation of content creation, which is generally barred by the First Amendment, is very problematic for a democratic society. In contrast, common carriage regulation of delivery can advance expressive freedom and be a desirable public policy. The lesson is that media regulation is not bad – only the wrong sort is.

Congress and the FCC once took this view very seriously. For example, they generally barred cross-ownership of carriage-obligated telephone companies and content-selling cable systems.[34] If kept separate, telephone systems operating fiber optic lines as common carriers would be more likely eventually to provide delivery services for new content suppliers who would provide competitive cable-type video content to households. Even though satellite companies now provide the primary competition to cable, the mandated separation rule certainly made sense originally.[35] And preventing mergers of these companies now enhances the possibility that cable companies will compete with phone companies to provide both phone and Internet service.

These same considerations also explain imposing total or partial common carriage and rate regulation on other content distributors – the U.S. mail, cable system operators, or, for some types of messages, even broadcasters. Because of the importance of the distinction between content providers and content delivery, Congress required, with subsequent Supreme Court approval, that cable systems carry local broadcasters for free if they so requested.[36] Similarly, Congress and the Supreme Court upheld requirements that broadcasters carry political candidates' paid advertisements during the election season.[37] Justices Brennan and Marshall, two Justices generally viewed as particularly sensitive to the First Amendment, suggested that the First Amendment itself requires the FCC to formulate rules to require broadcasters, as long as they carried product advertisements, to also offer some carriage of paid messages on controversial public issues, while other Justices indicated that they would leave the matter to Congress and the FCC.[38] In another context, after finding that local regulations required the cable system to operate in part as a carrier, the majority found that Congress's attempt to permit the cable system to exercise limited content control over the carried content was constitutionally impermissible. Specifically, the Court invalidated a law that allowed the cable company to "censor" indecency on PEG (public access, educational, or governmental) channels that the cable franchise agreement required the cable system to carry.[39] Other rules, such as the now abandoned Syndication and Financial Interest (Syn/Fin) rules, were also originally designed with the view that television, as a powerful content carrier, should be legally required to be more open to independent content creators.[40]

Regulating the delivery business on behalf of greater opportunities for content creators involves a policy judgment that distinguishes the market role of the two media activities. The judgment is that, though the First Amendment protects both, regulating delivery can benefit the communications order by reducing predictably concentrated delivery services' power over the hopefully less concentrated realm of content suppliers. These policies recognize that antitrust-*like* problems can exist due to concentration in media delivery even if other portions of the industry (e.g., content creators) are not concentrated. The policy sensibly rejects treating the communications industry as an undifferentiated whole.

The point here is that Compaine's industry-wide definition improperly combines delivery and content businesses. The complaint that Compaine defines the market too broadly, however, goes well beyond this objection. Most obviously, many media markets are geographically local.

A company that owns the only local newspaper and the only local TV station in a small town has undue power over local news (and, less important for this book's democratic concerns, possibly over local advertisers[41]) even though this combination would create hardly a blip in Compaine's industry-wide HHI. As I discuss below, even the FCC's recent deregulatory decision recognized that policy considerations require viewing each local area as a relevant media market.

Geographic uniqueness illustrates merely one facet of a more basic observation. Often, people will not view different media outlets or different content as ready substitutes. Many readers will distinguish the *New York Times*'s Metro section from the *Los Angeles Times*'s Metro section, thereby making geographic distinctions. New Yorkers may also be unwilling to quickly forgo the *Times*'s Metro section in favor of a New York screening of a Disney movie, or vice-versa, thereby distinguishing types of media. A price change in either the Disney movie or the *Los Angeles Times* may have little effect on a person's readiness to purchase the *New York Times*. Many advertisers also distinguish these media products – a grocery store in Los Angeles is unlikely to find either the Disney movie or the *New York Times* to be a plausible vehicle for advertising its current five-day sale of strawberries – and, of course, different content famously attracts different demographic groups, a prime concern of advertisers. Even without differences in geographic markets or format "type" – for example, "national magazines" – a price change in *Vogue* may not influence many consumers' decision whether or not to buy *The Nation*. Even in the smaller subcategory, "national magazines of opinion," a price change in *National Review* may have minimal effect on *The Nation*'s market. That is, for antitrust's policy of preventing power over price in, for example, the New York news market, Disney or the L.A. paper are irrelevant. On the one hand, their independent existence does not show the New York market is competitive and, on the other hand, one company owning all three does not indicate that any concentration exists. For the different concern of undue power in the public sphere, common ownership of Disney, the *Los Angeles Times, Vogue,* and *The Nation* as well as the *New York Times* is very relevant – but there is no reason to think antitrust standards revolving around power over price have any relevance to this concern or to the concern with undue power in local public spheres when evaluating local mergers.

Unless consumers' interests are oriented more completely to entertainment and diversion than these examples suggest, the FCC would be wrong to maintain, as it often has recently, that many different media outlets or products are part of the same market, implicitly treating them as interchangeable.[42] The Department of Justice and the courts have often – for example, in respect to newspapers[43] and radio broadcasting[44] – adopted the main rival view, that each media type is a separate product category. The discussion above shows that even this alternative is too broad. A magazine aimed at sheep ranchers will not compete with a cattle ranching magazine, where concentration may exist.[45] *Newsweek* or *Vogue* is unlikely to substitute for either ranching magazine. Whenever consumers find products not to be substitutable and providers cannot cheaply switch and supply the other, concentration should be evaluated for antitrust purposes in relation to very separate markets.

These observations only begin a discussion of identifying relevant markets for the purpose of finding market power over price. First, delivery and content creation often should be treated separately. They involve sufficiently separate activities that lack of market share in one says nothing about possible inappropriate market power in the other. Second, as to content, different media products are often not economic substitutes from the perspective of either audiences or advertisers. Differences may involve geography, subject matter, point of view, writing style, or language. The HHI for the industry as a whole is simply irrelevant to antitrust inquires. Compaine's invocation of it should be viewed as obfuscating any meaningful analysis of media concentration.

Thus, my first objection to Compaine's argument is that it trades on a misleading conception of antitrust. Even if he is right that conventional antitrust law provides a relevant measure of concentration, he has done nothing to show that under this standard there is no problem with current concentration. Of course, rejection of the media as a whole as the relevant antitrust category does not yet demonstrate that problematic power over price does exist. That issue requires empirical examination for which, in places, Compaine's book provides useful background data. And surely monopolistic power over price is objectionable and should be *a* policy concern. Still, it is not the only concern and usually not the most important concern. Next, I turn to Compaine's more important claim – that the Chicago School antitrust approach serves as a reasonable surrogate for advancing the even more important socio-political values. The critique will be two-fold. The first point, discussed in the next section, leads to consideration of an alternative antitrust criterion. The second, discussed in the following section, shows why even this alternative is inadequate to identify objectionable concentration.

POWER OVER PRICE FAILS AS A SURROGATE FOR ANTITRUST'S PROPER SOCIO-POLITICAL CONCERNS

Despite current preoccupation with economic efficiency, many judges and scholars see antitrust law as historically embodying major socio-political values or goals. In particular, they see "democratic" or political objections to concentrated power – objections to the power of the trusts.[46] In reference to the passage of the antitrust laws, the first Justice John Harlan observed that "the conviction was universal that the country was in real danger from another kind of slavery . . . the slavery that would result from aggregations of capital in the hands of a few individuals and corporations."[47] Judge Learned Hand saw in their passage "the belief that great industrial consolidations are inherently undesirable, regardless of their economic results."[48] Former Federal Trade Commission Chair Robert Pitosfsky stated that "it is bad history, bad policy, and bad law to exclude certain political values in interpreting the antitrust laws."[49]

If the goal is to maintain a society of small, competing firms even at the cost of economic efficiency in order to avoid dangers that concentrated power poses for liberty and democracy, this aim should have special force in relation to concentrated power in the public sphere. Concurring in the application of the antitrust laws to the Associated Press, Justice Felix Frankfurter explained: "A free press is indispensable to the workings of our democratic society. . . . And so, the incidence of restraints upon the promotion of truth through denial of access to the basis for understanding calls into play considerations very different from comparable restraints in a cooperative enterprise having a merely commercial aspect."[50]

Still, if antitrust laws have purposes other than restricting power over price, these purposes and perhaps their rationale need further explanation. Then, from the perspective of these purposes, the standards against which to evaluate mergers or monopolization need specification. Neil Averitt and Robert Lande offer one particularly promising suggestion: the true concern of antitrust law (as well as consumer protection law) is consumer sovereignty or, more specifically, consumer choice.[51] Antitrust law would be seen to be concerned not merely with *power over price* but also with *power over choice*. Consumers are freer if they can choose among many different competitors. In contrast, even if a single monopoly company in some market would offer more product variety, power shifts away from the consumer. Arguably, that company now *rules*. The single company chooses the choices; it has power over the specific variety of products to provide the consumer, whether or not it has power to raise price. But if many firms compete, no individual seller has power over the consumer. The consumer may also have more variety in the products from which to choose, but this is a different, secondary, empirical matter related (maybe) to welfare, not freedom. Given this vision of consumer sovereignty, the law ought to consider not just power over price but, more fundamentally, the capacity – whether or not used – to restrict or control consumers' choice.

Averitt and Lande agree with Compaine that *often* "price competition will serve as a reasonably good proxy for nonprice competition."[52] They explain, however, the economic reasons that this proxy will not apply in certain industry sectors. They specifically highlight "high-tech and media-related industries," with independent editorial power especially valued in the later.[53]

Two attorneys from the Antitrust Division, Maurice Stucke and Allen Grunes, took this point and ran with it. Stucke and Grunes connect Averitt and Landes's concern with consumer sovereignty to the political concerns that animate the antitrust laws. Stucke and Grunes argue that antitrust law combines, as Justice Black famously suggested in *Associated Press v. United States*,[54] with the values of the First Amendment to recommend a focus on maintaining a robust marketplace of ideas.[55] Antitrust law bars mergers that (unduly?) reduce competition or consumer choice in the idea marketplace. With this analysis, these authors more precisely formulate the concern with power over choice. They object to merged entities' power over the "idea" content provided to a consumer within the marketplace of ideas. Just as economic entities should not have the power (used or not) to limit a consumer by raising prices, they also should not have the *power* (used or not) to limit a consumer by restricting choice of content – in FCC jargon, power to restrict content diversity.

Some antitrust analysts will find counterintuitive a key step in this argument. How can concentration insufficient to create power over price be sufficient to create relevant power over content choices? If competition denies the firm power over price, the firm will be equally subject to the discipline of consumer preferences in providing the product. The reason a profit-maximizing firm in a competitive market has no power to raise prices is that it will lose customers to competitors. The same lack of power, these analysts might argue, applies with respect to detrimentally changing nonprice qualities such as content. But they are wrong!

Still, this objection to independent powers is influential and, as Averitt and Landes recognize, sometimes (but not always) right. The symbiotic relation between price and nonprice qualities explains the standard critique of price controls. Before the era of airline deregulation, legally set high *(minimum)* prices for airline tickets caused airlines to compete by substituting costly extras – good meals or fine service – where they would otherwise compete on price. The economic critique of this price regulation is that consumers, though pleased with these extras, presumably value them less (as subsequently shown by market competition) than cheaper tickets. Similarly, the standard (and in my view unsuccessful[56]) critique of price controls in provision of cable television is that mandated low *(maximum)* prices will result in a deterioration in program quality or service that most consumers prefer even at the higher cost. The general point is that products compete on both price and nonprice elements. As one decreases, the other also declines – and vice versa – a result embodied in the slogan, "You get what you pay for." The firm tries to find a profit-maximizing combination in response to consumer preferences. That is, in the absence of a firm having monopoly power, the market presumably establishes optimal combinations. Artificial control of one element by such devices as price controls will cause a movement of the other elements in the same direction, despite consumers' contrary preferences. By becoming a monopolist, an enterprise gains power to increase profits by increasing price or by reducing expenditures on nonprice aspects of the product. Typically, some combination of strategies is optimal for the monopolist's profitability. Artificial limits on one element will not return monopoly profits to consumers but merely cause the firm to try (less efficiently) to take these profits out by changing the other element.

At least in the media context, a key error in the logic that equates power (or its absence) over price with power (or its absence) over nonprice elements relates to the valance of different consumers' common reactions to qualitative changes in content. A profit-maximizing firm's power depends on *how* a change in either price or content affects people's willingness to purchase. Assuming the product stays the same, a price reduction predictably leads to some new purchasers, but typically does not cause any to abandon the product. (The converse is true for a price increase, putting aside often false, quality-signaling features of price where a higher price can occasionally lead to new purchases by supposedly signaling a better or more prestigious product.) Likewise, assuming price stays constant, for many products, the firm can increase the number of purchasers simply by offering a better quality product. But neither means of increasing the firm's customers is costless – the reduced profit margin from lowering prices parallels the increased cost of supplying a better product. Theoretically, the market determines which combinations of prices and quality create economically viable products.

This logic of an ideal price/product balance falters, however, in various situations. Most obviously, it falters if consumers disagree about whether the changed product is better or worse, a disagreement that is ubiquitous in respect to media content. True, if price is kept constant, more money spent on producing generally recognized higher quality content – money spent on better "production values," better writing, better editing – normally leads to some new purchasers without driving any away. Newspapers today complain about losing readers, but research evidence suggests that they can gain readers if they put more resources into journalism. The opposite typically occurs if content expenditures – such as the newsroom budget – are cut. But content has a second set of qualitative dimensions. Using the *same* expenditure, a firm can obviously create differently oriented content. The same expenditure can be made on sports news or national news, on pro-labor or pro-Republican commentary, rather than merely on local news. The firm could choose sitcoms aimed more at younger or older audiences. Changes such as these or related alternatives typically result in some new purchasers or viewers and the loss of some former audience members. Of course, given other media products in the market, there may be a profit-maximizing choice, a factor that allows a good economist to predict entities' rough array of content orientations.[57] The different contents are, in effect, different products, each with its own set of potential customers. As long as the market functions perfectly – that is, producing any product that consumers value more than it costs – a change by the firm to produce an alternative product could draw a new supplier for the old product. The problem with this solution relates to the typical monopolistic aspect of media products. The high first copy, low subsequent copy cost of media products (i.e., the declining average cost curve) results in the market *not producing many valued products*. Given this dynamic, and even if there were perfect knowledge about consumer preferences, profit maximization often will not dictate a unique choice of content. Market competition does not necessarily determine which of the valued products will and will not be produced. That *choice* is left in the hands of the producer. A change of content orientation could potentially lead to an equivalent gain of new and loss of old consumers (or of consumers of equivalent value to advertisers). If so, an equilibrium could develop with either content prevailing.

Moreover, many customers will, within limits, purchase either media product offered if it is the only one of the general type offered – the only local daily newspaper, for example – or if it is still the best from their point of view given the alternatives. Though the monopoly paper's audience may be smaller than the combined total of two competing, differently oriented papers, it would be higher than that of either individual competing paper. The nature of newspaper markets, however, especially given the role of advertising,[58] often means that only one paper will survive, and this prevailing paper could choose either content orientation. In any such situation, the firm has power over content (and even more power if it is willing to forgo the most profitable content) even when it has no remaining power over price – for example, it may have already used any power over price that it has. Thus, the market may support a single very profitable local daily with a republican, an objective, or a democratic slant but not support three or even two papers offering alternative slants. The owner gets to choose the news emphasis, editorial slant, or columnists. A profit-maximizing firm can have great power over content, that is, over cosumer choice, in addition to or even in the absence of power over price.

If media firms regularly have some power over content even when they have no power over price, even a merger that creates no power over price inevitably creates a new firm that has greater *power* over consumer choice than either firm had previously. The actual effect of the merger on consumers' content choices – the way that the merged firm will use its power – presents a complicated empirical and evaluative question. On the one hand, pre-merger, both entities often seek the same customers from the largest market category. Merger gives the two entities a profit-oriented incentive not to compete against each other. Thus, if it does not eliminate some products – mergers of local newspapers often result in closure of the least profitable – the merged firm might increase choice in respect to some content attributes.[59] For example, rather than two competing radio stations both offering "top 40" music, under joint ownership one station might change to classical or country or jazz, reducing competition with the other. On the other hand, the merger may simultaneously reduce other aspects of content diversity. Both stations, though with increased diversity in music format, may now both emphasize the most centrist styles of music within that format. They may both employ a smaller playlist. Or they may both adopt the general political cast of the owner. That is, even if profit-maximizing, the owner can choose the dimensions on which she will or will not distinguish the two entities. As the FCC said in another context, "it is unrealistic to expect *true* diversity from . . . [the merged entity]. The divergency of their viewpoints cannot be expected to be *the same* as if they were antagonistically run."[60] In one respect, however, the reduction of consumer choice is not empirically doubtful. The merger necessarily reduces consumer choice among content suppliers, that is, among those with ultimate power over content. From the democratic marketplace of ideas perspective that Stucke and Grunes emphasize, *this* restriction of consumer choice is a clear and significant loss. Whether the gains and losses in diversity produce a net benefit for society is not merely an empirical issue related to commodity preferences but also a normative matter related to the distribution of power.

Two hypotheticals can illustrate this power over content. Consider a merger of two radio stations in a ten-station market. If the audience share of the two merged stations is large enough, the merger could give the combination pricing power in the radio advertising market (assuming, as has the Justice Department, that radio advertising is a unique market). Often, however, this will not be the case. Pricing power will not exist. On the other hand, each firm had some power over content before the merger. Each could make some content choices without changing the size (or, more specifically, the value to advertisers) of its audience. The merged firm obviously has more power over content than either had independently. It will have at least the sum of the power each had by itself. The conclusion that now there is one less independent voice embodies this observation. The merger could eliminate the only evangelical, the only poetic, or the only leftist voice. Actually, the merged firm will have more than the sum of the power that the two had themselves, because the choices of other media entities in a market affect the economically viable choices available to any given media speaker. By controlling the purchased firm's choice, the purchasing entity increases its power over its *own* content as well as adding the power over its newly owned entity.[61] That is, power of the merged entity will normally be greater than the summed power of each by itself. Moreover, this increased power over content is independent of whether or not the merger creates any power over price.

Similarly, consider a local daily newspaper purchasing the only all-news radio station in a dozen-station radio market. Unless advertisers find *news* consumers (whether of newspaper or radio news) to be a uniquely identifiable and valued target audience, which seems unlikely for most advertisers, the merger is unlikely to have increased the firm's power over price of advertising or of the newspaper. On the other hand, the purchase quite obviously concentrates power over local news content. Of course, this power is not unlimited. Presumably, the firm cannot afford to lose too many readers or listeners by degrading the quality of news content too much. Likewise, it would be costly to adopt a viewpoint perspective that seriously offends too many prior customers (unless the "offensive" content picks up sufficient new customers). And the firm must avoid content decisions so extreme that they would actually lead new competitors to risk entry. Still, the merger surely increases the firm's *power over news choices* available within the community. Since both news vehicles previously had some power to choose news slant, for example, the political slant, the merged entity can coordinate these choices – possibly to increase diversity but also, with little likely loss of customers, to reduce it. The merger also necessarily reduces the number of *independent* professional news originators from which the public can choose. As with the radio station merger discussed in the previous paragraph, the quantity of power possessed by the merged firm is normally more than a summation of the power each entity had when independent. Before, choices were somewhat constrained by a need to react to – to compete with – the speech choices of the other news source. Now, whether out of a (benign?) desire to uphold decency standards or a (overtly objectionable) interest in dampening or blocking knowledge of financially, personally, or politically inconvenient information, the merger gives the firm greater power to reduce disfavored content. This power is largely new. Previously, if the one news entity heavily reported such information, that reporting would create pressure on the second to do likewise. Of course, if someone other than the offending party knows the information (that is, if it did not require extensive digging), she is theoretically free to spread it. In a free society, a person can gossip, leaflet, or post views or information on the World Wide Web. Nevertheless, all evidence suggests that a huge difference exists between factual presence of information somewhere within a community and its effective (widespread) or salient presence. Moreover, to the extent that the merger reduces the competitive need to engage in investigative journalism,[62] the merger may even reduce the information in the hands of anyone with any interest in its public communication.

The aim of restricting concentration of power over content, not just price, has animated congressional and FCC policy making. Congress enacted the Newspaper Preservation Act with an expressed intent to keep independent editorial voices alive. The law allows two papers in a single community (under statutorily defined circumstances) to enter into a Joint Operating Agreement (JOA), in which the papers can combine their business operations on condition that they keep their content operations entirely separate. In doing so, the law implicitly rejected the Chicago

School's emphasis on power over price. The whole point of a JOA is to increase the combined papers' power to extract revenue from advertisers and readers (as well as to reduce other costs of commercial competition), that is, to increase its power over price as a means to preserve *content* competition and consumer choice in editorially independent content. Similarly, the FCC long generally prohibited a single firm from owning multiple local broadcasters as well as local newspaper and broadcaster combinations – the two scenarios discussed above. In doing so, it never claimed that either scenario created power over price. Rather, the FCC sought to restrict a single entity's power over content and to preserve the public's choice among independent content sources.

The great merit of Averitt and Lande's analysis, as extended by Stucke and Grunes, is that by means of the notion of power over choice it connects the concern with greater audience choice of content *sources* to the goals of antitrust law. Sellers can have power over content choice even when they have no power over price. Consumer sovereignty requires legal restriction of sellers' power over content as well as over price. Competition increases consumers' choice among product originators or, more specifically here, increases competition in the marketplace of ideas. On the down side, these commentators leave unresolved the difficult task of specifying when lessening of competition is sufficiently substantial to be illegal under the antitrust laws. They rule out not all local media mergers, but all that have too great of an objectionable effect. They recognize that they provide no clear answers.[63] Nevertheless, their observations refute Compaine's key claim. They show that the Chicago School approach, emphasizing power over price and economic efficiency, is not a good substitute for the political and social values that antitrust law should also further. Even if Compaine had properly applied traditional antitrust analysis – failure to do so being his first problem as explained in the prior subsection – that traditional analysis is inadequate. The consumer choice interpretation of antitrust not only follows antitrust's historical rationale but also sees existing media ownership as much too concentrated.

Even This Enlarged Conception of Antitrust Is Insufficient to Account for the Fundamental Reasons (Discussed in Chapter 1) to Limit Concentration

Concentration that is acceptable from the perspective of one set of values is not necessarily acceptable from the perspective of others. Market power over price, as shown above, is only one possible concern. A second interpretation of antitrust law emphasizes concern with audience choice, which justifies dual objections: objections to power over either price or content. Both powers allow a firm to improperly restrict consumer choice. Even the second, more expansive interpretation of antitrust, however, is "commodity" oriented. It considers only how concentration can negatively affect the consumer's interest in the product choice. In that respect, even the broadened antitrust approach fails to focus on central objections to concentration.

Chapter 1 described media-specific reasons to oppose concentration. The first reason embodied the goal to create a more egalitarian, more democratic, distribution of power and influence within the public sphere. This *distributive* value does not presume that everyone wants to specialize in public communications, that each person should own or control a media entity, or that such an arrangement would be practical. Rather, the goal of maximum practical dispersal of ownership was to allow diverse groups to each have media entities aimed at the group's concerns and, ideally, owned or controlled by people with whom the group's members identify. The widest practical dispersion of media ownership also predictably increases effective communicative opportunities even for non-owning speakers. A non-owner would be less dependent on the power and biases of a few powerful entities in being able to present her detailed, complex view of policy or account of corruption to a significant portion of either elites or citizens. The aims of having more owner/speakers and more owner/gatekeepers can reflect people's *desire* for a more democratic distribution of opportunities for discursive participation. The aim is not for any particular diversity of content but for more dispersed control of public discourse with whatever diversity that dispersal produces.[64]

The second, *safeguard* rationale for dispersal of media ownership is also structurally based and democratic in aim. A community should not be subject to potential political or cultural manipulation by one or a few firms or owners and should have the safety resulting from multiple potential watchdogs. The third rationale observes that the economic nature of the media business typically leads successful firms to have high levels of potential operating profits. It then argues that dispersed ownership results in owners who are more likely to devote a significant portion of these potential profits to media products that produce valuable positive externalities rather than maximize the bottom line. Finally, ownership dispersal predictably provides other structural benefits – for instance, a structural reduction of conflicts of interest that undermine democratic or welfare contributions of content.

Both the Chicago School's narrow efficiency and the broader, alternative consumer choice antitrust analyses share an ultimate concern with the *provision of commodities to consumers*. In contrast, the three central values that chapter 1 emphasizes are better described as involving *noncommodified values* – structural values related to a favored process, to risk reduction, to more democratic distributions (of communicative power), and to collectively beneficial content. These benefits simply are not commodities that consumers individually purchase in a market. The benefits do have value to individuals. Choice of a desirable level for their provision, however, seems inherently a collective matter and ought to reflect discursively formulated values and defended predictions. That is, their optimal provision can result only from political choices (realized in legal rules), not market purchases. These noncommodity aims obviously support a much more stringent disapproval of media ownership concentration than do either of the two antitrust approaches.

The significance of these noncommodified values has not been lost on either governmental officials or scholarly commentators. In 1965, the FCC identified an obviously structural, not commodity value – "maximum diffusion of control of the media of mass communications" – as one of two primary objectives in broadcast licensing, the other being the socially inclusive but *partially* commodified objective of "best practicable service."[65] Like democracy itself, the FCC described "diversification of control" as "a public good in a free society."[66] To support its view about the distribution of broadcast licenses, the FCC then quoted from a Supreme Court antitrust decision, *Associated Press v. United States,*[67] involving newspapers. Justice Black had said that "the widest possible dissemination of information *from diverse and antagonistic sources* is essential to the welfare of the public."[68] "Maximum diffusion of control" became virtual boiler-plate, being quoted in 230 court or FCC decisions between 1965 and 1994.[69] The language ceased being employed only when, on the direction of a misguided Congress,[70] the FCC eliminated comparative broadcast licensing in favor of a more market-driven – and commodity-oriented – auction procedure. The obvious point, previously recognized by the FCC, is that a single owner is not a source antagonistic to itself.

These noncommodified values raise objections to ownership concentration where neither antitrust view considered above has telling application. All situations that Stucke and Grunes considered for stricter application of the antitrust laws involved media outlets that offer content to the same (or a significantly overlapping) set of potential consumers – for example, between entities in the same local community. This restricted context makes sense for a consumer choice framework. The issue is the content commodities that the consumer can choose. Increasing consumer choice, however, provides no obvious reason to object to combinations of media entities that operate in different geographical markets and serve different sets of consumers. In contrast, these combinations overtly conflict with the goal of maximum diffusion of control. The combinations undermine a more democratic distribution of power within the country's public sphere and endanger the other values discussed in chapter 1. These noncommodified structural, process, and distributive values provide reason to object to the growth of newspaper chains or consolidation in the cable industry and reason to severely limit ownership of multiple broadcast stations even if in different markets.

Maybe it should be no surprise that Compaine and even the more sophisticated antitrust analyses largely ignore the primary values at stake. Economic analyses are not inherently incapable of taking noncommodified values into account.[71] Still, many economists seem much more comfortable focusing on goods and services that hypothesized self-interested individuals purchase in a market, That is, they may find a commodity focus natural – implicitly adopting this extraordinarily value-laden and narrowly reductionist view of the social world! Their questions are: Is this commodity provided efficiently and priced fairly (Chicago School)? and Are there adequate *consumer* choices (broadened antitrust approach)? In contrast, consider other questions. Is media's communicative power distributed in ways that are democratically fair? Is it distributed in ways likely to lead to better and safer political and social processes – much like the goals sought with the constitutional structure of separation of powers? And is ownership distributed under rules likely to result in media owners whose journalistic, creative, and expenditure choices reflect the public's actual values and preferences better than do the choices of owners empowered under other ownership distributions? These questions all relate to what people want. They could also be understood as being about what a democratic society needs. Nevertheless, except maybe for aspects of the last question, these issues all involve values and preferences that a commodity-oriented economist is likely to ignore. That is, people can and do want and value – but do not as individuals purchase in the market – structures, practices, and processes, such as democratic voting and separation of powers. Often these desired noncommodity "goods" can only be obtained politically – through laws or government policies. These values and preferences, not commodity provision, should be the touchstone of media ownership policy.

Compaine is wrong in many of his subarguments. The first objection was that he wrongly applied conventional Chicago School antitrust analysis, for example, when he treated the entire information and entertainment creation and delivery industry as the relevant market. Second, he was wrong to believe that the narrow Chicago School antitrust analysis provides a desirable stand-in for broader social and political values that even he agrees should animate antitrust law. Most fundamentally, however, his view that concentration has not and predictably will not reach a level that should cause concern depends on simply ignoring the most serious objections to concentration. A broadened consumer choice antitrust approach, which clearly improves on the narrow economic approach, properly invoked antitrust history. The public, politicians, judges, and scholars had objected to the power of the trusts, the dangers of abuse of concentrated power, and the needs of democracy. This history, however, belies this broadened approach's continued commodity focus. Antitrust doctrine that takes adequate account of these historical concerns about power, process, and structure may be possible and should be welcomed. To do so, antitrust doctrine would need to abandon determinative reliance on commodity-oriented economics. My own guess, however, is that *adequate* legal recognition of the values described in chapter 1 will occur only through media-specific laws and regulatory policies. These laws, for example, would include those that existed when the FCC could say that, in a given locale, having fifty-one broadcast owners was better than fifty and that no enterprise should own more than a handful of stations.

THE FCC'S DIVERSITY INDEX

In 2003, the Federal Communications Commission culminated a congressionally mandated biennial regulatory review with an Order that would substantially relax restrictions on ownership concentration.[72] In doing so, it introduced a new analytic tool, the Diversity Index (DI). If wisdom were our star, this innovation could be placed in the dustbin of history – and it might be. In *Prometheus Radio Project v. FCC*,[73] the Third Circuit Court of Appeals found that the FCC had (in all respects relevant here) inadequately justified its Order and remanded much of it for reconsideration. The Court based most of its opinion on problems with the FCC's construction and defense of the DI.[74] Nevertheless, the Diversity Index merits examination. It represents precisely the type of reasoning found among those who see little problem with existing media concentration and who were powerful enough to control government policy making. Even some academic and activist critics of media concentration apparently believe that, if correctly reformulated, a new DI would properly employ social science to guide policy making.[75]

The FCC claimed that the Diversity Index provides its "media ownership framework with an empirical footing."[76] The goal is to restrict ownership in order to provide adequate *source* diversity. But the FCC's operative assumption was that, once achieving adequate diversity, the Telecommunications Act of 1996's[77] purported deregulatory presumption barred further legal restrictions. It also believed that further (unnecessary) legal restrictions on ownership would violate media owners' First Amendment rights to speak to as many people as possible. The Third Circuit rejected these limiting assumptions, finding that neither the act nor the First Amendment created any presumption against ownership restrictions. (Chapter 4 explicitly critiques the FCC's view of the First Amendment.) In any event, the FCC believed that in order to craft rules to prevent undue concentration, it must be able to identify when concentration was too great. It invented the DI to serve "as a tool to inform [its] judgments about the need for ownership limits."[78] Nevertheless, at best, the DI is a very curious measure. The FCC developed the DI in secrecy without the public notice that the law arguably requires.[79] Public scrutiny might have exposed as indefensible many of its key assumptions. More troubling, the DI probably represents a misguided but increasingly common empiricist belief that quantifiable facts can give answers to normative questions – and can do so without any coherent explanation for how the quantified facts even relate to the normative questions.[80]

The FCC explicitly modeled its DI on antitrust law's Herfindahl-Hirschman Index[81] (HHI). Its goal, however, was to measure diversity rather than market power. Thus, the FCC explained that it modified the HHI by adopting different assumptions reflective of this different goal. The two most crucial but also most questionable assumptions were, first, that relevant diversity roughly relates to the absolute number, irrespective of market share, of separately owned media outlets within a media category. (Why it did not include as a source each person in the population, each of whom is a source of communication to others, is unclear except that it would have shown the absurdity of the FCC's device for measuring concentration.) Second, the FCC assumed that radically different types of media entities combine to provide this diversity to the public. Thus, it included the Internet, radio, weekly newspapers, daily newspapers, and television in the single measure of diversity. It also had to identify a relevant content category and geographic arena. Reasonably assuming that the media's democratic role is what makes it special, the FCC focused on news and public affairs content. And given that it believed, contrary to many critics of media concentration,[82] that clearly the national level is robustly diverse, it focused on *local* news and public affairs media providers, as the area in which dangers should be identified.

With these assumptions, the FCC then constructed the DI. First, it assigned each media *type* a percentage share representing the extent people reported receiving local news from that type – 33.8 percent of the market to television, 24.9 percent to radio, 20.2 percent to daily newspapers, 8.6 percent to weeklies, and 12.5 percent to the Internet. I put aside its questionable methodology for assigning shares.[83] Then, to determine the importance of any particular media entity, the DI multiplies the importance of the media type not by the entity's market share but by treating each entity of the type as having the same importance for diversity. For example, if there were seven TV stations, each would count for 100/7, or 14.3. Thus, its share of the market would be 14.3 × 0.338 (the share of the market credited to television), or 4.83 percent. Then, as with the HHI, this number is squared – giving the hypothetical a score of 23.3. Finally, all the squares for all the media entities in the local market are added to get the DI – the seven TV stations making a 7 × 23.3, or 163.1 contribution. Again using the analogy to the HHI, the FCC then views the market as moderately concentrated if the DI is above 1,000 and highly concentrated for purposes of viewpoint diversity if the DI is above 1,800.

An examination of its consequences easily condemns the FCC's approach. To identify the diversity market, the FCC includes in its daily newspaper total all dailies in the market area – which, as it sees it, includes small dailies in suburbs and surrounding small towns. Thus, the FCC lists six dailies in Kansas City,[84] although the *Kansas City Star*, with a circulation of 271,500 and 87 percent of the total metro circulation as the FCC measures the metropolitan area, is the city's only significant daily. The other five, with circulations ranging from 2,000 to 14,000,[85] come from surrounding areas and often are not readily available within the city. To believe that Kansas City residents experience choice or diversity from the *Daily News*, a local paper with a circulation of 2,000, published in Richmond, a town forty-four miles away, borders on the fraudulent. (Similarly, in order to find twenty-one daily newspapers competing in New York City, the FCC includes a Trenton paper located sixty-five miles to the south and a Poughkeepsie paper located eighty-five miles to the north, neither of which I have ever seen in New York City and, in any event, are unlikely to provide significant local New York City news.) The FCC also lists nine TV stations (including noncommercial public TV stations) and 43 radio stations in the Kansas City market. On this basis, it finds robust diversity in Kansas City – it has a DI of 509.[86]

Using the DI, the FCC developed its new ownership rules. For a city such as Kansas City, these rules allow one company to own a daily paper, two TV stations (although only one among the top four stations), and nine radio stations. These new rules would permit the creation of a Kansas City media empire. Television audience shares are typically highly skewed. Not implausible would be a Kansas City market of nine stations with percentage shares of 34, 23, 14, 10, 7, 4, 3, 3, and 2. Under the new rules, the conglomerate could own two stations having a combined 41 percent share of the market. As the FCC calculates its DI, a merger between two independent TV stations and the independent newspaper would increase the DI by about 79 points to 588. Thus, the FCC's major conceptual innovation, the DI radar screen, would see hardly a blip due to a merger of the dominating *Kansas City Star*, the largest TV station, an additional TV station, and at least nine local radio stations – possibly the only radio stations providing significant local news. Diversity, the FCC believes, is not even moderately threatened by such a combination. In contrast, the Justice Department generally treats daily newspapers and television as separate markets. Even given the extremely doubtful proposition that the six papers the FCC identified are all in the same newspaper market, application of the Justice Department's measure would find that, even before the now allowed merger, the daily newspaper market has a HHI of greater than 7,569 (87^2 plus the squares of the percentage shares of each of the other six papers), well above the 1,800 that it treats as suggesting high concentration. And using the hypothetical audience shares noted above, even before the combinations that the FCC would now allow, the television market would have an HHI of 2,068, also indicating a highly concentrated market. With the combinations that the FCC would allow, the television market HHI could increase to 2,872 $[(34 + 7)^2 + (23 + 4)^2 + (14 + 3)^2 + (10 + 3)^2 + 2^2]$. That is, having found no threat to diversity, the FCC rules would allow the merger of the dominant media enterprises from two separate but already highly concentrated media markets, thereby creating an extraordinary media juggernaut.

The DI raises many serious but relatively technical issues. For instance, as sources of local news, the DI gives equal significance to media entities that are major local news providers and those that present no local news content at all. The fact that many radio stations exist in a market hardly creates diversity in local news if most radio stations present no news programming and the only newspaper, which owns the most watched local TV station, also owns the only radio stations that do provide local stories. Moreover, the FCC treats the TV station owned by the conglomerate, which is likely to be the main local news station,[87] as having no more importance for the purposes of diversity in local news than the many TV stations – 162 stations in the top fifty television markets[88] – that present no local news or public affairs programming at all. Counting these "no news" stations as providing diversity in local news quite obviously overstates the diversity that exists in a local news market.

A different problem follows from generalizing the reason that the FCC did not include cable as a local news provider. The FCC believed that few people receive local news from cable-originated local channels (partly because few cable systems currently offer such stations). Rather, the FCC believed that people mostly used cable to receive local news only due to its carriage of local broadcasters. As the Third Circuit pointed out,[89] the same is probably true for the Internet. The FCC provided no evidence that people receive substantial local news from the Internet other than news provided from a traditional news source, such as the Internet site of a local newspaper or broadcaster, which are already included in the DI. The existence of national Internet sites, such as Salon or the Drudge Report, hardly justifies the FCC treating the Internet as adding a significant source of diversity in local news. The FCC's approach is at best questionable.

Here, however, I want to highlight three conceptual problems with the DI that have the greatest policy significance: (1) including different categories of media in a single ownership analysis, (2) within a single category, considering all media entities of equal significance, and (3) implicitly claiming that the DI score has normative or policy significance as a measure that helps to identify when concentration reaches a level that undermines needed diversity of media ownership. As seen below, in many ways these problems with the DI both repeat Compaine's mistakes and ignore the policy values emphasized in chapter 1.

(1) Combining media of different types, as the FCC did, makes sense for some purposes, but not for others. In describing mergers that should be prohibited, all media should be included. All media combinations create unnecessary and potentially inordinate power in the public sphere. Considering all media entities of all media together also may make sense for corporate executives considering potentially profitable mergers. Cross-medium mergers can create synergies that are often functional from a profit perspective although usually dysfunctional from a public interest perspective. This last conclusion justifies the FCC's extensive cross-ownership prohibitions that its new rules would have largely abandoned.

For other purposes, however, combining different media in the same analysis is misguided. The Justice Department typically does not combine them for antitrust purposes. A newspaper and TV station, although their combination would clearly increase power in the public sphere, may not be very substitutable for advertising purposes. If not, the combination would not create power over the price of advertising. Therefore, the two should not be included in the same market for traditional antitrust purposes.

Arguably, an analyst should not treat media of different types as part of a single market for purposes of competition or consumer choice in a so-called marketplace of ideas (i.e., the broader commodified perspective considered earlier in this chapter). Many individuals rely almost entirely on one or two media categories for informational purposes. Identifying how much each medium is relied on in the aggregate hardly shows how much choice is meaningfully available to these individuals who do, and will probably continue to, rely mostly on a particular medium. If a person finds that, for her purposes, only newspapers provide adequate detail or scope of coverage or if she finds time only for radio, diversity *for her* requires choice within the particular medium on which she relies. Likewise, many other people do use multiple media categories but not for the same informational needs – weekly papers for cultural or movie reviews, daily papers for information about city problems and activities of local governmental bodies, and TV news programs for voyeuristic interest in fires, accidents, or crime and maybe sports highlights or weather. For these people, too, concentration in any category represents a potentially serious lack of choice in respect to specific informational needs. In other words, ownership of media entities of differing sorts can be objectionable for some purposes – most obviously for increasing concentrated power in the public sphere. In addition concentrated ownership within a single media category, despite the existence of many alternative media in other categories, can likewise be objectionable from the perspective of consumer choice and other antitrust (efficiency) values.

Fundamentally, the FCC misunderstood the significance of its own data about media usage. The appropriate perspective is that of an individual consumer rather than aggregated data. The FCC's choice to combine media into a single category is appropriate only if each or most individual consumers view these different media as plausible alternatives for serving the same information interest or need. There is simply no evidence for this doubtful proposition. And if not appropriate, the relevant category in which diversity should exist must be some category smaller than local media as a whole. Concentration within any media category creates undue power over these individuals. In a sense, the old FCC rules got it right. For purposes of providing individuals with source diversity, the FCC long enforced a "one to a market" rule within and between mediums. For the additional purpose of preventing undue power within the public sphere, local or national, the FCC severely restricted the total number of broadcast stations a firm could own nationally. The cynical thought is that the FCC expanded the media entities treated as within the market for purposes of calculating the DI merely to make finding objectionable concentration less likely.

(2) Even more problematic is the feature that most disturbed the Third Circuit: treating each media entity in a particular category as having equal significance.[90] This absurdity was illustrated above by looking at Kansas City. The Third Circuit drew its example from New York City. The FCC attributed the same 1.5 percent share of the media market share, generating a 2.2 contribution to the DI, to the Dutchess Community College's television station and the primary New York ABC affiliate station. The DI treated the virtually unwatched community college station as making a greater contribution to diversity than the *New York Times* along with the radio station it owns, a combination that adds 1.9 to the DI.[91] Worse, under the FCC's DI analysis, the ABC affiliate's merger with the *New York Times* would not only be unproblematic – it would add less than five points to the DI total – but would be even less problematic than the ABC station's merger with the community college station.

For the HHI, the whole point of squaring the market share is to emphasize the *disproportionately* detrimental consequences for competition of firms having especially large market shares. Squaring market shares represents this insight; it weights market shares in a nonlinear fashion. By treating each entity within a category the same, the DI does not emphasize but actually eliminates any significance of market share. Its squaring is meaningless except as embodying a slavish imitation but fundamental misapplication of the HHI approach. If the DI and the HHI are calculated for the same market (i.e., the same firms), the consequence is that it becomes virtually impossible to produce a DI score higher than the HHI.[92] For a given number of firms, the HHI is constructed to get the lowest possible score when each firm actually has an equal market share – the situation that the DI assumes by fiat. Given that without explanation the FCC adopts the same numerical standards (i.e., that there is a serious problem only with a 1,800 index score), its DI will never identify a problem not already found by antitrust regulators using the HHI. Again, the most plausible explanation is cynical. While the FCC wanted to appear, after extensive social science research, to have formulated a quasi-scientific standard to measure diversity losses that justify restrictions on concentration, it actually wanted to create a standard that *never* objects to a combination not already illegal under antitrust laws.

(3) There turns out to be a thoughtful possible defense of the DI, and the critique of this defense leads to the third, most fundamental objection: that the DI implicitly embodies a wrongly conceived conception of the value of diversity. Bruce Owen observes insightfully that "the choice of a method of measurement follows from the adoption of a goal or an understanding of the nature of a problem."[93] Owen offers to cash out this point in the context of media concentration. He argues that there are (at least) two identifiable concerns with competition in the media sphere: first, the economic (antitrust) concern with concentrated market power and, second, what Owen calls a Miltonian concern (in reference to John Milton's original defense of a marketplace of ideas method of finding truth[94]) or, more directly, a marketplace of ideas concern with diversity. Economists designed the HHI in an attempt to measure concentration in a manner that relates to the first concern. What measurement standard relates to the second?

At this point Owen's argument might be expected to replicate Stucke and Grunes's initially similar emphasis on consumer sovereignty in the marketplace of ideas when assessing media mergers. It doesn't. Unfortunately, Stucke and Grunes never identified a precise measure of objectionable concentration for their antitrust purposes – though implicitly they thought it would normally be more demanding than the conventional Chicago School economic criteria. Not so, says Owen. The premise of the marketplace of ideas is that people will be attracted to the best ideas offered and will increasingly shun the bad. Given this premise, the only important market or structural requirement is that people be able to offer ideas and others be able to access them. Concentration of market shares does not indicate a problem. Just the opposite! It hopefully indicates that people are finding the best ideas in the *agora*. The marketplace of ideas is working when people congregate around the best ideas.[95] Media enterprises grow precisely because people seeking truth (or wisdom) see their offerings as the best, as true. Properly functioning competition in the marketplace of ideas depends only on many voices being unrestricted in offering their wares, not on these voices necessarily having any success in attracting buyers, attracting audiences. To measure diversity or choice for purposes of the marketplace of ideas the analyst should, therefore, "simply count the number of (unweighted) sources."[96] The success or audience share of different sources has "no significance" from this perspective; rather, "all independent sources should be counted equally."[97]

Interestingly, presaging Owen, Compaine made the same point in an implicit challenge to reasoning like that of Stucke and Grunes. Compaine writes that the ultimate questions are: "Are there more or fewer voices *available to me*" now than in past decades, and Do I find gaining access to these voices easier or harder?[98] The fact that I do not want to pay attention to most of these voices, that the voices have minimal market shares, is entirely irrelevant. And as to whether one should think about industry segments or mass media as a whole in considering concentration, Compaine suggests the broader marketplace of ideas values support (or are at least consistent with) viewing "the broader mass communications industry . . . as the proper designation of the market"[99] – the conclusion that Owen likewise reaches when considering these free speech concerns.

Owen's intellectually elegant argument provides, I believe, the only available support for the DI's approach of ignoring market shares. The argument fails, however, for two reasons. First, although less important here, his claims concerning potential achievements of the unregulated "marketplace" of ideas are at best naïve. The view that the unregulated marketplace of ideas can be expected to arrive at anything reasonably treated as "truth" is simply implausible unless the result, whatever it is, is simply defined as "truth" by fiat – that is, because it resulted from this process. Then, however, the question turns to why the different "truth" resulting from some better designed process – for example, processes in which people were more equally able to participate – would not be preferable. Only misguided premises concerning the objectivity of truth, combined with extreme assumptions about the extent of human rationality, would justify a belief in the routine superiority of an unregulated marketplace of ideas for the purposes of reaching truth. Actually, people's views of truth and value normally reflect an inevitably complex and contextual combination of self-interest, tradition, and the receipt of psychological stimuli routinely manipulated by advocates, advertisers, and public relations experts at least as much as their views of truth reflect the rational power of arguments. In many electoral campaigns, for example, reversing the expenditures of two candidates would often also reverse the outcome.

I and many others have critiqued the marketplace metaphor based on the above points.[100] I further argued that the central justification for the constitutional status of *free speech* is captured not by the marketplace metaphor but rather by a commitment to respect individual liberty. Similarly, the societal *need* for a constitutional guarantee of free speech might be better captured by the image of the "dissenter," whose contribution to the social fabric Steve Shiffrin has so well portrayed.[101] (In contrast, the instrumental, democratic rationale for a constitutionalized *free press* rules out censorship but supports conscious structuring of the media marketplace to improve the media's overall quality and democratic efficaciousness.) Any realistic assessment of communications must recognize that power within the marketplace of ideas, power that reflects expenditures, ideological appeal, and various often unpredictable contextual considerations, will affect audience conclusions as much as will the wisdom of the offered messages. Of course, law should not restrict the views introduced into the marketplace – this is basis of the constitutional objection to censorship. However, ignoring media entities' power or influence, which is (imperfectly) measured by audience shares, is not simply naïve but an obfuscation. Different structures inevitably produce different subjective and social views, different "truths," but often – in the university, in courts, in legislatures, at board meetings, and in other collective projects about which people care – groups adopt formal or implicit regulations of speech in ways thought to improve resulting decisions' rationality, fairness, and wisdom. Any hope for the marketplace of ideas to lead to better conclusions depends on a structure that promotes more rational, inclusive, and insightful discourse. There is absolutely no reason to expect that an unregulated marketplace of ideas will lead to as wise or as good "truths" as it would if subject to thoughtful and democratic structuring – for example, structures that more widely distribute power within this marketplace. As long as purposeful suppression of views is (constitutionally) outlawed, purposeful, democratically supported interventions should be seen as less dangerous than the graver consequences expected from automatic reliance on nonintervention.

A second problem, though related, is even more fundamental. Owen's argument simply ignores the noncommodified, democratic, process, and distributive values that chapter 1 offers as the key reasons to object to ownership concentration. Basically, Owen swallows whole the view that the relevant values are those connected to commodity consumption (or, more specifically, commodity availability – although he labels these commodities "ideas"). He quotes as a major conceptual advance the suggestion that the value of diversity lies in the fact that "the greater the variety or breadth of media content, the greater the probability that *media consumers* can obtain utility or gratification from that content."[102] Even if ownership restrictions do not best further the instrumental value of providing for consumer satisfaction – though I argue that an unregulated market predictably fails to provide what consumers want[103] – Owen's claim simply ignores the noncommodified values that provide the basis for the central arguments for restrictions on media ownership. These noncommodified values make the distribution of power or influence – market shares – within the public sphere crucial.

This chapter has argued that popular perceptions are right to see the mass media as obviously and undesirably concentrated. Admittedly, there is an alternative perspective from which this is not true and that, in fact, finds that we currently have and will foreseeably continue to have an abundance of separately owned media. From this alternative perspective, regulation of ownership beyond that currently provided by antitrust law is at least unnecessary, probably undesirable.

This alternative perspective often does not stack up well against the facts of media concentration. It typically invokes a presently dominant but improperly narrow conception of antitrust law. Most important, however, this alternative perspective fails normatively. It, as well as the most prominent version of a broadened conception of antitrust law, fails to recognize the central democratic and noncommodified values justifying restrictions on media ownership outlined in chapter 1. Rejection of the main tenants of this alternative – and exploring its lacuna – has been the subject of this chapter. Nevertheless, the scholars who have offered the views rejected here have also suggested three additional reasons for finding media concentration unobjectionable. These reasons are the subject of the next two chapters.

THREE

Not a Real Problem: The Market or the Internet Will Provide

This chapter addresses two additional arguments – a market thesis and an Internet thesis – offered by those who reject current popular worries about media concentration. Their two arguments are: As long as traditional antitrust laws are enforced, the free market leads even large media entities to provide properly for audiences or, in any event, denies them any real power in the public sphere. Second, the Internet eliminates any reasons to object to media concentration. Each assertion is considered in turn.

THE MARKET CONTROLS AND PROVIDES

Ubiquitous among the many people who have a virtually mystical faith in free markets is the belief that within the market the consumer is sovereign.[1] Firms compete to give the consumer what she wants. Given this belief, it would seem to follow that liberal interventionism must be paternalistic or worse (e.g., rent-seeking). If the market is left unregulated, firms purportedly prosper only by giving consumers what they want – or, more precisely, what they want given their resource constraints and given a particular, contestable, commodified conception of "want." Firms that fail to do this – for example, because they are not good at it or because they try to do something else – will not succeed in the market. Bankruptcy quickly looms. If descriptively right, this first claim leads to a second: firms themselves have no real power; they must do what the market compels – which, according to the first claim, is to serve the consumer. Thus, there are two claims: that firms actually provide what people want and that firms (acting within the law) have no real power to do anything else.

Though the second point follows as a corollary of the first, the second could be true even if the first were not. "Market failures" (where the market does not successfully bring all the true costs and benefits of what the firm does to bear on its decision making) can direct firms to provide other than what people want even though the market still operates coercively on the firm. For example, in a realm without laws restricting pollution, the market might lead all manufacturers to produce more pollution and more of the goods they manufacture than they would if the amount that people would pay to reduce pollution could be brought to bear on their production decisions. In this case, the market would control without leading to consumers getting what they want. Then, only the second claim would be true.

This distinction between the two claims is important for policy purposes. If the first is true, it would undermine a main legitimate rationale for interventionist policies – specifically, for all policies that aim at promoting general consumer welfare. Even then, of course, interventionist policies might still be justified on distributive or community self-definitional grounds. But even if the first welfare-maximizing claim is false, the second premise – that the market controls and leaves the firm little discretion – could be true. In this scenario, there would be policy concerns about relying on the market but, maybe, little obvious reason for a policy concern about ownership distribution. Thus, for this chapter, the second claim is crucial. Although implicitly discussed earlier, the claim of consumer sovereignty – that the media supply what the audience demands – is so common, I here rehearse arguments from chapters 1 and 2 that show why both claims, though with emphasis on the second, are predictably and factually wrong.

The first claim (welfare maximization) fails because of huge and predictable market failures that result in firms not producing the media products that people want.[2] Major positive and negative externalities of different media products lead to charging people much less or much more for media products than they would if the media seller were charged for all the product's costs and compensated for all its benefits. Market determination of content systematically leads to too much production and distribution of content that has negative externalities and too little of content that has positive externalities. In addition are consequences related to the peculiar economic nature of intellectual "property." High first copy, low subsequent copy costs of media products create market dynamics that result in insufficient creation of particular types of media content. These two economic facts, plus several others, explain why media markets systematically fail to provide efficiency or welfare maximization, which market advocates regularly confuse with the profit maximization that these markets do encourage.[3] This divergence between serving consumers and serving corporate profits, between welfare maximization and profit maximization, provided chapter 1's third reason to recommend ownership dispersal: a belief that dispersal would more likely locate ownership in the hands of people less dominantly profit-oriented. This ownership policy aim, however, would be irrelevant if the second claim, that the market denies firms meaningful freedom of choice as to content, were true.

The second point, the "market determination thesis," has considerable pedigree even beyond the free market fundamentalism where it now seems most at home. The thesis constitutes a descriptive point of agreement between conservative economists, Max Weber[4] and many systems theorists following in his wake, and traditional Marxists – though these three groups differ in their evaluative assessment. The descriptive claim is simple: A competitive market structure generates pressures that dictate the behavior of enterprises operating in that market. To survive, a market participant needs to capture at least enough revenue to replace its capital – that is, it must at least cover its costs. The market-based firm must try to fulfill money-backed preferences of its customers as cheaply as possible – or, more specifically, at least as cheaply as do its competitors. If it fails to do this, it will lose its customers, thereby losing the revenue to cover its costs. This market dynamic enforces profit-maximizing behavior, thereby denying the enterprise any freedom except the freedom to try to be as profitable, as responsive to effective consumer demands, as possible. Consistent failure to achieve this market-dictated goal eventually means bankruptcy. Escape from the iron cage of rationality is impossible.

In the picture painted by the market determination thesis, real freedom of choice exists only in the realm of consumption – the realm Weber described as the household, which for *these* purposes is roughly comparable with Jurgen Habermas's concept of the lifeworld, where people individually choose on the basis of their values and coordinate behavior on the basis of discussion rather than through system-steering mechanisms such as money.[5] As noted, market advocates often praise the enforced responsiveness to consumer demands, sometimes asserting that it leads to allocating resources to their highest or best use. Radical critics often criticize particular (alienated) behavior dictated by (and distributive results produced by) this structure as well as the (false) needs or desires structurally generated. Putting aside their debate, the important point on which the market advocates and critics seem to agree is structural – whenever this market dynamic operates, the identity of the owners makes little difference.

To be more precise, those presenting this account recognize that some owners do not perform as the market dictates. Some may be naïve, stupid, or venial. Thus, it matters whether ownership is in their hands. The structural claim can only be that *over time* market dynamics educate the naïve, weed out the stupid, and defang the venial. The market leads eventually to the same (optimal) production irrespective of any initially assumed set of owners. In the long run, the market works to give us the media that best reflects people's market-expressed preferences – regardless of whether this cultural or political result is to be praised or condemned. If this market determination thesis is right, it would seem to imply that the distribution of media ownership does not create a problem of undemocratic or otherwise dangerous concentration of power because, at least over time, the market, not the owner, will largely determine the content of media production and distribution.

For present purposes, I do not dispute that this description of market dynamics, shared by conservative economists, Weberians, and Marxists, is generally true – that is, true in many circumstances.[6] Given my concession, unless this analysis of market dynamics is for some reason relevantly wrong in the media context, a policy concern with "who owns the media" is misguided. Therefore, a defense of a concern with media power as a justification for dispersing ownership beyond that accomplished through normal, proper application of antitrust laws requires some critique of this market determination thesis in the media context. Putting aside claims that this thesis is wrong everywhere, I consider three media-specific explanations for why it is relevantly wrong here.

First, entrepreneurial judgment will create variations in firms' content decisions. Even if the market effectively enforced a profit orientation, prospectively identifying the profit-maximizing content is an exceedingly difficult and continuing task. Even if all Hollywood studio heads sought only to maximize profits and would willingly sacrifice (all?) other values in the attempt, they hardly know how. Different content strategies are constantly tested. A decision maker's one correct decision does not mean that her next guess will be so. Different owners or managers constantly make quite different calculations. Each wrong guess deviates from market determination. To survive, a firm only needs to do roughly as well at making guesses as most others. Among owners who are roughly equally, but not perfectly, successful in identifying consumer preferences, their biases, which reflect their identities, will strongly influence the direction of their errors of judgments. This fact means that the distribution of ownership will affect the tilt of political or cultural biases or orientations that control the deviations of media content from that favored by consumer choice. The important point here is that normal entrepreneurial error leaves considerable room for different owners to make determinative content choices, choices that may be influenced in part by other goals such as personal ideology or by unconscious biases reflecting the same ideologies, without seriously sacrificing the profits needed to avoid bankruptcy. For this reason, the distribution of ownership matters.

The significance of this discretion implicit in entrepreneurial judgments is intensified by two related considerations. If some owners (or managers) are comparatively better than their competitors at finding profitable strategies, their success finances the option of "subsidizing" their other, non-profit-maximizing aims, aims that often involve choices about content. If either Rupert Murdoch or Silvio Berlusconi is good at being profitable, this merely increases the resources he can spend on being ideological. In addition, the market determination thesis is, at most, a claim about the long term. The ubiquitousness of judgmental errors increases the length of the short term, which can be relatively long – years or decades. This "short term" is obviously long enough to play a significant historical role in the lives of people or nations. Media owners' ideological or cultural choices may not be effectively profit-maximizing, but if they come sufficiently close, and especially if others are making errors, these owners' could still survive long enough to greatly and unequally distort the democratic public sphere.

Second, chapter 2 described circumstances where power over content may exist even if power over price does not. The high first copy, low subsequent copy feature of media products means that these products are in a crucial way similar to public goods. Given insufficient price discrimination, many media products will not exist even if they would produce more value (as measured by people's willingness to pay) than they cost. Those that do exist will not be equally satisfying to different people. Often one of several possible equilibria with very different media content could exist. Existence of any of various products could be profitable, but the nature of monopolistic competition sometimes means that only one can succeed. The most obvious example is in respect to daily newspapers, which in most American cities constitute a local monopoly. The town will usually support only one daily newspaper, no matter whether it has a Republican or Democratic orientation – leaving the choice of orientation to the owner of the prevailing paper. In fact, the owner may be able to make the choice without affecting profits. A change in content orientation will often cause some loss and some gain of customers, with those lost no longer being (well) served by any producer. If those lost and those gained are relatively equal in number (or purchasing power), the owner's choice of preferred editorial slant would hardly affect profits. Here, ownership clearly matters – it comes with great power within the public sphere. The more concentrated this power, the more troublesome from the perspective of either demagogic abuse or democratic distribution.

Third, and related to the previous point, is probably the most significant reason why the market does not determine behavior in the media realm even if it does so in many other contexts. Media markets typically involve a special sort of monopolistic competition[7] – unique products that do not have virtually identical substitutes and that are sold at a point where the marginal cost is less than the selling price (due to the high first copy, low subsequent copy costs). Of course, in this type of market, some products barely survive. And without adequate and relatively costless price discrimination, some cannot be profitably produced even though they would produce more value than they cost. More important here, however, is that successful media products are typically capable of producing monopoly profits. Even without barriers to full-scale market competition, many media entities are (potentially) extraordinarily profitable. Chapter 1 described the extensive empirical evidence of this profitability. Both daily newspapers and broadcasters are much, much more profitable (on an operating basis) than the typical publically owned manufacturing company. That chapter relied on this point to explain why it is important to get ownership in the hands of those committed to quality journalism and cultural creativity. Here the relevance of this point is more basic: this profitability allows for choice. Owners can take the potential operating profits out, generating unusually high rates of return, which is the primary accusation lodged at corporate newspaper chains and cost-cutting network TV news divisions. Alternatively, owners can "spend" these excess profits on public interest commitments to quality, on keeping prices low[8] (an availability that importantly contributes to the public sphere), or on content reflective of their personal ideological biases. These options explain the error of the market determination thesis. "Potential" profits allow for content choices on grounds other than profit maximization, with the owner essentially spending the "supra-competitive" returns on content choices.

Since chapter 1 already developed this point, one further example and a further note on the daily newspaper context should suffice here. André Schiffrin described how ownership has mattered in the book publishing world. He claims that, in the past, "serious" publishers found and then maintained the loyalty of very profitable authors.[9] The publishers would self-consciously use profits from these authors to sustain "good" but unprofitable books. Schiffrin proceeds to describe the elimination of this practice by the newly merged, huge corporate owners of the major publishing houses. Many, like Random House, now demand that "each book make money on its own and that one title should no longer be allowed to subsidize another."[10]

Both the old practice and the change described by Schiffrin are interesting. The standard model of pure competition expects firms in industries with a relatively large number of players, such as book publishing,[11] to be forced by competitive pressures to adopt a profit-maximizing strategy to survive. However, with monopoly products – which by law includes any copyrighted item – the potential exists for either the author or the publisher (or both) to obtain monopoly profits or, alternatively, to spend these potential profits on valued performances. In Schiffrin's tale, in former times authors who "make it" commercially often remained "loyal" to – that is, subsidized – publishing houses, thereby either unwittingly or consciously transferring some potential profits to these businesses and serving any public interest served by that publisher. Likewise, once having these potential monopoly profits, the publisher could choose either to take them out as profits or to use them to promote a more literate book culture. Ownership mattered! And Schiffrin reported that many publishers, with whom successful, loyal authors shared their monopoly product, actually decided to make non-profit-maximizing choices. Publishers consciously used this revenue to support serious but nonprofitable entries in their lists.[12] Like many of their "serious" authors, these publishers saw themselves as "paying" themselves, not in high salaries or fancy executive suites, but in the "currency" of freedom to publish the books that they wanted to publish.[13] This freedom was possible only because of the combination of the monopoly nature of the media product and the cooperation between loyal authors and publishers. Of course, some market fundamentalists might object that these non-profit-maximizing "expenditures" on editor-chosen books are socially wasteful. They are wrong. That might be true if profit maximization equaled welfare-maximizing media production. But it does not – as chapter 1's discussion of the various versions of market failure shows.

For reasons including considerable positive externalities associated with "good" books, the older behavior Schiffrin described was likely to move book publishing closer to (even if still far from) a social optimum.

Beneficial uses of potential monopoly profits are hardly guaranteed. Corporate conglomerate owners of the major publishing houses now dominate the industry.[14] Schiffrin claims that they differ from the former publishers in their priorities.[15] These conglomerate owners squeeze much higher rates of return out of their monopoly properties – targeting rates of 12 to 15 percent, where 4 percent had formerly been the industry average. In doing so, Schiffrin argues that these conglomerates have also abandoned earlier publishers' commitment to making books readily available to audiences by keeping prices down.[16] Profit maximization, however, is only one possible exercise of the choice available in this industry. While this corporate bottom-line goal now apparently dominates, according to Schiffrin, some potential profits are also sometimes spent to satisfy the new owners' political values, reflecting a new "intolera[nce of] dissenting opinions" and generally more conservative political views.[17] Note, however, that the complaint in this chapter is not that ownership uses potential profits for ideological purposes or that the ideology of conglomerate owners is conservative or intolerant but that the power to direct content in this way is concentrated rather than broadly distributed.

The opportunity to serve alternative or multiple objectives is even greater in some media sectors. As noted, high first copy costs create the conditions likely to produce local daily newspaper monopolies. This trend toward local monopolies is exacerbated by a general lack of dramatic product differentiation among papers, possibly due to the influence of advertising, which makes maximizing audience size, not maximizing the satisfaction (and willingness to pay) of smaller audiences, the most profitable strategy. Having more readers, not higher paying readers who want a particular orientation in the news content, gains more advertising revenue. Typically, an objective, nonpartisan (de-differentiating) voice that speaks equally to all segments of the community best serves this aim.[18] The result is a pattern of mostly one-newspaper cities. Despite very high "monopoly" profits,[19] potential competing papers find it virtually impossible to challenge the local monopolist. Considerable choice is then available to the surviving owners as to how to "spend" potential monopoly profits. Assuming that this potential is not simply wasted by an inefficient management, the owners can decide whether these potential profits will be "cashed out," used to provide for greater access to the paper by pricing it below the profit-maximizing level,[20] used to pay for quality journalism, or used to support other (often political or ideological) agendas of the owner.

Market dynamics push toward the first choice. Using calculations that capitalize a paper's potential earning, those most willing and best able to pursue profit maximization will typically be able to pay the most for an existing monopoly paper – but this higher price will then lock the purchaser into choices directed at achieving this profit-maximizing potential. Original or long-term owners have much more choice about journalistic practices. If, however, financial value becomes crucial because, for example, family heirs need to pay estate taxes or simply lose interest in the paper and prefer to cash out, a transfer of control to buyers prepared to favor profits over quality journalism or ideology becomes likely. This dynamic explains the continual complaint that new owners, especially the publicly traded chain corporations, impose higher and higher profit rate expectations on their local management, leading to the steady deterioration of journalistic quality.[21] To say, as is often said, that editors remain free as long as they meet the "numbers" – the corporate-demanded level of operating profits – is not saying much. They are free to provide as much quality as their "budget" permits, but much lower quality at much lower circulation levels than the paper could support. More to the point here, this dynamic illustrates the incorrectness of the market determination thesis. The market itself does not force this profit-maximization choice on media owners.[22] Rather, who controls and decides on priorities makes a huge difference. Contrary to the market determination thesis, which reflects the standard economic model, monopolistic competition allows the owner to choose among profit maximization, ideology, product quality (here journalistic quality), and greater – even if unprofitable – circulation.

Despite its impressive credentials, neither observation nor economic theory supports the market determination thesis's applicability to the media. Most successful firms engaged in producing and providing the public with media content have considerable choice over what they can successfully provide. Free market fundamentalists may continue to hold on to the premise that media firms operating in a market will provide precisely what audiences want and that if critics do not like the results, these critics' paternalistic complaints should be with public tastes, not media firms. There is, however, simply no reason to believe this claim. All evidence points the other way. Ownership (or control) provides for choice that can be used well or badly.

THE INTERNET AS A SOLUTION

Benjamin Compaine asserts that, at least from the appropriate perspective of the media as a whole, "there can be little disagreement that there is more competition than ever among media players" and that this point is obvious on the basis of "a single word, Internet."[23] Compaine ends his book with a dramatic statement: "Concentrated media power is breaking up."[24] As he sees it, the Internet changes everything. It erodes old bottlenecks, blurs the lines among media, creates convergence, makes "conventional industry classifications decreasingly relevant," and lays the foundation for "diversity, accessibility and affordability."[25]

Bruce Owen distinguishes two perspectives from which to evaluate concentration: an economic and a political perspective.[26] According to Owen, from the economic perspective, antitrust law purportedly provides a remedy for any undue concentration. In a long discussion (critiqued in chapter 2), he argues that from the political, or marketplace of ideas, perspective, the essential concern is availability – and lack of outsider blockage – of diverse content (that anyone wants to present) to anyone who wants it. If no one wants to provide or receive content reflecting a particular viewpoint, a democracy (and usually the society more generally) should not bemoan the fact that the view will not be considered. Owen then concludes that "evidence that people . . . use the Internet to acquire ideas and information effectively ends the discussion of the media concentration problem from a political perspective." Owen does admit that this conclusion would not follow if Internet gatekeepers limit access. He argues, however, that the combination of consumer demand for unrestricted access and competition "ensure that service provider access barriers cannot succeed."[27] Although recognizing that media concentration is still a problem in some arenas, another prominent communications economist, Eli Noam, concludes more generally that "[i]n the cyber-media future, scarcity and gatekeepers will be largely eliminated" and that "it is unlikely that media conglomerates combining all aspects of media will be successful in the long term."[28]

These comments illustrate a common refrain among deregulatory advocates that goes something like this: "In the past scarcity and economics may have impeded speech freedom and even justified some regulation. But the Internet is revolutionary! The era of communication poverty is history." Much like investors in the dot-com bubble of the late 1990s, these free market advocates fashionably invoke the Internet as eliminating all old problems.

This ubiquitous invocation of the Internet is misleading when not simply wrong. Most fundamentally, after recognizing that the Internet brings many changes, the question is whether these changes eliminate the reasons to be concerned with media ownership concentration. This question requires focus on the conceptual issue – what are the reasons for concern? These reasons determine what empirical evidence would count to show whether the Internet eliminates any problem with media ownership concentration. Before turning to the central issue, however, some observations about the Internet's current or predictable impact on media availability and consumption can provide a useful context for discussion. These observations consider: (1) some transformative consequences of the Internet for the public sphere, (2) the Internet's impact on media availability, (3) its consequences for the economics of the media, and, more important (4) its consequences for concentration and diversity of old media, new media, and "journalistic" media.

INTERNET EFFECTS

The Internet undoubtedly has transformative effects on the public sphere that potentially – or already – have great political and democratic significance. For example, Web logs (or "blogs") that form the so-called blogosphere provide important new loci for public discourse in a world where such loci in practice may have been declining. Also, the Internet surely has increased grassroots, distributed political as well as personal communications among those already organized or connected in the offline world. It has increased the capacity of organizations to reach out to new audiences and of individuals to find organizations they consider significant. In doing this, the Internet already has become an important democratic tool. It played a central role in temporarily propelling Howard Dean to the front of the race for the Democratic Party's 2004 presidential nomination. Even more significantly, it – as well as other "new" technologies such as cell phones – played a key role in helping to organize street demonstrations that have toppled governments elsewhere in the world.[29] That is, some uses of the Internet have helped to spread real political power to a broader popular base – power exercised in the street or in aid of grassroots fund raising. Moreover, bloggers have propelled issues, ranging from President Clinton's affair with Monica Lewinsky[30] to Dan Rather's allegedly improperly made report on President Bush's National Guard service,[31] to the political forefront. Whether such blogger power is more likely to thematize diversionary or serious issues and whether it is more likely to improve or skew public debate and the identity of the issues that become salient in the public sphere, as compared with that provided by professional journalists and media organizations, I venture no opinion here. Still, these communications-order gains (when they are gains) are different from – are complementary to, and may often be in part dependent on – the more traditional performance of the mass media. My tentative suggestion is that these particular developments have no bearing on any debate about the dangers or objections to media ownership concentration.

Compaine is clearly right, in at least some sense, when he says that "[t]he difference between the Internet and newspapers, books, records or television is that [the Internet] can be all those things."[32] The content provided by these other media can now often be received online in digital format. He is also surely right that the Internet requires some rethinking of when concentration exists. That point is mundane; technological change regularly affects the relevance of particular concentrations. Before movies, a person could see a dramatization only by attending a live performance. Before television, a person could see a movie only by attending a screening, usually at a movie theater. A firm that owned all the local theaters could determine which movies people in that locale could see. Today, a movie may also be available on free over-the-air television, pay cable, satellite video broadcasts, videotape or DVD rental or purchase, and, either now or soon, Internet streaming. Putting aside cases where the "format is the message" – as drive-in movies were for teenagers when I was a kid[33] – concentration within one traditional segment does not necessarily imply concentration in the provision of particular content. Substitutability is mostly an empirical issue and usually a matter of degree. The question remains: does the widespread availability of the Internet to both speakers and audiences create an abundance and convergence of media entities that erases any worries about concentration within the communications industry as a whole (all media entities), within a particular sphere (e.g., newspapers, television, cable, radio, or movies), within a particular geographic space, or within segments (e.g., delivery services or content categories such as entertainment, children's programming, country or classical music, textbooks, or news) considered more functionally?

Consider possible consequences of the Internet that could be relevant for this inquiry into the issue of concentration. Digital technologies can significantly reduce the cost or difficulty of making some media content.

These costs, for example, can sometimes be reduced due to use of online data searches and acquisition, digital cameras, or computer-based editing devices. Yochai Benkler has discussed how distributed knowledge within a networked world can make voluntaristic production methods as efficient as or more efficient than the hierarchical, commercial production practices that have long dominated.[34] Newly credentialed, branded forms of news media operating on a peer-to-peer basis may be possible.[35] To the extent that these projects develop and eventually serve the same function as traditional mass media, the development should be welcomed on grounds of a democratic distribution of opportunities to participate in the public sphere and should be encouraged by favorable legal rules.[36] Nevertheless, as long as traditional news and cultural media continue to dominate, as they do now, in performing (even if inadequately) their traditional roles, the mere possibility of this development has no obvious bearing on existing issues of concentration.

Despite these contributions as a facilitator of or input for journalism, the Internet largely operates as a distribution system – and consequences of its performance of this distributive function obviously require attention. The Internet enables easier pull (e.g., search engine), easier push (e.g., spam), and more routine distribution uses (e.g., regularly visiting ISP or other sites, blogs, or bulletin boards, having online subscriptions, joining group e-mailing lists, or sending individualized email). In themselves, distribution systems do not create goods – in this case, communicative content.

The Internet is often said to create a convergence of media forms – which makes sense if what is meant is that a person can obtain many media forms online while previously each had to be obtained separately. This does not support Compaine's claims as long as the policy issue raised by concentration is undue, undemocratic power within a particular content sphere or even the existence and nature of diversity. Rather, Internet-generated media *convergence* is somewhat analogous to retailing convergence within ubiquitous Wal-Mart superstores. There, a customer might be able to buy either a winter coat or a country ham. The superstore itself normally creates neither. Nor does the existence of Wal-Mart make winter coats the *equivalent* of or a substitute for country hams even if it is the place one goes for either. Moreover, the existence of Wal-Mart does not assure the creation of (good) country hams. Sure, the Internet has made access to various media products or communications much easier. But monopoly or otherwise undue power could still exist over creation of any type of content delivered by the Internet just as monopoly power might exist over any product sold at department stores. Like the coat and ham at Wal-Mart, an "online" report on peace negotiations in the Middle East is not particularly competitive with *The Simpsons* or *Desperate Housewives* in most people's preference functions. Neither the existence of competition in making nor the ease of online availability of both sit-coms and news programs online should reduce the democratic significance of concentration if only one or a few firms provide quality, well-researched, information about, for example, the Middle East (or about local government or about corporate affairs).

As someone who frequently checks both Alternet and the BBC online sites and whose friends check and on occasion report back to me on what they find on other sites, I recognize that the Internet does add to effective diversity. It does this primarily by dramatically reducing the time, cost, and consequent geographic limits of *distribution*. The convergence in methods of delivery, or the separate point, the greater ease of obtaining access, hardly means that the Internet creates a convergence in *creating* particular categories of content. As a converged distributive system, the Internet does not itself guarantee, within a single content category, multiple quality content creators from whom recipients can choose. Thus, a significant contextual issue is: how does the Internet affect creation, and how does it affect usage (especially consumption) of varying content? And, then, how do the answers to these questions affect the concerns with media ownership concentration?

Abstract economics predicts that the Internet's dramatic reduction of distribution costs will generate two simultaneous, but curiously opposing, consequences for media content. Which, if either, of these two effects will dominate may well depend on legal policy as well as on people's preferences and on technological developments. First is a simple diversity or "abundance effect." Reduced costs of getting content into an audience member's hands (or before her eyes) is likely to lead more people to create and offer potentially more diverse content to the public. That is, reduced distribution costs lower a significant barrier to entry into the commercial content market. Equally important, reduced delivery costs can enable a dramatic increase in opportunities for noncommercial and voluntary noncommodified content creators. The last fact is basically the story of blogging. Finally, as with any lowering of costs of providing a product, reduced delivery costs can result in lower prices for the ultimate consumer. The predictable result of lower prices is an increased total demand for the now less expensive media products. That is, reduced delivery costs can greatly increase participation in content creation, availability of diverse content, and total consumption of (or time spent on) this content.

Second is a more complicated logic of a potential "concentration effect." Any decline in delivery and copy costs intensifies the economic incentive to use (more) resources in making a more widely appealing first copy. The reduced distribution cost means that more of the potential returns from selling to the audience (or selling the audience to advertisers) is available to cover the cost of content creation. Each added audience member, obtained by producing a higher quality (or otherwise more appealing) first copy, is now more valuable to the seller/creator, leading to more investment in first copies. But note the consequence. The increased expenditures on first copies, as long as they do not necessitate a higher consumer price, tend to concentrate the audience on these "better" products. Thus, reduced delivery costs could cause a reduction of the number of diverse products – especially commercial products – that are available. In contrast, when delivery costs are higher, increasing the audience for a particular product is comparatively less valuable (because a higher portion of the audience's value is lost in paying for delivery). Instead of leading to efforts to maximize audience size (which translates into less products and more concentration), high delivery costs create some incentive to respond more specifically to relatively intense, more varied needs or interests for which there may be smaller audience segments but for which individual audience members will pay more to have satisfied. At least in the commercial realm, higher delivery costs predictably lead to greater diversity and more products being designed to reflect more specific audience desires. Higher delivery costs, in a sense, eliminate some of the economic advantages of mass production.

This tendency of lower delivery costs to lead to concentration can be expressed more formally. In this illustration, $F =$ resources spent on First copy costs, $\pi =$ profit, $A =$ Audience size, $P =$ Price (i.e., revenue per audience member), and $V =$ Variable costs per audience member, of which distribution and copy costs are a substantial part. I treat as an adequate description of the firm's costs: $F + V$. (In this model, other so-called fixed costs other than first copy costs can be assimilated to either V or F, but can be held constant and therefore ignored here.) Profit equals revenues minus costs, or $\pi = A \times P - (F + A \times V)$. The expenditures on first copy are seen more clearly by transposing the equation above to $F + \pi = A \times P - A \times V$, or

$$F + \pi = A(P - V)$$

Several observations about this formulation are pertinent. For a firm to be a going concern, $P - V$ must be positive, that is, it must be the case that $P > V$. Normally, it can be assumed that as audience increases, variable costs per audience member will either not be affected or will go down. If so, and if price stays constant, then audience should go up as first copy expenditures go up. That is, if P stays constant and V does not rise, A goes up as F goes up. This simple proposition follows from the fact that if the price is kept constant but more is spent on creating the product – which normally results in a better product – more people are likely to buy the presumptively "better" product. This obviously creates some incentive to spend more on F and attract larger audiences. The larger audience then allows for further increases in either F or π. This tendency is the "spiral effect" that often is said to lead to a monopoly for local daily newspapers.[37] As long as increasing F, which causes some increase in A, results in a greater increase of the right side of the equation, the firm will keep increasing F. Equilibrium occurs when an increase in F, although increasing A, does not increase $A(P - V)$ as much as the increase in F. That is, expenditures on F should increase as long as but only as long as $\Delta F < \Delta A(P - V)$. Eventually, a profit maximizing equilibrium should be reached. At that point, a further increase in audience would be too small to offset the increase in F necessary to obtain this increase in audience. That is, there will be an equilibrium point where $\Delta F = \Delta A(P - V)$.

The key change attributed above to the introduction of the Internet is that it causes a decrease in distribution costs, that is, a decrease in V. In leading up to the issue of how the Internet can be expected to affect audience concentration, the first question is how the Internet-induced decrease in V affects this equilibrium point. The equation indicates the obvious answer. Since V is now less, $P - V$ is larger than before. The larger $P - V$ means that in the equation, $F + \pi = A(P - V)$, the amount that the audience must increase, ΔA, to pay for a given increase in first copy costs, ΔF, goes down. The firm now has an incentive to increase expenditures on F beyond the prior equilibrium point, since this incentive exists even when it produces smaller audience increases than before. However, this greater expenditure on F results in a larger audience than before. The new equilibrium occurs at higher levels of both F and A. That is, a reduction in delivery costs, an important component of the variable cost, should increase the incentive to spend on F, the first copy, with the result that the media product will obtain a larger audience. Consequently, the Internet's decrease in delivery costs could lead to an increase in audience size for the media's largest products; that is, it could lead to audience concentration.

Other factors also predictably operate to concentrate Internet audiences. Probably the most important are network effects and branding, which were emphasized by Lincoln Dahlberg in describing the "corporate colonization of online attention."[38] As James Hamilton explains, both of these factors are especially important because media content is an "experience good" – that is, a context where "to know the good is to consume the good."[39] The now conventional observation about networks is that often the value of a good increases as others buy or possess the same good. Telephones, for example, are more valuable because people whom one might want to call also have telephones. Media content often operates similarly. Many people find last night's sitcom or this morning's news item more personally valuable to the extent that they can discuss it with others who have also seen or heard it. Likewise, people may experience a social or other cost from not knowing what "everyone" else knows. "Funneling" tendencies are an additional sort of network effect that often exist online. Google's search matrix prioritizes content according to how many other people have linked to the site – that is, Google intensifies a good's perceived value because of other people valuing it. Finally, branding should be particularly effective in concentrating consumers in relation to "experience goods." That is, if you do not know the good until consuming it – and even then have little basis for checking its quality (e.g., its accuracy), the good's reputation has considerable value. Reputation substitutes for lack of (or provides) preconsumption knowledge. And reputation is precisely what branding purports to allow a consumer to identify more easily.

Unsurprisingly, the *Digital Future Report* of the University of Southern California's Annenberg School Center for the Digital Future reports that Internet users are somewhat skeptical about whether online information is reliable – with the number who are skeptical possibly increasing with experience. It has never been the case that a person should believe a claim merely because it was published. Still, the obvious ease of publishing anything one wants online and the lack of controls reflecting either the standards of professional editors or the commercial incentive to maintain reputation make unknown sources found online particularly suspect. Predictably, the data in the *Digital Future Report* shows that the number of users who answer "yes" to the question of whether *most* of the information on the Internet is generally reliable and accurate declined from 56 percent in 2001 to 49 percent in 2003. More relevant to the branding point, however, is that 74 percent think that most or all information posted on established media or government Web sites is reliable and accurate but hardly 10 percent think so if it is an individual Web site.[40] That is, government and established media's branding seems successful. A person in search of reliable information will be much more likely to go to a site identified with the *New York Times* or CNN, for example, than one identified with an unknown individual, for example, identified as Ann's Blog. Moreover, although a search engine can help a person find information on a plethora of alternative sites, a person is likely, based on experience, to expect to find the reports she seeks on relevant "branded" sites even if it happens that Ann posted a report on the same subject on the same day. For example, a person would probably go to ESPN.com to find updated sports scores or to a BBC or CNN or *New York Times* site for news about Iraq. That is, channeling and branding contribute to concentration of audience attention.

Thus, the Internet should generate two opposing tendencies. On the one hand, lower distribution costs can facilitate the availability of new, more diversified commercial and noncommercial product offerings – what might be called its "diversity effect." On the other hand, these reduced "marginal" costs generate an incentive to make greater first copy expenditures that attract larger audiences, concentrating attention and thereby reducing the likelihood that small-audience content creators will succeed commercially. This second tendency, to increase concentration, might be called the "Hollywood effect." It corresponds to how Hollywood's capacity to spend huge amounts on the first copy long allowed it to dominate the world's movie industry.[41] The relative dominance of these competing tendencies is likely to vary depending on peculiarities of different content domains. I can offer a possible prediction, although one that could be foiled by various factors but that most likely will remain true at least without conscious policy intervention. The Internet is likely to lead to much more diverse content being more easily available to those who seek it and to many more sources of information (and opinion), but overall, concentration of audiences in the Internet world will be great and likely to be even greater than in the older offline world. For the moment, at least some evidence supports this prediction.

The Internet has led to a huge increase in the number of people who both try to communicate to the world and have the technological capacity to do so. In the past, most people could not realistically attempt to communicate regularly to the broader world. Most people did not own substantial media properties, nor had money to pay media entities

regularly to present their views, nor had the skills and resources to produce content regularly that media owners (or editors) would choose to
include. In numbers, the currently dominant form of "publishing" on the
Internet is "blogging." Although research by the Pew Internet & American Life Project found that even by November 2004, some 62 percent
of the approximately 120 million American Internet users did not have
a clear notion of what a blog was, at that time about 8 million of these
users claimed to have created a blog or Web-based diary accessible to
people the world over who have Internet connections[42] – though other
estimates of the number of Web logs exist. The *New York Times* in April
2005 referred to 10 million existing blogs;[43] a blog statistics site, Blog-
pulse, reports identifying over 17 million blogs (worldwide) in October
2005;[44] while Technorati claimed to be tracking 19.6 million blogs in
October 2005[45] and 24.9 million blogs in January 2006[46] – data that are
not so inconsistent given that the number of blogs has been reportedly
doubling roughly every five months.[47] Even though this rate of expansion is obviously unsustainable and somewhat greater than above reports
suggest, these data do indicate that my numbers will surely be out of date
by the time you read this.

It is another story when the question turns to how often these millions
of blog creators continue to post content or how often their blogs are
read by the 27 percent of Internet users who report that they read blogs[48]
or by the 9 percent who report regularly or sometimes reading political
blogs, blogs such as Daily Kos or Talking Points Memo or Instapundit.[49]
In a (nonrandom, volunteer participation) survey by Blogads of 17,000
generally heavy blog readers (median of ten hours a week reading blogs
and five or six blogs read a day), respondents were asked about each of the
forty-three most read blogs (those with reportedly 50,000 or more visits
a week) whether they read it twice daily or more, daily, weekly, monthly,
rarely, or never.[50] The most common answer to this question was "twice
daily or more" for three of the blogs, "rarely" for one blog, and never
for thirty-nine.[51] That is, concentration of audience attention seems
extreme – very heavy at the top of the most-read blogs with an incredibly
quick fall-off. Overall, these data suggest, first, a huge number of bloggers but, second, audiences concentrated heavily on only a few blogs.

Another statistics blog, The Truth Laid Bear (TTLB), provides data
on daily visits to the top 5,000 blogs it covers.[52] According to its data,
the top blog (Daily Kos) that it covered in late January 2005 reportedly
received 642,520 daily visits (interestingly down from 767,000 on a day in
October – but daily variations seem common and most widely viewed

blogs had an increase in daily visits during this period). A view of the concentration of audience attention (measured by visits) can be seen from Table 1. For comparison purposes, I have included for some of the ranks newspaper's average daily circulation, average daily readership, and online readership. Of course, for comparison, traffic measured as visits will overstate the number of unique visitors, given that some people will visit a blog multiple times during a day.

The data indicate, most importantly, that even though there are apparently millions of self-publishing bloggers, concentration of audience attention is extreme (and there is some evidence, not reported here, that this concentration is increasing). Of these millions of bloggers, most could probably reach larger audiences if they spent a couple of hours in the old-fashioned activity of distributing hand-bills in the town center – or, if allowed, at a shopping center.[53] Even better, if they really wanted to spread their views, they could become teachers or preachers (or journalists) and reach far larger audiences – and if good at the activity, they might even hold their audience's attention for much longer than does an average blog.

There is, however, an additional point to be made that is central here. The audience for blogs is not only concentrated, it seems to be much more concentrated – that is, have a steeper decline in audience – than is the audience for newspapers. This conclusion can be seen in the table by comparing the highest circulating paper and most visited site with the 100th highest in each category. Concentration of attention in newspaper was great – the top circulating paper had about twenty-one times the circulation as the 100th but not nearly as great as the concentration in blogs, where the top blog had almost eighty times the visits as the 100th ranked blog.

The above observation of huge concentration of attention in the blogosphere is only one perspective of how to measure concentration within a media realm and gives possibly the most conservative view of the extent of concentration in blog attention. The 100 daily newspapers with the highest circulation constitute about 7 percent of America's daily newspaper titles, while the 1,610 most visited blogs in the "ecosystem" of The Truth Laid Bear constitute 7 percent of the reportedly 23,000 plus sites that TTLB tracks.[54] Among this top 7 percent, the dropoff in visits is hugely greater among the blogs than it is in readership among newspapers, indicating much greater concentration among blogs. In the spring of 2006, the most read newspaper, USA Today, reportedly had just under 7 million daily readers, which was about thirty-one times

Table 1. *Web Log Visits and Rank vs. Newspaper Readership and Rank*

Web log rank[a]	Daily visits	Newspaper (at given rank)	Circulation[b]	Daily readership[c] (readership rank)	Online readership[d] (unique visitors)	Page views[e] (in millions)
1 (Daily Kos)	642,520	*USA Today*	2,154,539	7,080,055 (1)	9,731,225	133
2 (Overheard in UK)	457,291	*Wall St. J.*	2,091,062	5,147,255 (2)	2,491,772	47
3 (Gizmodo)	296,792	*NY Times*	1,118,565	5,043,815 (3)	12,765,423	453
4 (Defamer)	240,000	*LA Times*	914,584	2,392.096 (5)	4,307,571	48
5 (Gawker)	178,865	*Wash. Post*	732,872	1,817,325 (8)	7,838,720	135
11	102,896	*SF Chron.*	512,640	1,055,459 (16)	3,489,721	34
20	44,910	*Plain Dealer*	365,288	868,831 (20)	736,628	35
74	11,518	*Des Moines Reg.*	154,885	326,291 (75)	265,200	3
100	8,410	*Times (Wash.)*	102,255	263,386 (92)	1,138,612	9
626	1,000					
3148	100					

[a]Rank and daily visits data from http://www.truthlaidbear.com/TrafficRanking.php (accessed Jan. 25, 2006).

[b]Data from *Editor & Publisher International Year Book 2004* (referring to circulation as of Sept. 30, 2003).

[c]Data from Newspaper Association of American, Newspaper Audience Database (fall 2005 release), available at http://www.naa.org/nadbase/2005_NADbase_Report.pdf. Readership rank (number in parentheses) can be different from circulation rank.

[d]Data from ibid. The report says the "data . . . are based on Web usage during the month of July 2005." Though not entirely clear, this probably means that the totals refer to unique readers and pages viewed during the month.

[e]Data from ibid. The low readership of the online version of the *Wall Street Journal* presumably relates to it charging for access. I have no explanation for the high number of page views for the *Plain Dealer*.

the readership of the 100th ranked paper, *Florida Today*, at 226,000 readers. In contrast, Fark.com, the most visited blog listed by TTLB on June 7, 2006, with slightly over a million daily visits, was visited about 3,000 times as often as the blog at the bottom of this top 7 percent group, which received 350 daily visits. Moreover, since blogs tracked by TTLB are likely to be much more visited than the average blog, the drop-off rate among the top 7 percent of *all* blogs would be much, much greater. On a typical day, it is very likely that of the millions of blogs that reportedly exist – in early 2006 Technorati reported counting over 34 million blogs – over 99 percent will be lucky to receive one visit.

Below I offer a comparison of the concentration of online newspaper sites to the concentration of print editions that makes the same point: the online world tends to concentrate audiences. It also might be worth noting, given the regularly reported decline in newspaper readership, that the Newspaper Association of America found that "78 percent of adults in the top 50 markets read newspapers over the course of a week – representing 116 million readers" and in addition, "55 million [Internet] users . . . visited newspaper Web sites in November 2005," viewing 2.4 billion pages.[55]

In addition to rapid change in the "blogosphere," it should be recognized that the available data – gathered by different entities using different methodologies – is notoriously subject to question. For example, a study published by comScore purportedly based on actual monitoring of a panel of 1.5 million American Internet users gives information about which blogs are most popular. Although its data are very different from that provided by The Truth Laid Bear, the comScore data similarly shows a quite extreme concentration of audience attention.[56] ComScore reported that during the first quarter of 2005, the most visited site (Drudge Report) had 44 million visits (almost 500,000 a day on average), the second ranked site (Fark) had 10 million visits (about 110,000 a day), the third most-visited site (Gawker) had 4.1 million visits (about 46,000 a day), and the twentieth (Sportsbybrooks) had 711,000 visits (about 7,900 visits a day). Of the twenty most visited sites listed by comScore (based on its tracking of "actual" visits), only four (Boingboing, Engadget, Daily Kos, and Gizmodo) are among the twenty most popular sites listed by Technorati (based on links to other sites).[57] Drudge Report, the site reported by comScore reports to have over four times as many visits as any other site in the first quarter of 2005, was not included by Technorati as among the top 100 blogs (based on links to it by other blogs – although this may merely mean that link counts are a very poor measure of readership interest). Drudge Report was apparently not registered with TTLB, so there are no direct comparable data on site visits. But more troubling are direct comparisons of comScore's data with those reported by TTLB. (ComScore implicitly recognizes the statistical authoritativeness of both TTLB and Technorati by relying on them for some purposes.) Although comScore seems to be quite explicit about puffing the blogosphere for the purpose of generating interest among potential advertisers, thus creating a fear that it has an incentive to overstate blog readership, for those sites measured by both it and TTLB, comScore uniformly reported a much *lower* number of visits. TTLB measures visits only for blogs registered with it (according to comScore, TTLB measures 14,000 blogs, although, as noted above, other reports indicate that it covers 23,000). TTLB measured 767,000 daily visits to its most visited blog, the Daily Kos, in October 2005 (although only about 404,000 in April 2005).[58] Taking the lower April number, 404,000 per day, this still amounts to about 36 million visits a quarter (rounded to 90 days), while the comScore study listed Daily Kos as having less than 3 million visits (and less than 350,000 unique visitors) during the quarter – quite a disparity. Something seems wrong with the data.[59] Still, the general point remains. The data offered by comScore, like that offered by TTLB, suggest the same dramatic concentration of audience attention. According to comScore, the top blog has about a half a million visits a day, while the twentieth most visited blog receives less than 8,000 daily visits. That is, the most visited blog received over 60 times as many visits as the twentieth most visited blog. Compare this with the highest circulation newspaper, which has less than six times the 365,288 circulation of the twentieth ranked newspaper. Attention to blogs is simply not democratically (i.e., egalitarianly) distributed but is actually more extremely concentrated than is attention to other media.

Nevertheless, blogging and related Internet forms of communication are an increasingly important phenomenon. It would be a huge mistake to understate their potential contribution to the robustness of a democratic public sphere – to people's capacity to participate either as speakers or recipients of diverse content. However, unsurprisingly, the data suggest that extreme concentration apparently exists within the blog world. In any event, blogs' present or potential valuable role in the communications order may not reduce the reasons to object to concentration in the traditional news and entertainment (or cultural) media. The view of the Project for Excellence in Journalism (PEJ) is that, "for now, blogs are largely an echo chamber and commentary channel, rather than a 'news' source."[60] This may change over time, and in any event, this observation hardly means that blogs do not greatly enrich the communications order. But blogs may do so not by substituting for the crucial roles served by traditional media but rather by embodying greater participation in a public sphere. They also may have a positive impact on traditional media – sometimes scooping them, giving them new storylines that these traditional media find worth pursuing (or necessary to pursue – e.g., Monica Lewinsky), and making these traditional media more accountable.[61] In some circumstances, successful new online news media relying mainly on volunteers may be created – as illustrated by OhmyNews, a Korean online paper that relies largely on stories supplied by volunteer "reporters," that draws an estimated 2 million readers daily, and that reportedly helped to elect a reformer President.[62]

What about commercial, professional Internet sites? Does their existence make concentration of ownership in the traditional media irrelevant? Clearly, people are increasingly getting more news online. The PEJ reports the number of people who "ever" go online has stabilized over the last few years at roughly two-thirds of the population, while the percentage of these "Internet users" who go online for news three or more times a week has grown from 23 percent in 2000 to 29 percent in 2004.[63] These data indicate that old media still are and probably will continue to be of major importance. Some data suggest that people's growing attention to online news comes at the expense of fewer minutes spent watching television news. For newspapers, however, the primary change seems to be a shift from newsprint to online receipt of the paper's content. Daily newspaper circulation in 2003 of 55.2 million represents a decline of 7.6 million from the newspaper circulation peak in 1985 – but 55 million Americans visited a newspaper's Web site in November 2005.[64] That is, in terms of readers, as opposed to purchasers of print editions, there may have been no decline. If heavy reliance on online news means going to traditional media's Web sites, clearly this does not undermine any otherwise justifiable concern with concentration. Moreover, heavy news consumers in one medium – e.g., online – reportedly tend to be the heavy consumers of other media.[65] The significance of this fact, as well as the stability of the data about online usage, is unclear. If heavy usage of one medium means heavy usage of others, that might mean that "online" usage is not a substitute for, but either an addition to or method of receipt of old media – each serving different, even if related, functions. If this is right, again, expansion of online news access would not affect any reason to object to concentration in traditional media. And, of course, the expansion would not reduce objections to any tendency toward concentration in ownership of online media.

On the other hand, in various scenarios, online developments might relieve objections to media ownership concentration. They might, for example, if they represent the new availability of huge numbers of new journalistically rich, professionally created Internet "news sites" or if Internet access to traditional offline media reduces the undue or "concentrated" influence of *dominant* offline news enterprises. Neither possibility, however, seems to be the case. An examination of online news providers hardly shows a new dispersal of communicative power (deconcentration) within the media. Most of the most heavily used news sites turn out to be owned by offline brands and seldom add significant new journalistic resources. According to the PEJ study, seventeen of the twenty-five most viewed online news sites are associated with traditional news companies.[66] Of these twenty-five, eight are owned by one of the ten largest media conglomerates and fourteen by one of the twenty largest media companies. Of course, it should not be surprising that media conglomerates own the most viewed online news sites. The possibility of synergies suggests that offline media would have a huge advantage in providing online news content, leading to concentration of audience attention. The PEJ study reports that people view the four most viewed news sites – CNN, Yahoo News, MSNBC, and AOL – much more than the rest.[67] The drop-off is sharp. And of these four, Yahoo and AOL mostly merely post wire content (98% or more of their stories) from other news providers.[68]

Thus, the Internet changes the communications order – in some ways for the better and in others may be for the worse. Certainly, the Internet appears to be for many people an important location to receive news. Still, in terms of what audiences actually receive, the Internet mostly involves a few major news providers serving up wire news plus some major bloggers providing widely received but minimally financed news or commentary and a few already powerful old media extending their reach and dominance. That is, Internet news sites do not seem to represent extensive new investment in creating news content (as opposed to repackaging otherwise created content). It also does not appear that the Internet operates to substantially equalize influence among media entities; the number that dominate, that is, get the largest audience share, are even fewer than in the prior, exclusively offline world. Jupitermedia has been cited for the claim that "between March 1999 and March 2001 the total number of companies controlling 50% of all U.S. online user minutes shrank from 11 to 4."[69] Basically, the Internet can be viewed as further concentrating the public's attention on communications provided by a few owners.

Of course, all this could change. For example, given its availability online, people could spend more time with the newspaper from their original hometown, which they read before they moved to the "city," thereby maintaining cultural connections and, more relevant for the current discussion, equalizing power (audience share) among papers. This online reading of the small hometown paper surely occurs to some extent. Still, the concentration or "Hollywood" effect of reduced delivery costs seems dominant. In a review of the top 100 newspapers in 1999, James Hamilton found that the audience was much more concentrated on the most popular newspapers online than offline. That is, the largest papers had, as compared with smaller papers, a larger share of the total online newspaper audience than they had of the offline newspaper audience; again, the Internet increased concentration of audience attention.[70]

Clearly, something new is happening. The Internet greatly expands the types and sources of information to which people have easy access. Nevertheless, the tendency toward concentration is, if anything, more powerful than in respect to offline media. The American public as a whole appears to be receiving more of its information from fewer sources.[71] Finally, it should be noted that the major Internet sources mostly have the same owners that, according to critics of media ownership concentration, were too concentrated before – and are now too concentrated irrespective of – the Internet. Nevertheless, even if concentration is still great, maybe the Internet alleviates the *reasons* to be concerned about concentration. Thus, with this background, the inquiry can turn directly to the implications of the Internet for these reasons for concern.

DOES THE INTERNET ELIMINATE CONCERNS ABOUT CONCENTRATION?

The Internet's combination of easy publishing and unparalleled search capacities, both virtually costless (in out-of-pocket, but not time, expenditures) once a person has obtained a computer and a broadband connection, reduce concerns about access to already created communicative material that a person wants (and is willing to make some effort to obtain). Of course, not all created content will be available online, and some of this unavailability of information and culture will be due to legally authorized exercises of private power. The long battle over music downloading through peer-to-peer networks makes this problem evident. Copyright laws have and will likely continue to impede efforts to increase the free online availability of music. These laws also may provide the major impediment to making copyrighted books in libraries available (and searchable) by anyone with a computer. The result is not necessarily more income to anyone but merely a requirement of more inconvenient trips to libraries in hopes of finding the desired book and an inability to search easily for the most relevant content.[72] An additional form of potential private censorship would lie in major Internet service providers' use of content filters for either economic or ideological reasons. Technological design choices, for example, in relation to the form of search engines, inevitably skew for better or worse, the Internet's contribution to content availability. These restraints on availability and, maybe aspects of the skewing are potentially subject to legal regulatory control – although a question remains about whether the present power of large media owners blocks appropriate policy responses.

As valuable as the Internet's contribution to access of *already created content* is, lack of theoretically available media content has never figured as a major premise in critiques of ownership concentration. At least in discursively free, nonauthoritarian societies, diverse content that has already been produced is generally available. Anyone can go to the library or bookstore or other access points. The actual bogeyman in stories about lack of effective access to already produced content should be not media conglomerates but an inegalitarian societal distribution of wealth (or free time) or the education needed to know of the need for and methods of access. The Internet contributes to access. Now people's task of finding much already produced material – that which has been digitized and is searchable online – is easier and probably cheaper. But floods of information have long been available to those who are interested. To the extent that a commentator on the Internet's allowing anyone (on the favored side of the digital divide) to publish or to gain access to what has been published is trumpeting it as eliminating the problems that lead to objections to concentration, she uses a time-tested strategy of argument. She first misidentifies the problem and then shows that the problem, as she has misidentified it, has been solved – a great strategy for disingenuous politicians but not to be expected from scholars or serious policy analysts.

The real relevance of the Internet for the issue of ownership concentration involves the specific reasons why this concentration is characterized as a problem. Thus, this section considers the Internet's significance for three worries about concentration in the "old" mass media identified in chapter 1 (noted here in reverse order): its purported negative impact on (1) the creation of relevantly diverse, politically salient, quality content, (2) dangerous degrees of power over public opinion, and (3) a democratic distribution of communicative power to reach large and desired audiences.

Investment in Quality Content

A major reason to worry about media ownership concentration involves evidence and theoretical predictions that it increases media entities' bottom-line focus and that this focus reduces the likelihood that the media entity will forgo some monopoly profits in favor of "spending" more on creating quality content – that is, on journalistic or creative content that has more positive externalities and less negative externalities. Does the Internet significantly diminish this concern? It might do so, or alternatively it might exacerbate this worry, in at least three interconnected ways. It might increase production of quality simply by increasing the total available information resources that journalists or other content creaturs can use for quality production. It might do so by increasing the likelihood that either the old or new media entities will forgo profit maximization and invest more of their resources in quality content. Or it might do so by beneficially changing the incentives as to what content the media should develop and produce. Consideration suggests few reasons to expect any of the hopeful effects and, if anything, suggests that the opposite can be reasonably feared.

Before looking at these possibilities, the importance of resources devoted to quality content creation needs emphasis. Some significant news reports and great cultural content result from moments of inspired artistic and literary creation or unpredictable observations of newsworthy happenings or impassioned commentary. Most creation of quality content, however, involves regular application of considerable labor, talent, often costly production services, and other inputs including past mental or cultural creations that themselves may be costly if previously transformed into "intellectual property." That is, quality content typically requires investments of significant resources, meaning that it usually requires money. This point applies generally throughout the knowledge production sphere. Maybe the apple striking Newton's head led to a quick insight about gravity and certainly a couple of students working in a garage – named Bill Hewlett and David Packard as well as a second pair, Steve Jobs and Steve Wozniak – were able to change history, but a nuclear cyclotron or a pharmaceutical research program requires more resources and more planning on the road to producing meaningful knowledge. Any newspaper editor will report that although luck, dedication, and brillance help, increasing the financial resources dedicated to content creation normally improves the quality of the content produced. Admittedly, the Internet can either reduce the need for costly resources or increase their availability. Yochai Benkler properly warns against too easily accepting claims that quality production requires monetary investment. He describes how technological change, combined with a favorable legal background, can increase the potential for high-quality, efficient, peer-to-peer nonmarket production.[73] The greater involvement of people in this "distributed," voluntary process fits well with an ideal of a participatory public sphere. Effective reign of noncommercial motivations eliminates most market pressures to overproduce negative externalities and to de-emphasize content with positive ones. Policy makers ought consciously to favor laws that encourage these practices. But such matters are the subject of another book.[74] The concern here is whether now or in the intermediate future this production possibility or other changes wrought by digital communications significantly alleviate, in one of the three ways noted, concerns with concentration of mass media ownership.

The business model for online journalism may affect the resources available for quality journalism. The story, however, is not very comforting. If Internet news sites receive less compensation (from advertisers and directly from paying customers) per consumer than do offline news providers, the consumer shift to Internet access to news could reduce the resources available to support serious commercial journalism. In the worst-case scenario, Internet news providers could be reduced to redistributing wire content – which seems already to be the case for the primary portal access sites – or to becoming a morgue for content, sometimes otherwise unused excess content, of the site's offline traditional media parent. That is, Internet news sites may employ fewer journalists per news consumer. When this low employment is combined with lower offline revenue for their parents and competitors caused by the Internet sites drawing audience away from older formats, the net effect could be an absolute reduction in employment of the journalists needed to create professional quality news and public affairs content.

Data support this worry. Looking at a sampling that includes the most visited Internet sites, in 2004 the PEJ found that 58 percent of stories consisted of unedited wire copy, rising from 42 percent in 2003.[75] The PEJ study also found that 62 percent of online journalists, as well as 37 percent of national print, TV, and radio journalists, said that "the size of the newsroom staff had decreased compared with three years earlier."[76] The reported decline in online journalists occurred while revenue from advertising on the examined newspaper online sites had increased 34 percent from 2002 to 2003 and apparently as much as another 30 percent in 2004.[77] Despite the increasing prominence of the Internet as a place where people access news (even if largely created by old offline media) and as a place on which advertisers spend money, PEJ commented that it is "not clear whether the Internet will ever be as profitable as the old media." It then suggested that "if it isn't, most newsrooms may end up much smaller, and spread thinner than they once were."[78] The pessimistic conclusion is that "the economic base supporting the most difficult and expensive journalistic undertakings is eroding."[79]

Other aspects of the Internet may reinforce this same undesirable diversion of resources from journalism. As noted, the Internet is most fundamentally a distribution device. The hope might be that the cost saving involved leaves more resources, often supplied by advertisers, to be spent on content creation. However, another effect that has only recently begun to receive routine attention in the business world is the Internet's drawing down the relatively fixed pot of advertising revenue, potentially dramatically reducing advertisers' support of traditional media. (I would be the last to argue that advertisers' support of the media is acceptably benign, but there is no denying its financial significance.[80] This support has provided the media with resources to support serious journalism – a factor so important that Germany found the permissibility of commercial broadcasting to depend on it not having too negative an effect on the finances of newspapers.[81] Other countries have developed schemes to divert some of broadcasting's advertising revenue to newspapers.) The title of a recent news story, "Jobs Are Cut as Ads and Readers Move Online,"[82] signals the Internet's effect of reducing advertising's support of traditional media's expenditures on content creation. This story, which began with the report of seventy-five newsroom jobs being cut at the *Philadelphia Inquirer*, proceeded to report an expectation that advertisers will devote 15 percent to 20 percent of their expenditures this year to online advertising and that newspapers' rich classified advertising is currently being threatened by online sites, especially Google and Craigslist. In 2004, total ad spending was reportedly $141 billion. Of this, newspapers received $27.7 billion (local papers $24.5 billion, national papers $3.2 billion), while the Internet garnered $7.4 billion of advertising revenue,[83] an amount predicted to rise to $22.3 billion by 2009.[84]

If the diversion of advertising revenue to the Internet represented advertising revenue supporting online journalism – paying for content creation by professional journalists working for new online media – the change would be troubling for the owners of newspapers but not necessarily troubling from the perspective of the democratic functions of the press. However, there is no reason to expect that support of online journalism is the main use of online advertising. In addition to providing cheap and easy delivery, online search engines help people receive the content they seek. This feature is very beneficial in promoting information's effective availability (though, as noted above, it has not prevented the concentration of online audience attention). Despite this valuable role in providing accessibility, search engines do not create content. By the middle of 2005, Google and Yahoo! combined rivaled the three major prime time TV networks in advertising revenue.[85] Google had revenues in the third quarter of 2005 of $1.6 billion,[86] mostly from advertising. Even at this rate revenues equal $6.4 billion a year, already close to a quarter of the advertising received by all the country's newspapers combined. The advertising on search engine sites represents not just a transfer from traditional media to new media but, to a significant degree, a transfer away from the support of journalists and other content creators to the support of distributors of online content. This diversion ought to be troubling to a country that presently devotes too few resources to the journalist function, basically the third reason given in chapter 1 to favor dispersal of media ownership.

An additional way that the Internet could reduce worries about concentration is if it resulted in placing the decision of whether to devote resources to serious journalistic efforts in the hands of those firms most likely to do this rather than to maximize profits by skimping on journalistic quality. As long as most journalistic employment remains tied to the old media, this concern with the consequences of ownership concentration in these traditional media simply remains – the type of ownership that the firm has will affect the likelihood of desirable or undesirable resource allocations. As chapter 1 argued, undesirable effects predictably become more likely as ownership size increases and the type of ownership shifts toward shareholding of publicly traded shares. Alternatively, to the extent that increasing portions of total journalistic employment involve online commercial media, the problem caused by ownership concentration may well intensify for two reasons. These online media will often be owned by the same firms that generated the concern about too great a profit focus. Moreover, as noted, the total economic base to support the journalism may well be smaller. "Voluntary" media – blogging or structures such as Independent Media Centers[87] – may supply important new sources of information. Still, there is little reason to think that in the near term, merely because the Internet allows anyone to be her own publisher, the new noncommercial, volunteer-supported online news ventures will provide an adequate substitute for traditional professional journalism.

Last is the possibility that the Internet will itself create incentives that cause a shift in investment focus toward creating better quality information. As a distribution system, its most overt role, the Internet does not in itself directly create content. On the other hand, by making information and prior cultural creations so much more readily available to current creators, the Internet surely reduces costs for the creation of many, but not all, types of content. Significantly, it does so to varying degrees. This variability systematically influences economic competition. These cost reductions can affect competition among differing commercial content creations and between commercial and noncommercial content. They can also differentially affect the opportunities of various types of noncommercial content creators. Specifically, those types of content that the Internet allows to be more cheaply produced are now favored in their competition with other types of information. Legal (copyright and contractual) and technological self-help efforts to lock up much expression and sometimes information, making it available only for purchase, may limit the extent of the Internet's contribution to cost reductions. Still, predictably, some significant reductions remain at least for some types of content.

Of course, *any* reduction in the cost or difficulty of valued activities is *potentially* beneficial. Unfortunately, in practice, variable cost reductions are often not an unalloyed good. As the cost of creating certain content (i.e., products) goes down, the incentive to spend on competing high cost categories typically also goes down. In competition with the now more cheaply produced content, the noncheapened (or less cheapened) categories are less valuable to their creators/owners, with the result that their production will typically be reduced or abandoned. *If* the now disfavored categories are precisely the categories that typically produce greater positive externalities, the actual net social consequences of the potentially beneficial cost reductions could be negative. This could be true despite a net increase in the total quantity of content produced and consumed. Society can lose, for example, if the cost of creating drivel or fluff or diverting entertainment goes down while the cost of producing exposés or hard news stays constant.

An example closer to home may be interesting – although I would not want to generalize too quickly or even insist on the accuracy of my suggestion. My "unscientific" impression is that as facts and quotes are more easily found through simple Google searches, the factual detail of student seminar papers has increased while their overall intellectual quality – grappling with major issues and attention to high quality sources – has declined. If digital technologies generally, or the Internet specifically, reduces the cost of less socially valuable categories of news or information (was Clinton's affair that important?) more than it does for quality investigative journalism (the failure to report the savings and loan scandal in a timely manner, costing the country at least an estimated $150 billion[88]), there could be a consequent reduction of expenditures on this high-externality journalism. If so, the loss would be serious.[89]

Predictions about the consequences of the Internet for journalism and for the actual, effective societal receipt of quality information are hazardous and require great care. Online information surely sometimes aides the most valuable investigative journalism. I. F. Stone treated viewing government documents as typically more informative for journalism than interviewing the powerful. His successor today would probably make great use of online sources – and some current investigative journalists may be following his example. The Internet also empowers "volunteer" blogging, which has already made valuable investigative contributions.[90] The point is that the Internet and other digital technologies may contribute to or undermine making available high-quality diverse content. Still, nothing about this or other aspects of the Internet relieves the need for an ownership policy designed to get media ownership (of either the old or new media) in the hands of those most willing to make non-profit-maximizing investments in quality journalism or creative products.

Dangers of Concentrated Communicative Power

Concentrated communicative power creates demagogic dangers for a democracy, reduces the number of owners who can choose to engage in watchdog roles, may reduce the variety in perspectives among the smaller group of people who hold ultimate power to choose specific (varying) watchdog projects, and multiplies the probable conflicts of interest that can muzzle these watchdogs. No matter how positive the Internet's overall contribution to democratic practice, as long as relatively few companies (or individuals) control the media that are viewed, heard, or read by huge portions of the population, the danger of demagogic use of these media remains. Likewise, if these media control the bulk of the financial resources committed to journalism, the danger remains that too few will choose to engage in well-financed watchdog or investigative practices or that those that do so will have too limited a view about what problems or issues are worth investigating. This problem of too few (publicly effective) perspectives is exacerbated to the extent that conflicts of interest exist between possible investigatory topics or editorial perspectives and the conglomerate owners' other businesses (or these businesses' political interests). Media ownership concentration can deter major media entities from investigating or discussing major issues (as was frequently said to have occurred in relation to the Telecommunications Act of 1996) unless or until the issue becomes too obvious to ignore. In other words, despite the changes wrought by the Internet, a small handful of companies may continue to supply most of the financial resources for journalism (or cultural creation) and to control most of the audience attention. Nothing about the Internet suggests that this will not continue. In fact, the Internet may even intensify this problem with concentration. As long as this is so, this antidemagogic, safeguard reason for objecting to media ownership concentration remains undiminished.

DEMOCRATIC DISTRIBUTION OF COMMUNICATIVE POWER

A more democratic distribution of communicative power is possibly the most basic reason to oppose media ownership concentration. This distributive value has to do with speakers *actually* reaching audiences. Formal or technical capacity to reach audiences is not the issue. Overt governmental suppression of news or opinion is rare in modern democratic societies.[91] (Overt suppression may be less rare in relation to the exercise of power by private parties, as current bloggers are learning the old lesson that some employers can and will dismiss them for their off-the-job exercise of speech rights.[92]) People have long been free to cry out their views or hand out their leaflets on the town square – and to be mostly ignored just as their views are mostly ignored when put on their blog. The question here is whether the Internet has actually substantially broadened and equalized participation in the public sphere and the process of collective opinion formation. Or, alternatively, whether the Internet merely provides a means that potentially allows for such participatory results, but a potentiality that has not been and will likely not be realized for contextual and practical, often economic, reasons. My impression is that the Internet has done the first to some degree, though the evidence of online concentration of attention suggests that it has done so much less than its ardent supporters wish. Furthermore, there is no reason to believe that a real democratic distribution of communicative power has been achieved through the Internet or that it would not be furthered by reducing the concentration of traditional media.

Remember that the notion of "mass" in the idea of mass media means that the egalitarian distributive value cannot imply that each individual communicates equally or even broadly. Rather, the distributive goal is that each individual can reasonably perceive herself as part of groups that are not excluded, groups that cannot complain that they are disproportionately denied control of media of mass communication (combined with the real possibility of individually trying to become an effective speaker). And the distributive goal requires that no one can complain that the mass media are disproportionately controlled by narrow groups of which she is not a part. As to this distributive value, the Internet may reduce to some degree the concern with concentration. By allowing groups that are spread apart geographically to better access a single content site, the Internet makes a substantial contribution: it reduces some disempowering effects of diaspora. And by dramatically reducing distribution costs, the Internet makes more likely the existence of noncommercial, nonprofit media that serve smaller groups. But these distributive gains are limited. They hardly eliminate extreme concentration of audience attention on information provided by a few corporate entities or obviate the distributive rationale for dispersal. Concentration unnecessarily reduces the likelihood that any group will own or control substantial media properties. It increases the likelihood that individuals and groups will experience the media order as being dominantly controlled by the "other" – people not like them and not responsive to their concerns. Thus, despite all the positive practices stimulated by and opportunities created by the Internet, the Internet does not eliminate the force of the democratic distributive objection to media ownership concentration.

In an optimistic scenario, the Internet offers great gains to the communications order. Nevertheless, as long as the "old media" continue to exist and to play a major role in the communications realm – or even if existing concentrated media formats decline but their owners or new corporate owners take on life as massive firms refocused on digital communications – the three primary concerns emphasized in chapter 1 for objecting to ownership concentration have full force. Some aspects of the nature and economics of the Internet may even intensify these three concerns. Invocation of the Internet surely should not "end the discussion" with a conclusive "single word" – as suggested explicitly by Compaine and implicitly by Owen. At best, consideration of the Internet raises the empirical question of the extent to which the Internet reduces a comparatively few companies' share of the audience in relevant contexts and increases the number of independent, significant media outlets effectively accessed by diverse groups. Even as to this limited hope, the evidence is mixed, providing little reason for comfort.

The misguided invocation of the Internet as a total solution to problems of the communications order, including the problem of concentration, may be merely faddish. Claims of change – especially of revolutionary change – are perennially popular. Or these invocations of the Internet may merely reflect an intellectually sloppy failure to consider precisely the specific nature of the problems with the old order and precisely what solution the Internet, whatever else it does, offers to *these* problems. Nevertheless, a suspicion remains that this invocation of the Internet as a purported end of discussion primarily serves ideological deregulatory or other corporate purposes. Virtually no careful analysis actually shows that the Internet significantly reduces, much less eliminates, any of the major reasons for concern with concentration of ownership of the major producers of news and culture.

FOUR

The First Amendment Guarantee of a Free Press: An Objection to Regulation?

The democratic reasons for opposing media concentration described in chapter 1 could easily be taken as a summary of First Amendment values. Justice Hugo Black's canonical statement is that "[the First] Amendment rests on the assumption that the widest possible dissemination of information from diverse and antagonistic *sources* is essential to the welfare of the public."[1] Black's statement occurred in a case involving general antitrust law applied to an association of newspapers. In possibly its most famous broadcasting case,[2] the Court relied heavily and repeatedly on Justice Black's opinion, citing it in this media-specific case to justify the Court's central proposition that "[i]t is the right of the viewers and listeners, not the right of the broadcasters, which is paramount.... [It] is the purpose of the First Amendment to reserve an uninhibited marketplace of ideas in which truth will ultimately prevail, rather than to countenance monopolization of that market."[3] Likewise, in a continuously quoted passage from what many consider our most important First Amendment case, *New York Times v. Sullivan*,[4] Justice William Brennan read the First Amendment against what he called the "background of a profound national commitment to the principle that debate on public issues should be uninhibited, robust, and wide-open" and approvingly invoked Justice Learned Hand's view that the First Amendment "presupposes that right conclusions are more likely to be gathered out of a multitude of tongues."[5]

These statements seem to embody – they are certainly congruent with – the democratic principles described in chapter 1 calling for a wide distribution of media power and the recognition of the dangers in concentrated communicative power. It is hardly surprising that many media activists, especially the nonlawyers among them, often conclude that the First Amendment *requires* stringent limits on media concentration – as is constitutionally required in some Western European countries.[6] In contrast is a second view that the First Amendment does not require but does allow legislation aimed at limiting such concentration. A third view, that the First Amendment often prohibits such legislation, unfortunately has considerable currency today. The primary aim of this chapter is to show why this third view is wrong and the second is right.

THE FIRST AMENDMENT AS A LIMIT ON GOVERNMENT POWER: THREE PREMISES

In recent years, courts, the FCC, lawyers for media owners, and scholars have regularly invoked the First Amendment as a restriction on government's power to limit media concentration.[7] This chapter first describes this view of the First Amendment and then shows that it is misguided from the perspective of Supreme Court precedent, judicial prudence, and sound First Amendment theory.

In a dramatic case in 2001, the D.C. Circuit Court of Appeals in *Time Warner Entertainment Co. v. FCC*[8] heard challenges to FCC cable ownership rules.[9] The first rule limited cable companies from owning local cable systems that service more than 30 percent of the public within the country, thereby guaranteeing nationally the existence of at least four cable companies. A second rule[10] prevented a cable company from having an ownership interest in the programmers of more than 40 percent of its channels, thereby effectively restricting concentration by reserving 60 percent of its channels for programming by nonaffiliated firms. The court held that "the FCC has not met its burden under the First Amendment and, in part, lacks statutory authority" for these rules.[11] It reasoned that "the horizontal limit [the first rule] interferes with petitioners' speech rights by restricting the number of viewers to whom they can speak. The vertical limit [the second rule] restricts their ability to exercise their editorial control over a portion of the content they transmit."[12] That is, the court viewed the cable company as having presumptive rights under the First Amendment to buy other cable companies in order to reach more people and to control all the content delivered over its system. Government limits on concentration were, therefore, presumptively unconstitutional. The court added the suggestion that these First Amendment rights can be limited with adequate justification, but found that justification had not been demonstrated.[13]

Recently, the FCC has also viewed limits on concentration as raising serious First Amendment issues. It recognizes that the Supreme Court has been clear that regulation of broadcast ownership must meet only the relatively nondemanding "rational basis standard" – that is, requiring only that the law be "reasonable" or rationally related to a legitimate state interest. Still, the FCC emphasizes that "First Amendment interests are implicated by any regulation of media outlets."[14] It indicated that, for this reason, it would seek "to minimize the impact of [its ownership] rules on the right of speakers to disseminate a message."[15] Using the crucial First Amendment "scrutiny" notion of "reasonableness," the FCC says its decision in 2003 to reduce restrictions on concentration "turns in part on our determination that these rules in their current form are *not* a reasonable means to accomplish . . . public interest purposes."[16] Thus, the FCC explained that its change of rules to allow increased ownership concentration shows "greater deference to First Amendment interests."[17] Like the D.C. Circuit Court of Appeals, the FCC clearly saw rules limiting concentration as imposing a "burden on the freedom of expression," and, consequently, the FCC sought to serve public interest goals in a manner that limited concentration as little as possible.[18]

With varying degrees of caution, many scholars likewise point to First Amendment rights of media conglomerates as a reason to oppose media-specific limits on ownership. Ben Compaine, for example, began his discussion of the constitutionality of diversity-oriented regulation of media ownership by quoting Ithiel de Sola Pool's classic, *Technologies of Freedom*, for the view, evidently shared by Compaine, that media-specific regulation could cause "greater harm than any possible benefit that might be achieved" but that this harm could and should be prevented by court enforcement of the First Amendment.[19] According to Compaine, an antitrust approach that pursued overtly social and political antitrust objectives (of the sort endorsed in this book) in regulating media concentration could "collide with First Amendment protections." He cited this problem as a reason to rely on a purely economic (Chicago school) approach to antitrust or, presumably, to media ownership regulation more generally.[20] Less cautiously, others have argued that, under a proper interpretation of the First Amendment, many existing media ownership restrictions (that I argue are too lax) are unconstitutional for being too strict! Restrictions that these commentators would invalidate include those that, in contrast, the Third Circuit recently reinstated when it found that the FCC had not justified their elimination.[21] For example, Christopher Yoo identifies four existing ownership restrictions that constitute what he describes as "architectural censorship" – rules that have the usually unintended consequence of "degrad[ing] the quantity, quality, and diversity of programming available."[22] Yoo then expresses the hope, which he recognizes present judicial doctrine does not fulfill, that "the First Amendment would provide a basis for identifying and redressing architectural censorship."[23]

Were it not for the argument's considerable influence, the claim that legal restrictions on ownership concentration violate the First Amendment might be dismissed on its face. None of the laws or regulations prohibits specific communicative content – normally a defining feature of censorship of speech. Media companies have long raised First Amendment objections to laws that burden their business operations – but only to have the Supreme Court dismiss their claims.[24] Nevertheless, as noted above, recently First Amendment objections to media-specific ownership regulations have generated considerable traction. This traction makes sense only if at least one of two normative premises concerning press freedom is accepted and, especially in the case of the second, only on the basis of a third premise about the appropriateness of judicial activism. Here, I specify and explain these premises. In subsequent sections I argue that each of them has been rejected by dominant legal precedents and should be rejected based on sound (but contested) First Amendment theory.

Ultimate Beneficiary of Press Freedom

First is the issue of the identity of the ultimate beneficiary of First Amendment guarantees. If the ultimate beneficiary is the audience or the public – either as media consumers or as citizens who profit from a press that serves democratic needs – then whether ownership restrictions violate the First Amendment should depend primarily on whether the regulation and the government's capacity to regulate serves or disserves the public's interest in an ideal media order. Thus, relying on *Associated Press*, the Court in *Red Lion* said it is "the right of the viewers and listeners . . . that is paramount." Under this view, the press has those rights, and only those rights, that advance the public's interest in a free press. For example, *if* there were a reporters' privilege not to disclose confidential sources,[25] under this analysis, the privilege would exist not because reporters merit special rights on their own behalf. Rather, the privilege would exist only because recognizing it benefits the democratic role – the institutional integrity – of the press and thereby benefits the broader public.

Many who see ownership restrictions as constitutionally problematic adopt an alternative view. They see the ultimate beneficiary of press freedom as the owners, a view unsurprisingly presented by corporate media entities in many recent cases but more surprisingly credited by the D.C. Circuit in *Time Warner Entertainment*.[26] The argument is that ownership limits place a burden on potential owners' – usually corporate entities' – ability to speak to as many people as they could by buying new media outlets. (Of course, even with these ownership limits, these corporate media entities are as free as citizens are to use their wealth to pay other media entities to run their messages as advertisements. It is their business, not their speech, that these limits burden.) The proper meaning of press freedom varies depending on who its beneficiaries are assumed to be. If these corporate entities are the ultimate beneficiaries of the rights, ownership limits arguably directly restrict *their* expressive freedom. Media ownership limits directly and purposefully reduce not speech – neither speech content nor total quantity of speech is necessarily reduced and may be increased. Rather, they purposefully reduce the restricted corporate entities' capacity to speak as much as they might through buying media enterprises. Basically, the claim is that freedom of the press treats media entities themselves – usually corporate or otherwise multiperson, legally structured entities – as the central rights-bearing subjects. The content of rights is designed for their benefit, not the public's – the public may or may not benefit. On this assumption, structural rules that interfere with these entities' communicative efforts presumptively violate *their* First Amendment rights.

THE AIMS OF PRESS FREEDOM

A second constitutional critique of ownership restrictions is more instrumentalist. The free press guarantee can be understood as justified by its contribution to particular constitutional aims rather than as fundamentally providing for rights holders. Under this instrumental view, regulations that undermine these aims would be presumptively unconstitutional – that is, they would unless adequately justified by other important aims. Crucial to this argument are the aims identified as served by the constitutional guarantee. Constitutionality then focuses on empirical, pragmatic, or interpretative assessments of the relation of regulations to these aims, combined with a matter taken up below: how should a regulation's relation to these aims be evaluated, and who should do the evaluation?

Christopher Yoo's argument is mostly of this instrumental sort. His hope is that the First Amendment would overturn existing ownership rules that, he claims, have an often dramatic adverse impact on the "overall quantity, quality, and diversity of speech."[27] He argues that the courts' present failure to police "architectural censorship" amounts to a "disturbing abdication of responsibility."[28] His preference is for an effects-based constitutional doctrine – bad effects on speech presumptively justify invalidating a law, no matter what the law's purpose.[29] That is, he implicitly posits an instrumentalist aim of the First Amendment – preventing these adverse effects on speech provides a First Amendment basis for invalidating the laws.

Judicial Activism

The premises concerning either ultimate beneficiaries or aims of press freedom have much more telling force if courts should be active in reviewing and second-guessing political judgments about the structure of the media industry. To find a law unconstitutional under the First Amendment, a court generally must find that it is an *unjustifiable restriction*. This finding involves two elements. First, the law must limit First Amendment freedoms. The premises above allow finding such a restriction in two somewhat different ways. Second, the restriction also must be unjustifiable – or, more stringently, unjustified by the entity that established the restriction. Who makes this determination? One possibility is that Congress, whose members take an oath to uphold the Constitution, do so. But under the American system of judicial review, courts have the final authority. Then the question becomes: how (readily) do courts determine inconsistency with the Constitution?

One possibility is that finding a restriction, the first element, should largely end the inquiry. This First Amendment "absolutism" claims that restrictions on First Amendment rights, properly understood, are simply invalid. I say more below about this possibility, which I generally favor. Nevertheless, under widely accepted current practice, courts go to the second step and evaluate the law's justifiablility. In current legal language, this evaluation is said to be a matter of "scrutiny." Judicial *activism* consists of some degree of *heightened scrutiny* – that is, when being activist, the court imposes a higher justificatory burden on defenders of a law. Thus, the third premise is that structural rules are appropriately evaluated under a heightened scrutiny.

Activism here may seem appropriate. Even if judicial activism – and heightened scrutiny – is often criticized for allowing unelected judges to become policy makers in overturning decisions reached by a democratic political process, activism is arguably less problematic in the context of defending the First Amendment. Not only does the First Amendment embody an explicit, textual constitutional command, it is the constitutional embodiment of fundamental individual rights or of rights considered essential to a democratic society. Possibly the very *legitimacy* of governmental power depends on protection of speech rights – the right to dissent from majorities. Democratic majorities may be adequate for determining what dominant majorities want. They may, however, be systematically suspect in their willingness to protect dissenters. In any event, even incidental burdens on individuals' speech freedom – so-called content-neutral restrictions – should and do receive heightened scrutiny.

THE ULTIMATE BENEFICIARY (OR BASIS) OF PRESS FREEDOMS

Utilitarians sometimes argue that the ultimate justification of all rights is (or should be) the benefit to society as a whole and that this premise ought to be crucial in interpreting constitutional provisions. In contrast, the probably more dominant reading of constitutional rights such as freedom of speech, guarantees of equal protection and due process, freedom from unreasonable searches and seizures, and freedom from cruel and unusual punishment is that these rights should usually or always trump mere utilitarian (and other instrumentalist) considerations. These rights are "side constraints" that limit the means by which the collective permissibly pursues the welfare of the whole. They are fundamentally rights of individuals. The legitimacy of government depends on the government recognizing rights that respect the dignity and ultimate moral significance of *each* individual – individuals whom the state in turn asks to voluntarily obey the nation's laws. It is sometimes said that these rights are "inviolate."[30] In this view, the ultimate beneficiary of constitutional rights is the rights holder.

With respect to freedom of the press, the *overt* right holders are press entities, entities such as Time Warner or News Corporation or Clear Channel or any other collective entity that chooses to be the "press." The reason that owners argue that telephone companies presumptively cannot be prohibited from owning cable systems is that this limitation interferes with the companies' freedom to be the press and to speak. Thus, a natural reading of the First Amendment might see press entities as the ultimate beneficiary or holder of press freedom.

A crucial step in this argument, however, is quite odd and, I think, lacks appeal. It is possible today – maybe more so now, with the development of Internet blogging than at any time since the demise of the colonial printer – to conceive of a press or communication entity as involving only a single person investigating and then communicating by writing, speaking, and delivering content. This romantic image of the single individual certainly does not describe the modern norm, and when they exist these individual activities might more readily and appropriately be conceptualized as exercises of speech freedom. Virtually any modern press enterprise – and even more so those of huge conglomerates such as Time Warner that encompass multiple magazines, cable systems, broadcasters, film studios, theaters, Internet sites, and more – involves multiple decision makers whose authority within the enterprise is determined by a combination of participant agreements and legal rules, including property, contract, and corporate law. Put otherwise, the press plainly consists of legally structured institutions. Legal structuring of institutions is often necessary even for their identification, much less their functionality. Legal structuring of individuals, in contrast, is hardly commonsensical. Its normative acceptability was arguably largely abandoned with the repudiation of slavery and slavery's analogues.[31] Of course, like all institutions, the press consists ultimately of morally significant individuals. It is a logical mistake, however, to treat the press entity – the overt rights holder – as an individual. Attributing ultimate or inherent moral significance to legal structures – to institutions – is, at best, perverse. Rights as limits on policy choices that further the collective welfare, although possibly justified because of the moral significance of individuals, hardly seem worth defending merely for the benefit of the legally created institutions whose significance presumably lies in the service of society. Thus, if there is a way to conceptualize the ultimate beneficiaries of press rights as other than the press, that approach would seem appealing.

In fact, not only does normative theory offer a different and better conception of the press, but the best reading of history and Supreme Court precedent embodies that different conception. Almost universally accepted is the view that a free press is an essential *institution* of democracy. This view provides an obvious reason to put its protection into the Constitution and to treat press freedom as a structural, not a rights, provision. The Constitution is mostly not about individual rights – although most of the Bill of Rights may be. Justice Potter Stewart, though without being able to explicitly bring along a majority of the Court,[32] read the Press Clause to protect a democratic "fourth estate."[33] He saw the Press Clause, unlike the free speech guarantee, as a structural provision, operating much like "separation of powers" provisions to protect freedom and democracy. The basis of the Press Clause is not an "inviolate" right exhibiting respect for the individual person but an "instrumentalist" evaluation of the best way to set up a democratic country. When Justice Stewart noted that the press is the only "business" to receive explicit constitutional protection, he was not so much observing an anomaly as pointing to the instrumental rationale for the constitutional guarantee. The system is most secure if each "estate" is guaranteed the institutional integrity that allows it to persuade, struggle against, or expose the other branches.

This instrumental rationale does not in any way exclude recognition of press rights, but it does determine their content as well as their point. Thus, Stewart famously emphasized the need for what I have called "defensive press rights"[34] that protect the integrity of the institution. His best example was reporters' right to keep their sources' identity confidential, that protect the work product and institutional boundaries of this "estate." In contrast, Stewart rejected what I have labeled "offensive rights" – claims that other branches have a *constitutional* duty to aid this fourth estate, for example, by giving the press a special constitutional right of access to other branches or their files. The availability of this access, he thought, is better left to democratic decisions such as those embodied in freedom of information acts. The Constitution sets up the struggle among the different "estates," while guaranteeing that no branch undermine the institutional integrity of the others. Most emphatically, the key to press rights lies in their being implicit in proper recognition of the institution's instrumental, democratic role.

This instrumentalist, democratic interpretation of the constitutional status of the press explains this chapter's initial quote. Justice Black exhibited absolutely no sympathy for the Associated Press's claimed right of freedom from structural regulation. Enforcement of the law may have forced AP members to associate with, or speak to, entities with whom they would choose not to associate or speak, but the law did not censor – it did not prevent the Associated Press from choosing content or from communicating it. Black explained that "the First Amendment, far from providing an argument against application of the Sherman Act, here provides powerful reasons to the contrary."[35] In rejecting the Associated Press's autonomy-like claim to control its own operations and its associations with various newspapers, Justice Black explained that "[s]urely a command that the government itself shall not impede the free flow of ideas does not afford non-governmental combinations a refuge.... Freedom of the press from governmental interference under the First Amendment does not sanction repression of that freedom by private interests."[36] Essentially, the corporate entity has no rights inconsistent with the preeminent instrumental goal of having the "widest possible dissemination of information from diverse and antagonistic sources, [which] is essential to the welfare of the public."

Justice Black's analysis easily provides a basis for Justice White's statement for the Court in *Red Lion* that it is "the right of the viewers and listeners ... which is paramount."[37] Of course, to ground the status of the press on this instrumental value does not mean that the press does not have some rights that can be treated as absolute as certain individual rights are – it only means that the rights have different ultimate justifications. Censorship of the press's communicative content must be ruled out for the press to play its democratic role, just as censorship of an individual's speech must be ruled out for the individual to be free.

If, controversially, there are any differences between what an individual and the press can say or refuse to say, the differences must be found in the origin of the rights, in the first case in expressive liberty and in the second in the press's instrumental democratic, informative, and cultural roles. For example, individual freedom might require that the individual be free to repeat, or give, to a friend words already expressed and copyrighted by a third person – a right imperfectly recognized as a "fair use" of copyrighted material.[38] In contrast, a legislative body[39] could reasonably conclude that some intellectual property rights, rather than limiting the press's democratic role, often would provide incentives that promote a robust communications order and democracy-serving media entities. This legislative judgment, however, may be empirically plausible and consistent with the press's democratic role *only if* the intellectual property rights do not restrict any press entity from reporting all facts or ideas. They should provide commercial property rights only in unique (but non-newsworthy) expressive combinations of words. This distinction between not restricting individuals' noncommercial copying while restricting the press's copying the same expression might be embodied in the difference between an individual's constitutional speech freedom and the press's protection in the Press Clause.[40]

Likewise, an individual's free speech right to refuse to say things she does not believe is, as the Court recognized, intrinsic to the constitutional notion of individual liberty.[41] Punishing a schoolchild for refusing to salute the flag violates her expressive freedom.[42] In contrast, not only does common carriage status require telephone companies to carry expression that their owners or directors may find heinous, but the Court has also upheld requirements that both broadcasters and cable systems carry content they would reject.[43] On the other hand, if reporters have *any* right not to disclose the name of sources,[44] it is obviously not based on any inviolate notion of individual liberty as recognized for the child who would not salute the flag. Rather, the reporter's right not to speak must be based on instrumental evaluations of the requirements of institutional integrity – defensive press rights – needed to protect the press in the performance of its "watchdog" or other democratic roles.

The difference between the two theories of press rights occurs not in their equivalent objections to censorship of content but in the context of structural regulation – an arena basically irrelevant to the free speech rights of individuals. The constitutional attacks on structural regulation seek to analogize the media to the autonomy of individuals. The Court, however, has never supported this move. *Red Lion* obviously adopted the democratic rather than the press-as-holder-of-rights-on-its-own-behalf interpretation. Despite *Red Lion*'s repeated reliance on *Associated Press*, most commentators (and subsequent court cases) treat *Red Lion* as limited to the broadcast context, where the First Amendment is purportedly at its weakest. Recurrent language in Court opinions and academic scholarship (unreflectively) assumes two separate First Amendment media traditions, with the broadcast model being secondary and less constitutionally protected. Nevertheless, a historical examination of the Court's treatment of the print media finds no evidence of a real inconsistency with *Red Lion*'s instrumentalist reading of the Press Clause or its willingness to uphold structural regulation. The purportedly opposing print tradition turns out to rely on only one case, *Miami Herald Publishing Co. v. Tornillo*,[45] which struck down a requirement that newspapers give electoral candidates a right to reply when criticized by the newspaper. As currently interpreted, even this decision does not support a second tradition.

Language in *Miami Herald* emphasized First Amendment protection for what might be called "editorial autonomy." The Court said that the statute amounted to an unconstitutional "intrusion into the function of editors," which includes "the choice of material to go into a newspaper" as an aspect of "editorial control and judgment."[46] I largely put aside the issue that this emphasis on the rights of "editors" rather than "owners" leaves open. With a possible sideways glance at the European notion of protecting "internal" press freedom, which protects the journalistic and editorial roles from undue limitation by owners,[47] certainly the Court's language supports the possibility of structural regulation to promote editors' independence from limitation by owners. Such protection would be only a small extension of a controversial lower court decision (other decisions reach arguably conflicting results) that held that the First Amendment does not bar application of sex discrimination laws that restrict a newspaper owner's freedom in the choice of its editor in chief.[48]

If *Miami Herald* protects some editorial (or owner) "control and judgment," this protection could result from a very plausible vision (though not precisely the vision advanced in this book) of the democratic role of the press – namely, that the government must be always disabled from making press entities into more inclusive (neutral) forums for debate. Extensive access rights might undermine the institutional integrity needed for the press to perform its democratic roles. The press must be allowed to be vigorously partisan in a manner that an access statute undermines.[49] That is, *this* objection to the right-of-reply law would be grounded not on the press having rights on its own behalf, like those of an individual, but only on its having rights based on its instrumental value as explained by a particular democratic theory.

Regardless, the "editorial autonomy" reading of *Miami Herald* has since been largely repudiated. The Court had originally offered an additional basis for its decision. The statute "exacts a penalty on the basis of the content" – specifically, the law penalized the paper's initial criticism of the candidate by requiring it to then print a reply.[50] The Court routinely invalidates suppressive content-based regulations. Doing so in *Miami Herald* on the grounds of the statute's content discrimination was especially appropriate, the Court explained, because the penalty's deterrence effect could interfere with the democratic role of the paper. The statutory reply right might lead editors to "conclude that the safe course is to avoid controversy," to avoid the initial criticism, with the result that "political and electoral coverage would be blunted or reduced."[51] Quoting *New York Times v. Sullivan*, the Court concluded that the statute "inescapably 'dampens the vigor and limits the variety of public debate.'"[52] Thus, the content-based penalty provides a second ground of decision.

Subsequently, emphasizing this penalty analysis, the Court implicitly rejected the editorial autonomy concept of press freedom. Congress passed a law that, within prescribed limits, requires cable systems to carry local TV stations.[53] Cable systems challenged the law in *Turner Broadcasting v. FCC*.[54] They argued that cable systems, like the newspaper in *Miami Herald*, have full First Amendment rights – a claim that the Court basically accepted. With this point in their favor, the cable systems continued by correctly arguing that the "must carry" rules unconstitutionally interfered with their "editorial control." On the "editorial autonomy" reading of *Miami Herald*, the cable systems had an apparently foolproof argument. Nevertheless, the Court balked. It explained that the "editorial independence" protected in *Miami Herald* was independence from being penalized on the basis of content.[55] Penalizing the paper's initial content choices, the Court observed, constituted the flaw in the right-to-reply law.[56] Since the cable system could not escape the "must carry" obligations by making particular content-based choices, no speech was penalized or deterred. This conclusion constitutes a direct rejection of the "editorial autonomy" rationale of *Miami Herald*. Without this rejection, the Court would have been unable to escape Turner Broadcasting's claims. Essentially, the Court said that the "right to reply" law operates like censorship, which is forbidden, while "must carry" rules constitute structural rules. (The Court did give careful scrutiny to these structural rules before upholding them,[57] but that is a story for the next section.)

Despite explicitly reciting the differences between print and broadcast media, *Turner I* implicitly repudiates reading *Miami Herald* as constituting a commitment to a print tradition that makes structural regulation a presumptive violation of a print entity's right to be free of structural regulation. And despite the popular belief in such a tradition, it receives direct support from no other Supreme Court holding. Of course, lack of case law support cannot be definitive. Its absence may represent normative or interpretative error or merely a lack of litigation raising the issue in cases that reach the Supreme Court. Certainly, in the twentieth century the government has been much more involved in regulating broadcasting and cable than print media, and these areas have been where most litigation has occurred. Still, the Court has upheld structural regulation in the print context in the few cases where constitutional controversies arose.

Early in the twentieth century, Congress passed a law requiring newspapers periodically to publish identifying information and always to publish an indication that material included for compensation constitutes an advertisement. Failure to comply would result in loss of valuable second-class mail privileges. In a decision handed down before the development of any robust First Amendment jurisprudence, the Court perfunctorily rejected a newspaper's First Amendment objections to the statute.[58] Clearly, the statute interfered with "editorial control," that is, the "choice of material to go into a newspaper,"[59] but the Court was not concerned.

Later in the century, as noted, *Associated Press* not only upheld antitrust laws – structural regulations – as applied to the print media, it also gave a stirring explanation for why doing so served the First Amendment. A skeptic, however, might suggest that this reasoning applies only to general laws, not media-specific laws. Of course, *Red Lion* belies that view. After a series of great cases developed modern (very protective) free speech doctrine,[60] the Court reached the same result as *Associated Press* in a media-specific case. In 1978, in *FCC v. National Citizens Committee for Broadcasting*,[61] the Court decided that newspapers could be subject to newspaper-specific limits in their opportunities to obtain broadcast licenses. It held that the FCC rules restricting newspapers were "reasonable." On the basis of an FCC finding that some communities were and others were not especially well served by newspaper-broadcast cross-ownership, the Court even upheld applying different structural restrictions to different newspapers – allowing the combinations in some communities but not others.

Similarly, the Newspaper Preservation Act (NPA)[62] is a media-specific structural law dealing with ownership. The NPA purposefully advantages some papers and, in practice, competitively disadvantages others. It exempts certain financially troubled papers from an antitrust prohibition on combining into a single business unit – a "joint operating agreement" (JOA) – as long as the combination keeps the papers' editorial operations entirely separate and independent. Some members of Congress argued that the law would "stifle competition in ideas by crippling the growth of small newspapers."[63] Benefits from keeping competing city dailies alive seem real, but the law's disadvantageous effect on some competing papers is also clear. On this later ground, disadvantaged suburban competitors of two city dailies that were entering into a JOA challenged the law's constitutionality. The Ninth Circuit Court of Appeals, however, upheld the act largely based on the NPA's good purported purpose of trying to keep independent editorial voices alive.[64]

In summary, if the corporate media entity were a rights holder on its own behalf, it might have a sound First Amendment objection to an ownership regulation that purposefully interfered with its ability to reach some potential audiences. Fortunately, no significant theory of the constitutional basis of the Press Clause supports this conceptualization of the rights of the press. The dominant theories, which uniformly see the press as having an instrumental democratic role, suggest the opposite. And virtually all the Supreme Court's holdings – and the opinions' ringing statements – suggest the opposite. Even *Miami Herald*, the lone case that might support such strong rights, did not use imagery of a corporate rights holder – its reference was to the editors. More important, as the Court now tells us, that case invalidated not a structural regulation but a direct penalty of content – a constitutional evil under any First Amendment theory.

UNDERMINING FIRST AMENDMENT AIMS

Ownership restrictions also might be found unconstitutional if inconsistent in effect or purpose with the goals of the First Amendment. An argument for this conclusion requires resolving two matters. First, what makes the law unconstitutional – inconsistency in purpose, in effect, either purpose or effect, or both purpose and effect? Second, a finding of inconsistency requires knowing the goals or aims of the First Amendment. What are they? In addition, there is a third issue – how activist should courts be in their evaluations of these theoretical issues and the factual matters related to them?

PURPOSE/EFFECTS ANALYSIS

For good reasons, constitutional law mostly finds violations of basic rights only on the basis of an "impermissible governmental purpose," with the notion of purpose construed broadly and interpretatively. Enforceable constitutional provisions mostly direct the government how to act, not what to achieve. People mostly have "rights" to proper respect – for example, to respect as equals and as autonomous agents – not particular outcomes. Government presumptively and, optimistically, mostly has good ultimate aims. Importantly, though, impermissible purposes can lie in knowing use of objectionable means as well as in bad ends. Possibly, the central premise of civil libertarians is that government should use only acceptable means even in its pursuit of good ends. Government should not try to achieve even worthy ends by torture, coerced confessions, improper searches, taking property without compensation, denying a person's equality, or, especially relevant here, by censorship.

In contrast to the objection to bad purposes, the government has no duty to subsidize or otherwise promote the development of information or data despite the effect this lack of development has on people's ability to engage in communication. Moreover, the Court has repeatedly held that the government can keep information secret as a means to pursue legitimate ends. It cannot, however, pursue the same ends by prohibiting and punishing publication of the same content.[65] That is, there is no objection to trying purposefully to maintain secrecy. And there can be no objection merely to the *effect* of stopping a person from communicating particular information – that effect is accomplished equally by the government not developing the information, by keeping the information secret, or by prohibiting its publication. Objection can be raised to particular means of accomplishing this end – by *purposefully* prohibiting speech. Trying to promote national security by prohibiting dissenting speech is impermissible, but promoting security by raising taxes to hire soldiers is fine. This would be true even if the taxes reduce the resources dissenters have available for their dissenting speech. The constitutional problem is with purposefully restricting speech, not with that effect if it results from keeping secrets or raising taxes.

Here is not the place to review the comparative constitutional significance of government purposes and effects, which has proven incredibly complex, nuanced, and contested[66] – and has spawned excellent scholarship. The choice between purpose and effects analyses has been most debated in the context of Fourteenth Amendment "equal protection" – where some version of purpose analysis has prevailed.[67] In the speech and press arena, laws that on their face or otherwise overtly prohibit or burden particular categories of protected speech almost by definition purposefully use constitutionally "bad" means. Their "purpose" is to suppress speech whether or not in service of some more legitimate end. Unsurprisingly, these laws are typically[68] held unconstitutional. Actual or potential speakers also often object to facially content-neutral laws that negatively *affect* their speech practices.[69] Here, however, the government typically has a justification entirely unrelated to a "bad purpose" of suppressing speech. If, however, a determinative bad purpose is found, the law is struck down. The typical doctrinal approach applied in these cases has become the *O'Brien* test. The Court upholds the law: (1) "if it furthers an important or substantial government interest; (2) if the government interest is unrelated to the suppression of free expression; and (3) if the incidental restriction on alleged First Amendment freedom is no greater than is essential to the furtherance of that interest."[70]

Obviously, the *O'Brien* test requires difficult judgments about which people will differ. Look at the test, though. In practice, the most telling element has been the second – and requiring a government interest unrelated to suppression is overtly a search for a "good purpose." This is where the real action of invalidation occurs. In contrast, both the first and third elements of this test seem "effects"-focused. Courts, however, are normally and properly disinclined to substitute their view of importance for good-faith assertions by political branches, which presumably reflect popular (or, sometimes, lobbyists') views. This policy deference guts the significance of the first element except as a requirement that the asserted "good" purpose be comprehensible in the context. Likewise, the final element requiring that the law "be essential" to further the interest has potential to be a major lever in a balancing "effects" analysis. Occasionally courts seem to give it that role, although practice in this regard is hardly uniform. Many scholars see the requirement as playing an "interpretative" role. Laws are seldom struck down using this third requirement *except* where circumstances justify a suspicion that the regulation actually has, even if superficially deniable, a "bad purpose" of suppressing speech or was adopted with at least an unconscious contempt for speech interests, a contempt that itself should be constitutionally objectionable.[71] These suspicions about attributable bad purposes are sustained when government could achieve any plausible legitimate aim by means that do not have the bad effect on speech. In other words, this third element helps to smoke out some purported benign purposes as not actually explanatory. It operates as an interpretative aide to the central concern: uncovering and outlawing bad purposes.

Normatively, the choice between a purpose or effects analysis ultimately depends on a view of the role of constitutional guarantees in a democratic system. Are constitutional guarantees designed to rule out, even in the government's embodiment of the popular or majority will, means and ends that deny respect to people as equal, dignified, and autonomous agents? And to prohibit disregard of the requirements of the constitutional structure? These are requirements specified by the "purpose" inquiry. Or are constitutional provisions designed to (at least presumptively) assure certain especially valuable results or outcomes as the government goes about governing – the goal of the "effects" focus? Of course, it is certainly possible that the provisions do both, may be to different degrees. It is also possible that some constitutional provisions are best understood as raising one inquiry while others raise the other. The question for this chapter is: which approach is right for interpreting the Press Clause?

Several pragmatic points have relevance. First, recognizing that many laws unavoidably have consequences for speech – often the same law has *both* good and bad effects from a speech perspective – "effects" analyses almost inevitably lead to a balancing of a law's bad impacts on speech against the good it does, both for speech and for other societal interests. For a court to engage in this balancing not only requires it to substitute its evaluative analysis for that of legislative bodies but to do so with virtually *no* guidance[72] from the Constitution or even any serious constitutional theory. Second, to begin the balancing, the court must make crucial empirical predictions. Although knowing that there will be effects on communications is often easy, the more precise knowledge of their extent and nature needed for any sensible policy balancing will often be very obscure. Predictive accounts are typically highly disputed and dependent on complex empirical inquires. Given the ease with which people – and judges – can disagree about both the empirical predictions and evaluative assessments, validating this subjective approach allows for an extraordinarily activist judiciary. Moreover, it would be activist in precisely the realm – policy or evaluative judgments – that in a democracy is arguably much more appropriate for legislative bodies or popularly responsive officials, and activist in an area for which it has no particular institutional competence. Given the inquiry's lack of precision, any decision maker's conclusions are as likely to reflect ideological inclinations as anything else.[73] Judges coming from conventional backgrounds and possessing conventional values can often follow a practice of applying rules or clear standards even in ways protective of dissidents or unpopular outgroups whom the judges personally disfavor. This protective response, however, seems much less likely in the case of open-ended "effects" balancing where typically a conventional world view provides the primary basis for judgment.

Thus, judicial case law and in my view normative analysis both recommend that a "bad purpose" inquiry be the center of the First Amendment analysis. An effects analysis turns courts into unguided policy-making entities and places them in a role that should be reserved for legislative bodies. Admittedly, my normative view on this issue is controversial – disputed by some judicial activists on both the left and right, as the earlier discussion of Christopher Yoo's article illustrates.[74] Here, however, I move on to an even more crucial inquiry: what makes a "purpose" bad under the First Amendment?

Aims of the Freedom of the Press Guarantee

Any determination of the constitutionality of ownership regulations must measure the challenged regulation against aims or purposes attributed to the constitutional guarantee. Unless a law or policy conflicts with these aims, there is no ground for constitutional objection. But care is needed in describing the constitutional aims or purposes. After the initial attribution, the argument becomes comparatively easy.

Thus, someone who wants a law invalidated regularly attributes to the Constitution aims with which she believes she can convincingly show the law conflicts. Someone who wants to uphold a law or practice attributes to the Constitution goals that the law either serves or, at least, aims with which the law does not conflict. I do not mean to suggest bad faith in either case. Typically, the same firmly held values behind the person's wish to have the law struck down or upheld have also influenced her good faith beliefs about the aims or purposes of constitutional provision.

MISGUIDED THEORIES. At one time, speaking through Justice Oliver Wendell Holmes, Jr., the Supreme Court attributed to the speech and press guarantees the *main* aim of preventing prior restraints on speech[75] – which in England had taken the form of an administrative prescreening of publications that Blackstone had railed against as constituting a denial of what he meant by press freedom.[76] Subsequent punishment of a newspaper for *truthfully* exposing corruption of government officials, according to Holmes, created no constitutional problem. This extraordinarily narrow view of the aim of the First Amendment has long since been abandoned, though remnants remain, as illustrated by the *Pentagon Papers Case,*[77] where the Court repeated the view that prior restraints are *especially* problematic.[78]

More recent examples of implicit attributions of aims to the First Amendment abound. Christopher Yoo expressed the hope that the First Amendment would provide a basis for courts to strike down ownership rules that he believes – there is great room for factual disagreement here – reduce the "quantity, quality, and diversity of speech," an *effect* that he calls "architectural censorship."[79] Given his complaint (about this purported effect) and his solution (invalidation under the First Amendment), he implicitly[80] attributes promotion of, or at least not allowing laws that detract from, the "quantity, quality, and diversity of speech" as an aim of the First Amendment. Without this attribution, Yoo *might* have good policy objections to ownership regulation, but his constitutional analysis would collapse.

On its face, however, Yoo's attribution is remarkable. Certainly, the fourth estate and checking function theories of the Press Clause's guarantees have no necessary relation to the *general* quantity, quality, and diversity of speech. The optimal result in serving the checking function is to deter misfeasance and malfeasance corruption. This aim could be achieved by having a press that has a sufficient reputation for exposure that it *deters* wrongdoing of the powerful – thus, reducing the need for the press's own speech although with a press standing ready to provide more exposés if needed. The aim here is functional, not commodity-based. Even the fourth estate role, which suggests the relevance of the quantity and, even more, the quality of political discourse, on which Yoo did not even pretend to dwell, is more nuanced about the circumstances of production and reception that make these communications valuable.

Why might Yoo think – and many others likely agree[81] – that the aim of the First Amendment is to avoid laws that reduce the quantity, quality, and diversity of speech? The error has various explanations, but in my view one is particularly on point here. Many people, especially many economists influential in the legal academy, assume first that public policy should promote things people value. (So far, so good – unless "things" is too objectified and excludes processes, structures, distributions, and relationships and unless "promoting" is understood as maximizing, which seems to require a single metric on which to measure properly incommensurable things.) They next assume the propriety of an econoministic premise. The claim is that in theory and, at least in the case of products or services sold in the market, in practice, value can often actually be measured by how much people are willing and able to pay for it. (Here, the analysis is more dubious.) Then comes the crucial error. Without careful thought, they implicitly equate these things of value with objects or rights that a person can possess or services that she can obtain (rather than also include processes, distributions, and relationships). Thus, in the speech/press context, they assume that what people value is the communicative content that they receive. Obvious, right? People want more (and better) speech (or pictorial, musical, or other media) content. Essentially, people value "commodities" that take the form of media content. Given this commodity framework, the First Amendment protects this interest in receipt of diverse and plentiful commodities against not only content-based censorship (a claim that can be justified on many grounds) but also other impairments (unless these impairments are adequately justified). Interestingly, the dominant First Amendment metaphor, the marketplace of ideas, suggests the centrality of receipt of diverse commodities.[82] We need a good marketplace, which apparently produces precisely what was identified above: more and better content choices.

The conceptual errors of this commodity interpretation of value[83] and, even worse, of its use in interpreting the First Amendment, are many. Critics of this interpretation hardly deny that people want commodities. They add, however, that often people also want and value democracy and personal safety and fulfilling friendships and a host of other noncommodity "things" to which the nature of the media order contributes. Thus, a critic could observe that commodity interpretations typically take an audience's, not a speaker's, view of the value of communications – even though, phenomenologically, the notion of "freedom of" speech and the press would seem fundamentally about *activities* of speaking and publishing. Audiences are, of course, often (but not always) very significant, but they are phenomenologically incidental to the activity. In practice, many people affirmatively value these activities, not just the commodities they receive.

Possibly more to the point here, the critic would go back to the arguments for press freedom – its relevance to democracy and good government, and its watchdog and fourth estate roles. People do value constitutional separation of powers (i.e., separate legislative, executive, and judicial branches). They value democratic procedures. But why? High on the list is probably that separation of powers safeguards liberty, and people value liberty. Or these democratic processes or structures involve people in, or at least allows their involvement in, processes of self-determination, and people value such activity. Any collective political order that denies people this opportunity of self-government gives grounds for complaint. Or maybe people believe that democracy in the long run leads to other outcomes that they value. In any event, democratic procedures and separation of powers require the use of resources, but their very nature precludes their purchase by individuals in a market. The same is true about many aspects of what is valued in relation to press freedom.

The market fails to provide for these values for many reasons, not the least because separation of powers and some democratic procedures are necessarily public goods – one person cannot have it without others also having it. Egalitarian premises also would make purchase of these goods by individuals in a market unfair. The nature of these values may even be intrinsically inconsistent with market processes – their value degraded by *monetarized* trades. Of course, choices – "trade-offs" – are still possible. Jane might reluctantly sacrifice her relationship with Bob because of her love of Pat – but hopefully not simply because Pat is willing and able to pay more. A person might – I think unwisely – be willing to give up democracy or freedom for a promise of security. She should not give up her vote, however, for a bribe. The very value of storytelling in a family, like voting in a democratic election or love in relationships, should make it inconsistent with market payments. The point is not that separation of powers or democratic procedures do not have costs. People sometimes conclude these costs are too high to make them worth it. Nevertheless, the valuation process will and should involve discursive and collective – that is, political, not market – judgments.

The commodification focus of more quantity, better quality, and more diverse media products simply does not engage the democratic values underlying press freedom. Many government policies normally considered constitutionally optional can purposefully add to or subtract from the quantity, quality, and diversity of media output. Consider subsidies for publication or postage; consider provision of government information; or, conversely, consider limitations on access to government files, records, and facilities; consider provision for higher quality public education. Almost every aspect of governmental communications and cultural and educational policy, national or local security practices, and protections of informational privacy purposefully affect the quantity, content, quality, or diversity of communications that is publicly available. An effects focus brings within its scope a constitutional analysis of a virtually unlimited range of policies. Raising or lowering the federal funds interest rate a quarter point could have an effect on communications. Surely, the First Amendment should not be understood to require a specific governmental fiscal policy. Thus, the objections are two-fold. Neither a commodity focus nor an effects valuation provides a proper interpretation of First Amendment aims or purposes.

A PROPER DEMOCRACY-ORIENTED THEORY. Once democratic process values are seen as central to the First Amendment, objections that regulation reduces rather than increases the availability of communication commodities is simply beside the point. But this does not necessarily imply abandoning evaluations of the purposes (or effects) of government media policies, including instrumentalist policies related to media ownership concentration. An emphasis on democracy merely establishes a different yardstick against which the evaluation should take place. But this yardstick cannot be applied without a more precise characterization. If press freedom is guaranteed to protect or support the press in its performance of a "checking function" or a "watchdog role," then that democratic aim is the standard. A bad purpose is to purposefully undermine the performance of that role; a bad effect is to affect its performance negatively. But such an interpretation is too abrupt. While freedom of the press is almost universally thought to be an essential element of democracy, the nature of the democratic roles of the press is not clear without inquiry. Only the results of that inquiry can provide an appropriate yardstick against which to measure government policy. But think: identifying the democratic role(s) of the press depends on what is meant by, what is valued about, democracy. Different conceptions of democracy are probably best served by different media structures. These different conceptions may even lead to different interpretations of the meaning of press freedom. Thus, to know whether either restricting concentration or allowing it interferes with press freedom requires a theory of democracy.

Unsurprisingly, democracy is a contested concept. This topic was taken up briefly in chapter 1. The emphasis there on an egalitarian sharing of democratic political power, specifically including communicative power within the public sphere, responded to only one set of democratic theories. That emphasis most overtly embodies a *liberal pluralist* view of democracy. It sees democracy as aiming to achieve outcomes that fairly compromise – that is, more or less proportionately achieve or advance – the potentially conflicting interests of all people or groups within the polity. This liberal pluralist theory could be contrasted with a major alternative. *Civic republicans* treat a common discourse aimed at the public good as definitive of democracy. This discourse should be inclusive and civil, aiming at real agreement rather than fair compromise. Though this inclusive, public discourse could easily be distorted by the media's commercialism – or by ideological or self-interested biases of either monopolistic commercial or governmental entities – concentration itself does not undermine and might even serve this discourse. Elihu Katz has argued that a state monopoly on broadcast media in Israel beneficially involved the country as a whole in a public discourse.[84] James Curran, although disagreeing with Katz on many points, also favors policies that assure a robust core media. He suggests a public broadcast system for this role, serving roughly to provide a basis for an inclusive common discourse.[85]

Defending a "discourse theory of democracy," Jürgen Habermas explains that a democracy requires both discourses aimed at uncoerced agreement (the republican ideal) and discourses aimed at fair bargains (the liberal ideal).[86] Habermas argues that it is inaccurate to assert that people are never motivated by or able to find a common good, but that it is equally naïve to believe that people will not often have separate, sometimes opposing, interests that lead to disagreement or that in such cases they should not aim at fair bargains. Democracy involves a complex mixture of republican and liberal discourses; I have labeled this conception *complex democracy* because it complexly combines liberal and republican premises.[87] Invoking Nancy Fraser's conception of counterpublics or subaltern public spheres,[88] my elaboration of complex democracy also emphasizes the importance of subgroups' cultural, self-definitional discourses, as well as strategic discourses *internal* to subgroups, both of which are necessary if democracy is to avoid an undemocratic domination of smaller, structurally weaker, or otherwise marginal subgroups.

Each theory of democracy has different implications for the democratic rationale for press freedom and for the constitutionality or desirability of restricting ownership concentration. The liberal pluralist should find such restrictions beneficial, maybe constitutionally required. Each group, maybe each subgroup, needs its own media at least to report when public issues impinge on its interests, to aid in recruitment to its views, and to mobilize its constituency. For the civic republican, these ownership restrictions are probably unnecessary and potentially objectionable, for example, if they undermine a community-wide "common discourse" – although this republican does worry about commercial corruption of dominant media. Thus, civic republicans should favor relatively heavy regulation of the concentrated private or governmental media in order to ensure its inclusiveness, civility, and maybe public relevance. The FCC's "fairness doctrine," which purportedly required coverage of controversial issues and the airing of "all" (reasonable) sides of the issue, is an obvious republican policy. Moreover, civility was assured by the licensee's responsibility for and control of this coverage.

My view, however, is that complex democracy is normatively the most appealing and empirically the most plausible theory of democracy. In recognizing that both republican and liberal discourses are needed, there is some tension with chapter 1's argument for maximum dispersal of media ownership. A complex democrat is likely to conclude that *some* community-wide media entities are needed for common discourses. In effect, democracy creates competing claims – the need for empowerment of individuals and groups in their own discourses and for collective discourses. Responding to these competing claims is a proper subject of policy making, which should determine whether one or the other discourse is more in need of support and how different media, different structural orders, can best provide for these different democratic needs. These issues of policy are taken up in chapter 5. In contrast, for the purposes of the constitutional discussion, although concentration could serve a common discourse, a real danger exists that concentration could undermine pluralist and subgroup discourses. It all depend on the empirical circumstances. This danger should justify however much restriction on mergers as is thought appropriate in order to provide for adequate opportunities for dispersed, pluralistic discourses. Facts may overwhelmingly show that too much concentration has or has not already occurred. If market processes lead this danger to materialize, regulatory limits on ownership concentration serve democracy. For the *constitutional* discussion in this chapter, however, all that is needed is the possibility that a legislative body could reasonably judge that undue concentration has occurred or might occur. From the perspective of complex democracy, judgments about the ideal amount and content of regulation cannot be resolvable on principle. Rather, these judgments will depend on complicated and debatable empirical evaluations of circumstances. For this reason, no clear abstract (constitutional) principles determine which policies are best – which will serve the democratic role of the press. Instead, constitutional doctrine appropriately leaves the matter to legislative assessment because the *better* theory of democracy requires reliance on the legislature's greater sensitivity to variable empirical factors.

Though not my preferred argument, the same deferential conclusion could be reached by a different route. Where normative theorists disagree as to what is the better conception of democracy (and history and legal precedent show no clear constitutional commitment), the choice among theories of democracy should not be mandated by courts under a purported constitutional interpretation. Rather, the public should choose through political debate and struggle their preferred conception of democracy. A central arena for and result of this debate and political struggle is the choice of preferred media policies.

JUDICIAL ACTIVISM: THE PROPER LEVEL AND FORM OF SCRUTINY

The constitutional text is primarily a blueprint for the organizational structure of government. In the first instance, it is not directed to the courts and is mostly not about individual rights. The Constitution, however, does specify limitations on, and occasionally mandates, exercises of governmental power. Bound by oath to support the Constitution, obviously members of both houses of Congress and the President must take positions on its meaning.[89] Although less often noted by lawyers, this blueprint can also guide citizens in determining whether their government acts legally – that is, in accordance with *their* interpretation of the Constitution.[90] They may decide to replace officials or to ignore laws if they conclude that the officials act inconsistently or that the laws are inconsistent with the Constitution's meaning. In any event, the judiciary's role can only be interstitial. Some meanings will not have been and, in the case of many issues relating to impeachment, for example, sometimes cannot be decided by the courts. Certainly, officials' or private people's interpretations, when they occur, are unlikely to be always consistent with each other or to correspond to the courts' interpretations.

Nevertheless, in our political order, the institutional role of the courts in determining the operative constitutional law, as well as influencing other actors, is immense. The question arises: how actively should courts intervene in imposing their interpretations in place of those of other actors? On one view, the matter is simple. In deciding cases, judges have an obligation to the parties before them to do their best at interpreting and applying the law, including the Constitution when it is relevant.

Most commentators conclude that the matter is more complex. They often argue that judicial review raises considerations of legitimacy – federal court judges are unelected – and of competence. Many theorists recommend, and most observations of the Court suggest, that the degree of activism varies not only historically but also depending on the context (e.g., less in relation to the military) and the constitutional provision invoked (more in relation to Equal Protection than the Commerce Clause). My general perception is that recent liberal Justices usually defend activist intervention but seldom engage in it, while conservatives regularly condemn but often practice it.[91] This broad debate about the propriety of judicial activism can, however, be put aside here. This section's two narrower questions are: what level of activism does legal precedent indicate should apply to evaluating legal regulation of media concentration, and what level of activism does the best theory of the First Amendment recommend?

PRECEDENT: PRELIMINARIES. Under current First Amendment doctrine, the degree of judicial activism often reflects the level of so-called scrutiny that courts apply to a law and to the government's justification. Courts and commentators often divide scrutiny into three levels described by legal code words: rational basis scrutiny, intermediate scrutiny, and strict scrutiny. Nevertheless, using differing levels of scrutiny has been subject to serious and pervasive criticism by various Justices and commentators, initially in the equal protection arena.[92] Historically, scrutiny analysis was not used in First Amendment analyses, and its recent adoption there has likewise been subject to severe critiques, prominently illustrated by those of Justice Kennedy.[93] Therefore, before discussing current scrutiny analysis, I briefly note an alternative to this relatively recent and arguably misguided scrutiny innovation.

If the First Amendment is read to rule out certain governmental purposes – that is, as a directive to government not to aim at certain consequences – the judicial inquiry would be: Does the government have this prohibited aim? If it does, the conclusion is: unconstitutional! No matter how good a justification the government otherwise has or how purportedly necessary the law is to achieve that good end, the purpose to use this bad means (or to have this bad end) – for example, to censor speech or to undermine the institutional integrity of the press – is impermissible. If an unacceptable purpose is not found, the law is upheld. No balancing! The inquiry is concerned with not the importance but with the permissibility of the government purpose. Remember, however, that the "forbidden purpose" analysis refers to having those purposes as either ends or means. Most limits on speech – prohibitions of racist speech, of reputation-damaging false speech, or of speech that creates some danger, for example – have highly proper ultimate ends. As one judge pointed out: "The constitutional protection accorded . . . is not based on the naive belief that speech can do no harm."[94] The central premise of civil liberties is that the government should advance its worthy ends only with legitimate, even if less effective, means, rather than with purposeful restrictions on speech.

Automatic invalidation of laws on the basis of an impermissible purpose to restrict constitutionally protected speech is historically very explanatory of much case law. Many of our greatest speech-protective First Amendment cases, including *New York Times v. Sullivan* and *Brandenburg v. Ohio*,[95] would probably be decided differently under an honest application of current scrutiny analyses.[96] Public figures' capacity, sometimes even their willingness, to serve the public can depend on protecting them from false, reputation-ruining characterizations. State libel laws offered this protection. In *New York Times*, the Court inquired whether the rationale of the First Amendment covered the outlawed speech. Finding that it did, without more analysis of the justification of the restriction, the Court protected the speech. In contrast, current scrutiny analysis would observe that liability was necessary to serve high public as well as individual interests and, on this basis, presumably should uphold the law.

Speaking for the Court, Chief Justice Rehnquist more recently used an almost identical analysis. He held unconstitutional the imposition of liability for intentionally subjecting Reverend Jerry Falwell to intense emotional distress by publishing a cartoon implying an incestuous drunken rendevous between Falwell and his mother in an outhouse. Rehnquist found the rationale of free speech encompassed satire and parody. Like Brennan in *New York Times v. Sullivan*, Rehnquist protected this speech without weighing the again very real, significant government interest in protecting public figures from potentially disabling personal attacks and without considering whether there were other ways to protect the injured person.[97]

Similarly, *Brandenburg v. Ohio*, the leading modern "clear and present danger" case, established a requirement of both an intent to create and a likelihood of creating imminent lawless action as prerequisites to outlawing the danger-creating speech.[98] But neither the *imminence* of nor the *intent* to induce lawless action seems crucial to the "compelling government interest" in prohibiting speech almost certain to lead eventually to lawless actions.

In these three cases, the law's legitimate ultimate purpose was to prohibit reputation-ruining, injury-causing, or danger-creating speech. The laws, however, purposefully restricted protected speech as its means to achieve these ends. Once the Court found that the rationale of the First Amendment encompassed the forbidden speech, without more scrutiny, it protected the speech, leaving society to respond to the real harms by means less direct and less effective than the restrictions on speech. In contrast, scrutiny analyses in each instance could easily find the government interest to be great and the speech restriction to be the most direct, only really effective means to serve the interest. On this basis, an honest application of scrutiny analysis must uphold the restriction on speech. That is, scrutiny analysis is likely to justify the "wrong" results in these landmark speech-protective decisions.

Despite the possibility of the above form of analysis, many Justices and commentators find purposeful restrictions *potentially* justifiable. They purport to "scrutinize" the justification offered by the government and sometimes also evaluate the severity of the restriction on core First Amendment rights or aims. Their scrutiny represents a form of balancing. The previous paragraphs showed that this balancing is not intrinsic to a "bad purpose" analysis. It is, however, virtually inevitable if courts use an "effects" criterion. A negative effect on First Amendment rights or aims *cannot* be conclusive. For example, an income tax that left Mary with less money to place ads in the local paper promoting the Kyoto treaty is likely to have an *incidental* negative effect on her protected, politically salient speech. An absence of subsidized child care could leave Jane with insufficient time for leafleting for abortion rights. Nevertheless, surely the appropriate *constitutional* response (legislative or policy-making responses are a very different story) to their complaints is: "tough." Effects of laws are ubiquitous. *All* laws believed to have a net negative effect on First Amendment rights or aims cannot be unconstitutional.

PRECEDENT: DOCTRINAL SCRUTINY ANALYSIS. Given the current doctrinal emphasis on scrutiny, the question can be asked: what level of scrutiny does precedent recommend for evaluating structural regulation of the press generally or ownership concentration specifically? It turns out the answer is not entirely clear. While case law outcomes at the Supreme Court level remain deferential, doctrine is apparently inclining toward a more activist posture. With one interesting exception involving cable franchises, noted below, the Supreme Court has never upheld a constitutional challenge to structural media regulations – although it strikes down *purported* structural regulations that actually operate by overtly penalizing content. That was the story in *Miami Herald*, discussed above, where the right of reply law operated as a penalty on the paper's criticism of Tornillo.[99]

Nevertheless, the Supreme Court rarely faces media structural regulation cases. Especially rare are media-specific structural regulations involving newspapers, which purportedly receive the greatest constitutional protection. Many observers believe that newspaper structural regulations would receive heightened scrutiny and often be struck down. (Given the historical role and function of newspapers, many imaginable, *purportedly* structural, regulations of newspapers may be hard to understand without attributing to them a bad purpose of muzzling a strident press. If so, the constitutional objection would reflect not current scrutiny analysis's concern with the strength of the government purpose but rather the badness of purposeful interferences with the structural integrity of the press.) Contrarily, I suspect that most of these same observers believe that the Supreme Court would uphold the Newspaper Preservation Act (NPA) against a First Amendment challenge, just as the Ninth Circuit Court of Appeals has done.[100] This view exists even though the NPA is clearly a newspaper structural regulation that, as members of Congress explicitly recognized, disadvantages some newspapers in its attempt to further its conception of media diversity – specifically, by keeping an independent editorial voice alive.[101]

From the effects perspective, which judicial activists usually favor for reviewing media structural regulation,[102] "bad effects" on the media created by general laws and media-specific laws should be indistinguishable. Lawyers for the print media long followed this logic. They often challenged general laws based on the law's effect on the media entity. Nevertheless, the Supreme Court, without considering any application of heightened scrutiny, had no problem rejecting these challenges. *Associated Press*, discussed earlier, involving general antitrust laws, is possibly the most obvious illustration, but the same result applies to labor and other laws.[103]

Nevertheless, the view persists that the First Amendment operates as a serious restraint on governmental structural regulation of the media. In suggesting that the First Amendment might limit stringent enforcement of generally applicable antitrust laws, even one of the best current telecommunications scholars, Howard Shelanski, could in 2006 assert that "the Supreme Court has *consistently* held that economic regulation of *media ownership* should be subject to intermediate scrutiny under the First Amendment" unless conditions justifying even stricter scrutiny were present.[104] This consistency is a myth. Shelanski cited only two cases, which I discuss further below, to support his claim: *Turner Broadcasting System v. FCC*, which is the sole Supreme Court case to apply intermediate scrutiny in a media structural case (rather than quite routinely upholding the law if seen as reasonable) and which does not even involve regulation of ownership, and *FCC v. National Citizens Committee for Broadcasting*, a case that repeatedly, including on the pages to which Shelanski referred, required only that the ownership restriction be reasonable, applied none of the usual rules of intermediate scrutiny, did not require any fact finding to support the rules' reasonableness, referred to how ownership restrictions supported First Amendment values, and certainly did not say it was requiring intermediate scrutiny. Clearly, the case was much more deferential than Shelanski suggested.

Still, the now widespread view is that media-specific laws are constitutionally much more problematic. Since general laws can have the same effects on the press, this view makes sense if and only if these laws are seen as likely loci of constitutionally objectionable purposes. Nevertheless, this view that media-specific laws are treated by the Court as problematic is wrong. Here too, the Court has traditionally been deferential. Possibly the most pertinent case, is *FCC v. National Citizens Committee for Broadcasting*.[105] Newspapers were subject to a restriction not applicable to individuals or most other businesses. In the area of the newspaper's operation, it (generally) could not own broadcast stations.[106] The Court rejected newspapers' First Amendment challenge and instead found this regulation of newspapers "reasonable" – a legal code word suggesting rather minimal scrutiny. Maybe the Court upheld the structural regulation only because it involved the opportunity to obtain a broadcast license and the Court routinely upholds restrictions placed on broadcast licenses. Little reason in logic or precedent, however, compels this narrow reading. No Supreme Court case until 1994 shows any greater scrutiny applied to any structural regulation. Moreover, with the one possible exception mentioned next, no Supreme Court decision has found any media structural regulation unconstitutional.[107]

Los Angeles v. Preferred Communication[108] is often (incorrectly) taken to have invalidated a structural regulation. Los Angeles awarded exclusive (i.e., monopoly) cable franchises. The economics of cable service means that usually total costs are much lower if only one company lays cables. Head-to-head competition among franchisees is likely to be economically "ruinous" and unstable, and, therefore, monopoly status may be natural. Meaningful competition is most likely to come – as it mostly has – from those who exploit different technologies, for example, telephone lines or satellites, to deliver competing multichannel programming, with this difference in method relating to some meaningful product differentiation as well as different prices. In *Preferred Communication*, the Court actually neither invalidated the exclusive franchising[109] nor identified the level of scrutiny that should apply. Rather, it reasonably said that the challenge to this government grant of monopoly status raised a real First Amendment issue. Such a monopoly grant, the Court said, might be unconstitutional unless the city could show insufficient physical or economic resources to support more than one cable system.[110] The Court did not indicate whether a showing that multiple systems would involve wasteful expenditures that would cause a decline in content quality or a rise in price to the consumer means that "insufficient" economic demand exists. Nevertheless, the Court in *Preferred Communications* approved in principle a First Amendment challenge to a structural regulation. This case, however, should provide little cheer for constitutional activists and is arguably unproblematic from the perspective advanced in this chapter. For any commentator who believes democratic values require diversity, a First Amendment challenge to the government establishing a media monopoly is virtually the opposite of the challenges to most structural rules, certainly challenges to rules restricting concentration.

Finally, consider *Turner Broadcasting System v. FCC*,[111] decided in 1994. Cable companies challenged rules that generally required them to carry local over-the-air broadcast stations.[112] After concluding that cable was more like newspapers than broadcasting for First Amendment purposes, the majority applied intermediate scrutiny with little apparent thought or comment on the fact that this level of scrutiny was greater than that previously employed in any media structural regulation case. Maybe the majority thought it was being deferential – it was as compared with the dissent, which wanted the Court to apply strict scrutiny because it viewed the carriage requirement as content-based. Alternatively, this level of heightened scrutiny may reflect the Court's current automatic inclination to categorize virtually all First Amendment cases as involving either a content or noncontent regulation, with strict scrutiny reflexively applied to the former and intermediate scrutiny applied to the latter. This recent practice arose, however, in the context of the speech of individuals. Whether *Turner* indicates a willingness now to be more activist in the media structural context is unclear – although as noted below, lower courts have interpreted it so.

Despite the heightened scrutiny, the Court still upheld, after further fact finding below, the "must carry" rules.[113] Continuation of this practice of upholding media structural laws could be – should be – the case's most meaningful legacy, and its scrutiny can be seen as toothless.[114] Alternatively, a more worrisome and activist possibility involves the incredible malleability of intermediate scrutiny.

The potential malleability is evident in *Time Warner Entertainment*,[115] a truly remarkable decision of the D.C. Circuit. Time Warner challenged a regulation that required cable systems to reserve at least 60 percent of their channels for cable content providers (networks) in which it had no meaningful ownership interest – much like the reservation of "must carry" channels in *Turner*. As in *Turner*, the challenged regulation required the cable system to carry channels it did not own. But rather than taking its lead from *Turner*'s holding, the court relied on *Turner*'s intermediate scrutiny to find this requirement unconstitutional.

Consider! The lower court invalidated a regulation imposing essentially the same type of burden, carriage of channels that the cable system would choose not to carry, that the Supreme Court approved.[116] The Supreme Court should have little trouble finding that the same interests in promoting source diversity and reducing excessive power in the marketplace of ideas that justify "must carry" rules also justify a similar mandate to cede control over some channels to independent content providers.

The three major differences between the two cases cut in favor of more easily upholding the regulation at issue in *Time Warner*. The "set-aside" requirement in *Time Warner* left the choice of specific cable networks to carry with the cable system, requiring only that it not own them. This difference eliminated any possible objection, available in *Turner*, that the rule required the cable system to carry content to which it substantively objects. O'Connor's dissent in *Turner* also objected that the "must carry" rules were content-based because the government premised the carriage obligation on the value of local content, especially local news, provided by the "must carry" stations. Whether or not her characterization is persuasive, it had no application to the "set-aside" law in *Time Warner*. Finally, Justice O'Connor noted the "danger in having a single cable operator *decide* what millions of subscribers can or cannot watch" – a danger similar to but less than that in *Time Warner* of having a single company both *own* and *decide* what millions see. She then suggested that "Congress might . . . conceivably obligate cable operators to act as common carriers for some of their channels, with those channels being open to all through some sort of lottery system or time-sharing arrangement."[117] Except for leaving cable operators greater discretion, the regulation did basically what O'Connor recommended. Thus, the regulation that the D.C. Circuit struck down in *Time Warner* presumably would have been approved by the Justices in both the majority and the dissent in the Supreme Court. How did the D.C. Circuit go so far wrong?

The Circuit Court in *Time Warner* repeatedly cited *Turner* but never mentioned the actual dispute involved or the holding in *Turner*. Rather, it cited *Turner* exclusively for *Turner*'s approval of, and method of applying, intermediate scrutiny. The Circuit Court concluded that the government had not met intermediate scrutiny's requirement of showing that the regulation "does not burden substantially more speech than necessary to further those interests."[118] This behavior illustrates my claim: scrutiny's inherent malleability allows divergent results even though the laws, and their purported burden on First Amendment rights, are strikingly similar.

THEORY. First Amendment theory offers a much simpler answer to the issue of activism: it is not appropriate here. Unlike an individual whose autonomy should be inviolate, the rationale for constitutional protection of the press – of media entities – lies instrumentally in their service to democracy. Other than the lone pamphleteer or maybe today's blogger, media entities are created against a background of law and are inherently legally structured. If this structure is measured by its effects on the media order, given that most inadequacies in the press's performance that are identified by media scholars relate to predictable consequences of the market, an effects-based activism probably would hold market structures and regulation by the market unconstitutional. Not only can one not expect courts to follow that logic, it is misguided from the start. The constitutional theory advanced here is that unconstitutionality should depend on unconstitutional purpose. Whatever else can be said about the reliance on a market, it is difficult to conclude that its purpose is to undermine a press capable of serving democracy.[119] Given that purpose analysis only invalidates when there is no legitimate purpose to explain a means of regulation, few non-media-specific laws will be in danger. They can seldom be coherently interpreted as solely designed, even solely applied to the media, for the purpose of undermining the media's service to democracy.

Of course, some purposeful executive actions might improperly intrude into the institutional integrity of the press. That characterization represents the press's claim about the government compelling disclosure of confidential sources or "appropriation" of other aspects of the journalist's work product – information that would not exist other than for the journalist's media role. The central issue, though, should turn on whether the press clause protects *that* aspect of institutional integrity, not on a scrutiny-based effects analysis. Likewise, constitutional objections might be made not to government payments to journalists or media entities for carrying government messages but to government payments for representing the messages as the press's own. Unlike properly identified government advertising, this subterfuge interferes with (arguably "abridges," to use the language of the First Amendment) the institutional integrity of the press in providing for public discourse.[120] The claim that these practices violate the press clause, however, is not based on scrutiny tests, which typically *begin* with what is considered a presumptive violation and which then ask whether the violation can be justified. Rather, the claim goes to interpreting the Press Clause to determine what governmental aims or means are prohibited. The question here is what the answer is in respect to structural regulation.

Thus, theory looks to identify bad purposes in relation to the press performing its democratic or more general instrumentalist roles of providing for free, robust, informative, inclusive public discourse. "Bad" would be a purpose to undermine press performance or to undermine its institutional integrity or, maybe, to compromise its integrity for other social goals. (This last possibility is the objection to mandated disclosure of sources or payment for placement of government messages that falsely appear to be the press's own message.) Generic activism, so implicit in effects analyses, is inappropriate here – though not because courts should not demand the government meet constitutional requirements but because courts should not be engaged in second guessing legislative bodies on institutional design or policy judgments not ruled out as impermissible by the best interpretation of the Constitution. In contrast to most censorious penalties of message content, most structural regulation will not have a purpose to undermine media performance.

Still, theoretically bad purposes can exist in relation to structural regulation. To find out whether this is the case requires an initial identification of what constitutional theory identifies as the proper role of protection of the press. Only then can an observer see whether the purpose of a regulation is inconsistent with the press's constitutional status. What is the rationale for protection? To protect the press in providing a free and democracy-serving communications order? Well, yes, but what does *that* mean? The mundane response is that this is contested even among the most intelligent scholars; therefore, courts should stay their hand. The trouble with this response is that the same is true for most interpretive constitutional issues. In one view, the courts' assignment is to find and adopt the best, the wisest, answer to the issue of constitutional interpretation that they face using the best, most legitimate, methodology they can find. Contested issues – as constant dissents in Supreme Court opinions illustrate – are an ubiquitous, accepted part of the judicial process and do not justify judicial passivity. In any event, if they do justify passivity, as some think, this has no special bearing on the issue in the media context but is rather a generic reason favoring passivity in judicial review.

Here, the discussion of complex democracy in the previous section becomes relevant. If the ideal form of democracy – the form that properly guides constitutional interpretation – is, as I argued, complex democracy, the argument for judicial deference on media structural issues becomes much more powerful. Complex democracy recognizes multiple roles of the media. Different roles are often best served by different, potentially conflicting, structural rules. Complex democracy also recognizes that the determination of which roles are most in need of nurture represents a contextual policy conclusion that is likely to vary over time. Given these two points, no invariant or abstract constitutional principles could possibly determine the proper aim to be furthered in the choice of structural rules. Even if rules' empirical consequences for media performance were clear, which is seldom the case, as long as the ordering of proper aims is indeterminate, there is no basis for finding particular structural choices unconstitutional for failing to further these aims. Legislative policy-making bodies have the responsibility to make good faith judgments, embodied in law, about which aspects of the media require special, overt nurture. That is, the best interpretation of the Press Clause – that media structural rules should (among other things) serve complex democracy – runs out before particular policies are determined.

The propriety of deference to media structural regulation contrasts with not only the actual existence but also the arguable theoretical propriety of activism in protecting individual speech, where an aim is to protect the freedom of the dissenter in the face of majoritarian conventionalism.[121] Whatever the appropriate general views about judicial activism, the best substantive interpretation of the Press Clause directs courts to limit themselves to invalidating rules or practices that are inconsistent with all reasonable conceptions of the media's democratic role. Courts should invalidate political, informational, or cultural censorship and structural rules that can be reasonably shown to constitute attempts to undermine the media's capacity to perform its democratic role. Courts, however, should not second-guess "good faith" (i.e., "reasonable" or "rational," as minimal scrutiny requires) legislative or administrative judgments about the structures that best serve the needs of a democratic society's varying groups of citizens and consumers.

In sum, First Amendment objections to media ownership regulations are groundless. Admittedly, these objections make sense under particular assumptions: if the First Amendment gives to press owners, usually corporate entities, rights grounded ultimately in their own status as owners, or if the purpose of First Amendment rights is to achieve particular, usually commodity-oriented, aims related to supplying content to the public. Even then, to become legally effective, these assumptions, especially the second, require a judiciary willing to be particularly activist in this context. However, neither assumption nor the required activism receives any support in dominant First Amendment precedents. The Supreme Court has explicitly or implicitly rejected these premises whenever invoked by a corporate media entity.

These assumptions are also rejected by the best – in fact, by virtually all – theories of either the First Amendment in general or the Press Clause in particular. First Amendment theorists generally read the Press Clause (or, in some cases, the Speech and Press Clauses combined[122]) from the perspective of its special structural role in service of democracy. To justify any special rights of press entities or journalists requires at least a demonstration that the specific right serves the press's democratic role. Better, these rights should be shown to be implicit aspects of the institutional integrity of a press capable of performing its democratic role. Purported objections to restrictions on ownership concentration do not fit this paradigm. As the Court has recognized at least since Justice Black's statement in *Associated Press*, with which this chapter opened, all values embodied in the press clause count in favor of restricting concentration.

Invoking the First Amendment as a reason to limit ownership regulation serves some corporations' economic interests. But it does not serve the First Amendment, democracy, or thoughtful evaluations of media policy. Raising such First Amendment objections simply obscures the real policy issues properly at stake.

THE FIRST AMENDMENT AS REQUIRING LIMITS ON CONCENTRATION?

Periodically I am asked, usually by media activists, not lawyers, to participate in litigation challenging corporate media mergers as violating the First Amendment. This chapter's opening quotations from Supreme Court opinions can be easily read to support such challenges. Thus, the question here is: should courts rely directly on the First Amendment to block (or undo?) objectionable mergers?

Most American constitutional lawyers would immediately say "no." They would observe that the provisions of the Constitution of the United States, with very few exceptions,[123] are directed at government. Lawyers call this point the "state action" doctrine. Usually, only the action of the state – the government – not of private individuals or entities can violate the Constitution. Specifically, only the government can violate the First Amendment.[124] Media mergers between two companies – however bad as a matter of policy – cannot violate the First Amendment.

This common lawyerly response is too quick and too myopic. Respected legal theorists have argued that, even if private parties cannot themselves violate the Constitution, the government's willingness to allow private parties to achieve their private ends through having the government enforce its laws – and maybe even the government's failure to adopt particular laws, including property-related laws – can be a constitutional violation.[125] The First Amendment certainly could be read to require the government to regulate the communications order as a means to achieve or avoid particular constitutionally salient results. Any law that contradicted these mandates would be, to that extent, unconstitutional. In a legal challenge to a media merger,[126] courts could reject the merger partners' reliance on a "governmentally backed" legal order that permitted constitutionally objectionable mergers.

Pragmatically unthinkable? Not at all. Western European democracies have long believed that a strong public broadcasting system is necessary to prevent (market) censorship.[127] Given this view, the German Constitutional Court held that the German Constitution mandates the provision of the services of public broadcasting. It also found that a mixed system that includes private broadcasting is constitutionally permissible *only if* private broadcasters are subject to considerable regulation, including regulation aimed at promoting diversity.[128] That is, some constitutional democracies read their free press guarantees to require activist constitutional review, including invalidation of over-reliance on the market and requirements that government regulate private ownership. More directly to the point, constitutional courts in France, Italy, and, by implication, Germany have held that their respective constitutions require limits on media concentration.[129]

Doctrinally unobtainable? Not at all. As noted, nothing in the structure of the American "state action" doctrine requires a different result. This activist requirement is not so far-fetched. In a First Amendment suit to force television networks to accept advertisements raising questions about the Vietnam War, two dissenting Justices indicated that they would find that the FCC violated the First Amendment by allowing broadcasters to adopt a general policy of noncarriage of paid messages relating to controversial social issues as long as the broadcaster continued to accept advertisements for commercial products.[130] Though the majority rejected Justice William Brennan and Justice Thurgood Marshall's argument in that particular context, three of the other Justices did so on grounds that did not repudiate applying the First Amendment to a failure to regulate private broadcasters.[131] Rather, their view was substantive. They concluded that the government's choice to allow the existing editorial autonomy was constitutionally permissible. That is, the "no state action" claim is not a very persuasive basis to avoid finding media mergers unconstitutional. Some other substantive explanation is needed before rejecting the popular view that media mergers can in themselves violate the constitutional guarantee of a free press.

The real reason to reject this affirmative use of the First Amendment is precisely the argument made in this chapter. The theory of complex democracy leads to an interpretation of the ideal democratic media order as performing different, somewhat conflicting functions. These functions include providing for a democratic distribution of communicative power (as emphasized in chapter 1), providing for common societal discourses, and performing a "watchdog" role. No abstract principle determines the proper balance or trade-offs among these functions. The best constitutional interpretation leaves judgments about these trade-offs, as well as the empirical judgments about how to achieve the preferable balance, to policy analyses – the task of legislative and administrative, not judicial, bodies. A conclusion that allowing most mergers of privately owned media companies best serves society is a conceivable judgment, although I think – and this book argues – that it is a wrong one. If judicial activism with respect to ownership policy is rejected, the best explanation is an understanding that the First Amendment leaves to legislative or administrative bodies the responsibility to make judgments on these issues. The next chapter turns to suggestions about how these bodies ought to exercise this responsibility.

FIVE

Solutions and Responses

I t is now time to take stock. Chapter 1 provides three main reasons to favor maximum feasible dispersal of media ownership. This dispersal provides for a presumptively more egalitarian distribution of power within the public sphere, reflecting normative premises of democracy. Dispersal also provides various democratic safeguards – both safeguards against undemocratic, potentially demagogic abuse of power and safeguards in the form of likely better performance of the media's watchdog role. Finally, a major cause of media dysfunction reflects market incentives to focus maximally on the bottom line rather than on quality and media that people value. Structural economic theory and sociological theory, both reinforced with empirical evidence, suggest that media conglomerates, especially publicly traded media conglomerates, are more likely than other ownership patterns to exhibit this collectively dysfunctional profit-maximizing behavior. Chapters 2, 3, and 4 consider and reject counterarguments that assert that media concentration is not today a real problem or that restricting this concentration creates First Amendment objections. In response to this final point, however, chapter 4 emphasizes a theory of complex democracy that had been only marginally discussed in chapter 1. Complex democracy supports not only the argument of chapter 1 for maximum dispersal of ownership but also a reason to favor inclusive and presumptively larger media entities capable of supporting societal-wide discourses. With this background, which media policies related to ownership are best? That question is the subject of this chapter.

The first issue is identifying ideal ownership restrictions. Two initial observations should be made. Even the most stringent ownership dispersal requirements cannot be expected to fully meet any of the three concerns raised in chapter 1. Moreover, although this chapter is primarily about ideal policies, the reality is that ideal ownership policies are unlikely to be fully enacted. These points suggest considering other policies that are appropriate in addition or as alternatives to any ideal. Finally, I offer a postscript that responds to a different point. Each of the three rationales for ownership dispersal is independent of the others. Thus, the postscript will briefly focus on each separately in considering relevant policies. Overall, this chapter and the postscript aim primarily to stimulate ideas, which justifies describing only the general direction rather than the exact detail of the proposals.

A media firm can expand by gathering more audience for its existing media entities, by founding new media entities, or by purchasing existing entities. (I use "entity" to refer to a specific outlet – e.g., a paper, station, cable system – and "firm" to refer to the overarching corporate owner. With maximum ownership dispersal, the two would be the same.) Theoretically, each method of expansion could be subject to legal limitation. Legal policies could also be directed at the conditions under which each is permitted. Each regulatory approach, however, raises somewhat different policy issues and, despite chapter 4's assertion of broad governmental power to regulate structure, possibly different constitutional issues.

To illustrate the care required for wise policy thought, I begin by showing why society should reject the first, most direct, means of regulation – limiting a single firm's audience reach – and, except in limited circumstances, should reject the similar notion of prohibiting a media firm from expanding by founding new media entities. Only then do I turn to consider seven, I believe desirable, broad approaches to regulation of ownership concentration. Specifically, the law could (1) use antitrust laws (or, as more often described in Europe, competition law) to restrict concentration, (2) require specific governmental approval of proposed mergers, (3) prohibit media mergers that increase the level of concentration in the media and prohibit most mergers of media and nonmedia firms, (4) require that permitted media mergers keep alive independent editorial or content voices, (5) require that some or all media mergers be approved by journalistic or creative employees, (6) use tax, subsidy, and related preference policies to encourage the creation of media entities by or their sale to favored categories of owners, for example, sales that increase local owners, minority owners, or smaller owners who do not already own other media entities, and (7) impose special responsibilities on dominant media entities.

FLAWED REGULATORY LIMITS ON OWNERSHIP

LIMITING REACH OR AUDIENCE OF A MEDIA ENTITY

Possibly the most direct way to disperse media ownership would be to mandate fragmented audiences. A single media entity could be prohibited from selling to more than a specified number of people or to more than a specified percentage of the potential market in its locale of operation. For example, a rule could provide that no newspaper could sell more than a million copies. Or, since that limit would be relevant for only a few national newspapers, an alternative or additional rule might bar selling to more than a fixed percentage of the audience in its market area, say, a 25 percent maximum household market penetration. This entity-based audience cap itself would not prevent the same firm from owning competing papers. It could be modified, however, to do so or to restrict a firm from *owning* media entities whose combined audience share exceeds the audience cap. Although this audience cap would not directly guarantee the existence of competing papers, it would leave an unfilled market into which they would predictably enter. Similar but differently calibrated rules could apply to other media. In markets with more than one radio and television station, a rule could provide that no firm could have more than twice the audience share of its nearest competitor, thereby guaranteeing some dispersal of audiences.

Though this proposal might seem quite radical, in a slightly modified form, it is not entirely unprecedented. Nicholas Kaldor, a prominent British economist, once proposed taxing British newspapers' advertising at a rate that would rise with circulation and then redistributing the tax revenue in amounts corresponding to circulation but ceasing when a paper reached the "ideal" circulation level.[1] Essentially, the plan would penalize (but not prohibit) being larger than the maximum size legislatively deemed to be desirable and subsidize the growth of smaller papers. In 1981, Italy adopted a law, apparently never adequately enforced, prohibiting a company from owning newspapers controlling more than 20 percent of the national or 50 percent of a regional newspaper market.[2] Limits or penalties for excessive audience size are certainly thinkable.

A distinction should be noted, however, between applying an audience share rule to limit internal growth and using it as the basis to restrict mergers. The second is quite common. Although not a hard and fast rule, using a maximum percentage market share as a rule of thumb for identifying objectionable mergers is routine in enforcing antitrust laws. Likewise, the FCC, under direction from Congress, barred ownership of cable systems that potentially reached more than 30 percent of the national cable audience, although the D.C. Circuit invalidated the chosen percentage in a decision criticized in chapter 4.

The difference between using an audience percentage cap as a standard for merger control (or as a basis for a subsidy policy) and for restricting internal growth should make the latter offensive to policy makers. Restricting entities' internal growth in effect tells some members of society, some potential audience members, that they cannot see or hear some popular media – a popular book, song, movie, or newspaper – that other consumers are permitted to see or hear. Sure, policy makers can say that the limit is imposed for a good reason, such as to promote competition or diversity. A legislative body, however, should find this limit on audience members' personal *freedom* to be totally offensive.

This limit on audiences also probably violates the First Amendment, a suggestion that merits comment given chapter 4's claim that *structural* regulation of the media, as opposed to *content* penalties, creates virtually no serious First Amendment problem unless the regulation involves an impermissible purpose to undermine the press's democratic role. The Supreme Court has held that media-specific ownership or merger restrictions, which limit a firm's practical capacity to reach larger audiences, raise no serious First Amendment issue but, instead, serve First Amendment values. The proposed audience cap uses an arguably more direct means to pursue virtually the same aim of dispersing ownership.

The constitutional difference between the two policies can be seen by evaluating the complaints that each of two parties – media audiences and media owners – could raise. Remember that the democratic rationale of *press* freedom emphasizes the audience, not the speaker – the value of audiences, of citizens, receiving communications. Of course, media professionals or media entities hold any actual press rights (e.g., reporter's privilege or freedom from censorship), but the theory of the press clause is that these rights are in the service of the ultimate beneficiaries, the audience or public. With that background, what complaints can media entities or owners make on their own behalf? They have, chapter 4 showed, no complaint about structural regulations unless these regulations can be shown as a subterfuge for censorship or an attempt to undermine media performance. They have no grounds for complaint about any structural rule aimed at improving the communications order. Of course, as individuals, owners have speech rights not to be blocked from speaking. They have, for example, the same right as other individuals to use their personal wealth to pay media entities to include their views in the form of an advertisement. Media owners or media entities do not have, however, any right to the structural arrangements, including ownership structures, that most favor their speaking. As a matter of speech rights, they have no basis for complaint about structural rules unless adopted for a censorious or otherwise illegitimate purpose.[3]

Turn next to the rights of audiences. An audience member has a presumptive right to have the government not attempt to prevent her from receiving communications – certainly, to prevent her from receiving communications the content of which someone has a general right to make. Of course, many general laws as well as media-specific structural laws that determine the identity of owners *affect* the communications she receives. These laws inevitably disfavor those audiences who would prefer messages from media controlled by someone other than those that existing rules identify as the media owners – and inevitably favor those who want communications from the identified owners. No audience member, however, can have a constitutional right to the structure that most favors her preferred communications. (The right would necessarily conflict with others having the same right given differences in preferences.) The structural choice can sensibly be made only on policy grounds.

Throughout my constitutional discussion, I have emphasized the central civil libertarian premise that the government must not merely pursue legitimate ends – of which ownership dispersal is an instance – but must use permissible means. Constitutional violations most often occur not because of effects or objectionable ultimate goals but because the government chooses impermissible means. Laws restricting mergers and laws imposing audience caps purposefully use qualitatively different means in their pursuit of their similar dispersal goal. Audience caps *purposefully limit some people's access to an entity's speech*. Merger restrictions *purposefully make a choice among possible owners*, a choice that favors some, usually "weaker," potential owners. Of course, the legal regime necessarily determines the identity of media owners as well as the possessor of all other property. Merger law is simply a self-conscious element in this determination. This necessary "distributive" determination is not made, however, on the basis of impermissible purposes – for example, to suppress or punish particular content (which would be equivalent to censorship). Rather, merger rules choose between potential owners on the basis of wanting to disperse opportunities within the public sphere (or to increase economic efficiency or serve various other legitimate goals). In contrast, the audience cap directly and purposefully limits some audience members' access to protected speech. It bars some potential audience members from receiving (because the media entity is prohibited from providing) communications after too many others have received it. Because audience rights are basic in interpreting the press clause, this purposeful restriction on audience access is a constitutionally impermissible means to pursue even legitimate objectives. (The cap also in effect favors wealthier audience members who can outbid poorer audience members for the desired but restricted communications – an additional perversity of this proposal.)

PROHIBITION ON A MEDIA FIRM CREATING NEW MEDIA ENTITIES

Existing media companies (or specifically defined categories of firms, e.g., already "large" firms) could be prohibited from opening new media outlets or beginning new media enterprises. As noted below, this approach has played an interstitial role in the United States in the context of broadcast media. In other countries, more ambitious versions have been tried on occasion. For example, in 1947, a purported commitment to pluralism and prevention of press ownership concentration led postwar France to limit any individual or firm to ownership of a single newspaper, thereby implicitly prohibiting a newspaper from starting a new one. Nevertheless, though credited with slowing down press concentration to some extent, this French law apparently was soon "widely ignored."[4]

Unlike the constitutional rationale for rejecting audience caps, respect for listener or audience rights does not make a limit on existing media creating new media entities unconstitutional. This limit does not legally prevent any audience member's access to media communications that do exist. It does not censor content. It does not prevent any person or commercial entity from initially deciding to operate a medium of expression, although it may require a person or firm to choose which type of media enterprise to operate or to become. Rather, this limit on creating new media entities operates more like other structural (and distributive) rules. These rules all partly determine (in combination with human choices) which communications entities will exist and who owns them. Of course, some listeners would prefer the communications that would exist under one structure and one set of owners, others would prefer those that would exist under an alternative. Individually, however, listeners surely could have no right to the existence of their preferred structure. Rather, as a group, they can act politically in seeking laws to create the structure they collectively find most desirable. They also have a right that the government not purposefully suppress or undermine the communications order. But structural rules that can be seen as reasonable attempts to improve the communications order, especially its democratic quality, should be and virtually always are constitutional.

The key point is that the rationale for press freedom is not that corporate entities have rights on their own behalf. Rather, the communications order should serve the public, which requires that the communication order be subject to noncensorious government structuring designed to make it operate better. Censorious reasons for preventing firms from creating new "presses" obviously would be contrary to press freedom. Likewise, the government presumably should not be able to restrict creation of new media entities simply on the ground that people already receive too many communications. As the Court has said, "in [a] free society ... it is not the government but the people individually ... and collectively as associations ... who must retain control over the quantity and range of debate on public issues.[5] The public sphere should be as broad as people want. In *Los Angeles v. Preferred Communications*,[6] discussed in chapter 4 and the one structural case where the Court indicated serious constitutional doubts about a structural regulation, the Court concluded that a government prohibition on creation of *any* new competing cable systems could violate the First Amendment unless the ban was appropriate due to insufficient "physical capacity and economic demand."[7] Still, an objectionable rationale for regulation – a purpose to create a monopoly – does not discredit structural regulation generally. The law should seek to make the public sphere as functional for its democratic tasks as possible. As long as a prohibition on certain categories of firms creating new "presses" can reasonably be seen as an effort to serve this functional aim, the law should generate *no* constitutional objections. The Supreme Court arguably implied this view when it said in *Red Lion*, quoting an earlier decision: "to deny a station license because 'the public interest' requires it 'is not a denial of free speech.'"[8]

Unsurprisingly, principles historically at work in American communications law allow restrictions on particular entities from creating new communication entities whenever the restriction can be reasonably seen to serve the communications order. To prevent ownership concentration, the FCC has denied the only current qualified applicant a license to create a new broadcast station, leaving the slot open for future applicants. The FCC's duopoly rule, an early policy against concentration of local station ownership, began with such a denial in 1938.[9] Telephone companies were long prohibited not only from buying a cable system but from starting and operating a cable system in the area of their operation.[10] Essentially, the law gave the company a choice. It could be a common carrier phone company or a cable content provider – but not both. The FCC also imposed a national cap on ownership of cable systems, which would have prohibited sufficiently large cable conglomerates not only from merging with other cable companies but also from starting a new cable system. Although the D.C. Circuit found the limit too restrictive given the particular mandate Congress had given the FCC, Congress clearly judged that prohibiting very large cable systems from either building or buying new systems was a desirable policy measure.[11] Nothing in the D.C. Circuit's opinion denied that a proper limit on either building new cable systems or buying existing systems would violate the First Amendment. Similarly, at the local level the FCC's cross-ownership rules prohibit even print media from creating certain new media. The rules prohibit a company not only from buying but also from receiving a license to build a new broadcast station in a locale where it also owns a newspaper. The Supreme Court in 1978 seemed little troubled by this prohibition when it unanimously rejected newspapers' constitutional complaint.[12] These examples clearly suggest that prohibiting a company from starting a new media entity is not ruled out as a matter of constitutional principle.

Each of the above examples of narrowly prohibiting a category of media firms from starting a new media entity, even though others were allowed to do so, seemed plausibly justified. Other possible applications of this type of restriction may also be justifiable. Weekly newspapers owned by entities other than the owner of a town's monopoly daily paper can add valuable diversity and reduce dangerous concentration. Time has shown that firms other than the dominant local daily are often willing and able to start these weekly papers. Prohibiting dailies from creating new weeklies in their area of operation in an attempt to further their own power could make sense.

Combined with a prohibition on purchasing existing media entities, a broad general prohibition on existing media firms creating new media entities would be a direct way of restricting ownership concentration. Nevertheless, it seems misguided as a *general* approach. Three policy objections are primary. First, contrast this approach with prohibiting mergers. Prohibiting mergers typically preserves an existing speaker. This proposal most directly merely prohibits creation of a new media option, usually a much more difficult policy to justify. Second, as a practical matter, often only an existing media firm will be willing and have the expertise to create a new entity to serve a particular unserved or under-served area or group. Third, sometimes the firm that best combines expertise, available resources, and ambition to create really new media products, that is, the firm most likely to provide either technical or content innovations, will be an already existing media firm.

Of course, these have all been contextual arguments. Sometimes, an entirely new firm will create a new media entity if, but only if, existing media firms are prohibited from doing so. Moreover, sometimes there may be grounds to regret new creations. Nothing guarantees that new successful entities, even those that develop profitable new innovations, will be socially beneficial – but that is a separate problem. If the problem of innovations that would be profitable but socially undesirable is real – for example, because they operate in a manner that transfers wealth from the poor to the rich or because they lock society into a pathway that is difficult and expensive to redirect – the problem might justify, at most, certain legal regulations of innovation. A law that bluntly and broadly prohibited the companies most likely to be innovative from creating new products does not seem sensitive to the occasional contexts where an innovation would be unwise.

POLICY PROPOSALS

1. ANTITRUST LAW

Outside areas where law requires either a license or franchise, United States legal history provides few illustrations and little guidance for concentration policy other than that resulting from general antitrust laws[13] and a specific exception to it, the Newspaper Preservation Act.[14] This approach is valuable and should be strengthened in its applications to the media realm. As chapter 2 argued, history's indication of the importance of democratic concerns with concentrated power and promotion of consumer choice justify somewhat different and more muscular enforcement of antitrust limits on mergers than occurs presently under the dominant Chicago approach. One response to problems of concentration is an invigorated antitrust enforcement that recognizes that antitrust's "general" concerns themselves justify more intense "media-specific" applications. Nevertheless, primarily because of antitrust law's essentially "commodity" orientation, even ideal vigorous enforcement will be insufficient to respond to the problem of media concentration. This inadequacy follows from the high importance in the media sphere of values related to process, to distribution of power, to structural democratic safeguards, and to hoped-for deviation from market dictates – which were the central concerns chapter 1 raised about media ownership concentration.

Two observations illustrate this inadequacy and the need for media-specific regulation. First, existing antitrust ownership limitations have focused on competition in the product sold, which in the media realm often seems primarily the sale of audiences to advertisers. Often, antitrust law's commodity concern is power within the advertising market. Recent, belated moves by the Antitrust Division of the Department of Justice to restrict extreme concentration of ownership in local radio markets occurred more or less when the purchasing company would control more than 40 percent of the radio advertising in the locale.[15] Second, because the concern is with power over commodities, not with power within the public sphere, antitrust laws provide virtually no limits on national concentration among sellers of media products that are not themselves primarily national. Newspapers, broadcast stations, and cable systems primarily operate locally. Common bemoaning of the twentieth century's move toward increased chain ownership of newspapers has lead to considerable research examining whether such ownership produces bad consequences.[16] Nevertheless, since newspapers in different locales are not in the same market, antitrust laws are irrelevant to the issue. They have never imposed any restrictions on chain concentration as opposed to combinations of locally competing papers.

The same point was made by the D.C. Circuit. It found unduly restrictive the FCC's national cap restricting ownership of cable systems to those that reach no more than 30 percent of the national cable audience.[17] The court reasoned that since cable systems (seldom) compete against each other for audience, concentration of ownership creates no anticompetitive effect in relation to audiences. Although the court recognized the possibility of monopsony power in the market for purchasing cable content, it found no reason to fear that consequence until an entity owned more than 60 percent of the country's cable systems – or, more precisely, controlled more than 60 percent of the cable audience. That is, the court believed that antitrust-like anticompetitive dangers would not exist as long as the country has at least two owners of the currently dominant way to see television. The FCC's rule, the court said, was unduly restrictive since it required that nationally there be at least four owners of cable systems.[18] The court's conclusion, of course, would be wrong if Congress's policy concern was, as it might have been and chapter 1 suggests it should have been, to disperse communicative power in the national marketplace of ideas.

Antitrust enforcement still might be valued, even as part of a dual regulatory regime with a media-specific component. First, different agencies, for example, the FCC and the Department of Justice, typically respond to different objections to ownership concentration and either objection could be relevant when the other was not. Enforcement by multiple agencies can also offer advantages if enforcement within one becomes lax. The second agency may take up some of the slack. Restrictive FCC regulation of ownership long made antitrust laws largely irrelevant to broadcasting ownership. Beginning in the late 1990s, however, as the FCC sought to abandon any serious policing of ownership concentration, the Justice Department applied antitrust laws to block mergers that created undue concentration among local radio broadcasters.[19] Obviously, either side at any moment can be more stringent. Moreover, procedurally, it may be easier to sustain objections under one set of laws or the other. As I write this, Germany's commission on media concentration announced that it was rejecting Axel Springer's plan to purchase ProSiebenSat.1 because the purchase would give it too much "power over public opinion." The German antitrust authority had also indicated that it would probably reach the same result on grounds of concentrated power in the advertising market. Importantly, though either regulatory body can be overruled, the authority with power to overrule is different in each case, providing a further safeguard on concentration.[20]

In any event, the notion of applying antitrust laws to media mergers is uncontroversial – although controversy often exists as to particular applications. An appropriate conclusion is that strengthened antitrust enforcement constitutes a desirable but insufficient response to media ownership concentration.

2. REQUIRE GOVERNMENT APPROVAL FOR MERGER

A method to slow or stop undesirable media mergers is to require prior government approval of any media merger either as an adjunct to the antitrust law or as an independent requirement guided by other, possibly more stringent, approval standards. In the United States, the Hart-Scott-Rodino Act requires corporate entities to present the government with antitrust-relevant information prior to most *large* corporate mergers.[21] Approval gives merger partners some reason to expect that the government will not later challenge the merger as illegal.[22] Similar merger review procedures exist in more than eighty countries.[23] Unlike in the United

States, the specific concern with media concentration has led some countries to impose a special, stricter review process or to apply different analyses in the media context. In Germany, the anticartel law has a lower size threshold (measured by revenue) for strict review of media mergers than for other commercial mergers. Considerations specially related to the press purportedly guide the evaluation – but the German's review has apparently had at best limited effectiveness in slowing concentration.[24] In Britain since 1965, mergers of economically viable newspapers that would result in a proprietor controlling circulation of over 500,000 a day require pre-merger evaluation – as do other media mergers at the discretion of the Minister for Trade and Industry. Again, however, this approach has apparently accomplished little. Out of forty evaluated, only one press merger was rejected between 1965 and the late 1980s.[25]

Requiring pre-merger review, combined with media-specific conditions or presumptions against approval, possibly carried out by two different agencies using different criteria – for example, by the Antitrust Division of the Department of Justice and the FCC – could have merit. The British and German experiences, however, warn against expecting too much. Still, clear standards that embody a strong presumption against mergers could increase the chances of obtaining meaningful results.

The primary policy problem, and possible constitutional problem, with this approach lies in the government discretion intrinsic to an approval/disapproval process. Discretion creates three dangers. First, without adequate guidance by clear standards, administrators may bow too quickly to carefully crafted arguments from corporate advocates for approval of mergers even when the merger actually disserves the public interest. Second, officials' exercise of discretion may primarily reflect partisan inclinations. It is hard to ignore suspicions that politics entered into the Thatcher government's approval of Rupert Murdoch's takeover of the *Sunday Times* as well as the less financially troubled *Times*.[26]

Possibly, review by an independent judiciary could police against the worst political abuses. An appellate court found an unconstitutional abuse of *legislative* discretion when Senator Kennedy got Congress to adopt a narrowly designed law to stop the FCC from extending a specific temporary exemption from the cross-ownership prohibition.[27] This story of judicial intervention, however, may not be so comforting. It may involve the court overthrowing a congressional correction of an agency abuse. Kennedy's efforts were apparently aimed at an improperly partisan decision by the FCC under the

Reagan-appointed FCC chair, Mark Fowler. Fowler's FCC had granted Murdoch an exemption to a bar on local cross-ownership that allowed Murdoch's company to own both a Boston television station and newspaper, the *Boston Herald*.[28] In supporting the "corrective" legislation, Senator Hollings quoted a statement that Fowler purportedly made at his retirement party: "The greatest gift I gave to anybody as Chairman of the FCC was an 18-month waiver to Rupert Murdoch."[29] Still, in themselves, occasional unwarranted politically based merger approvals, as arguably occurred to favor Murdoch, leave the situation no worse than if no approval requirement had been in place to restrain mergers.

The third problem with official discretion, possibly the least obvious but most serious, is its capacity to distort editorial policy in a firm's effort to gain approval for its merger or other business plans. This structural arrangement undermines the independence of the press. Reportedly, Knight-Ridder directed its cartoonists at both its *Miami Herald* and *Detroit Free Press* not to lampoon Attorney General Edwin Meese during the period before Meese exercised his discretionary authority to allow or disallow the *Free Press*'s proposed joint operating agreement with another Detroit paper.[30] Similarly, though hardly known for his liberal politics, Murdoch's occasional kid-glove treatment of liberal politicians is usually explained by purported hopes to gain government approval for his corporate ambitions. After Murdoch's British papers oddly supported Tony Blair's candidacy, Blair's Labor government "proposed relaxing TV-ownership rules in ways that would benefit News Corp."[31] That is, the need to get discretionary government approval increases the danger that the watchdog will avert its gaze and employ nonjournalistic considerations in choosing content.

The capacity of governmental discretion to censor, favor, or distort speech has lead to a First Amendment requirement in other contexts to strictly limit or to eliminate that discretion. Permit requirements for parades or use of parks are allowed in principle but are routinely struck down if the rules give officials any discretion in granting the permit and, thereby, give the officials power to censor or favor particular people or particular content.[32] At a minimum, these constitutional principles warn that governmental approval authority should be bound as strictly as possible by rigid, clear standards. Nevertheless, the context of structural regulation seems somehow different from that involved with parades and assemblies. Possibly, this reflects the complexity of structural interventions. Generally desirable structural rules would seem to be appropriately waived when their application in specific cases thwarts their instrumental goals. In any event, the existence of waivers to media ownership restrictions has not produced successful constitutional objections. Instead, in this context, the Supreme Court has observed that their availability "underscore" the "reasonableness" of the rules barring cross-ownership "as a means of achieving diversification."[33]

Nevertheless, relatively discretionary waiver opportunities create real dangers of partisan abuse by the grantor and, equally troubling, of opportunistic self-censorship of the supplicant. As noted, the Newspaper Preservation Act empowers the Attorney General to allow business-side mergers (joint operating agreements, or JOAs) that would otherwise presumably violate the antitrust laws. Although the power is circumscribed by rules or standards, observers have been unconvinced that these have been (or maybe could be) objectively applied. Approval purportedly depends on a paper not being sustainable without the JOA. The apparent availability of buyers for the *Seattle Post-Intelligencer*, however, made approval of the JOA there questionable.[34] Similar doubts about the approval of a JOA between the *Detroit News* and *Detroit Free Press* have been reasonably raised.[35] Still, the Supreme Court's point stands. The possibility of deciding either way can aid in achieving instrumental goals. The widespread international practice of requiring pre-merger review supports this conclusion. The addition in the media context is that review should be in service of democratic anticoncentration principles as well as the usual efficiency concerns of antitrust. To require approval, with various presumptions against granting it or at least with opportunities to oppose it, would be an improvement on comparatively unrestricted mergers.

3. PROHIBIT MERGERS THAT INCREASE CONCENTRATION OR INVOLVE TAKEOVER BY NONMEDIA FIRMS

Adoption of any media-specific merger limitations will reflect political struggle and compromise. The present discussion aims to describe elements of a purportedly ideal policy, recognizing that further matters not considered here are likely to justify refinements and that power dynamics inevitably would lead to other modifications.

The most stringent merger policy would simply prohibit all transactions that combine existing media entities. Even if an existing owner is unwilling or unable to continue operations, some group (or individual) can normally be expected to coalesce and be willing to take over a going concern, that is, any entity that does or is likely to produce operating profits. For local media, people in the area served by the media entity may be willing and able to combine to take it over. If no one else will pay more, often existing employees would rather take over the enterprise than lose their jobs – and would be willing and able to pay more than the scrap value of a closed facility. Of course, prohibiting purchase by another media entity would reduce, possibly drastically reduce, the entity's sale value. For this reason, existing owners are likely to strongly oppose such a restriction. Media policy, however, *ought* to be concerned with the quality of the communications order, not the wealth of (usually) already wealthy existing owners. At most, ownership creates a presumption of control of operations. Nothing about either press freedom or the idea of ownership implies any particular rights related to *market* alienation.[36] Rules about ownership alienation is a proper subject of public policy.

This rule could reduce the incentive to create new communication media due to the lower expectations of profit from an eventual sale. But I expect not only that this effect is more hypothesized than real, especially in the media context, but also that this reduced incentive has good as well as possibly bad consequences. Chapter 1 emphasized the desirability of getting ownership into the hands of people more committed to journalism or the creative role than to profit maximization. This rule does not directly burden the opportunity to start media entities. If it reduces the financial rewards to those who create the entity merely in order to be able to sell, the rule increases the likelihood that founders will be committed to their media enterprise and to journalistic or creative roles – a presumptive gain for the quality of the communications order. This approach also directly embodies the values of dispersing ownership of media entities.

By excluding existing media owners from purchasing, the rule will exclude some potential buyers who would bid more to buy (and would presumably increase operating profits to pay off the debt). It will thereby often lead to ownership by people less willing or able to maximize profits. Of course, this is part of the point. Chapter 1 emphasized that profit maximization comes at the cost of the highest quality or maximally welfare-serving media operations. This rule creates an opportunity for new owners who would emphasize journalistic or creative quality – but also, unfortunately, for those simply less capable of quality operations. Which category will dominate cannot be predicted with certainty. The main point, however, is that the rule prevents ownership changes that increase concentration.

There are, nevertheless, two problems with the simple directness of this proposed ban on media purchases by existing media owners. First, the rule could prevent ownership changes that reduce the level of media concentration. It prevents a large media conglomerate from selling one of its media operations to a smaller media firm. Sometimes, only such a smaller media firm will pay enough to convince the conglomerate to sell. Here, the rule prevents sales that reduce concentration and increase dispersal. In doing so, the rule may also unnecessarily reduce the flexibility and dynamism of the media order.

In contrast to the prior point about the rule being too strict, it may also be too lenient. Many nonmedia commercial entities have economic incentives to be media owners. They can often benefit greatly by favorable portrayal of their products, by favorable coverage of their views on legal/legislative issues, or simply by increased political power due to a capacity to reward or punish local electoral candidates or incumbents with the extent and nature of their media coverage. These benefits, however, conflict with journalistic integrity and various democratic roles of the media. Ownership by nonmedia firms also predictably compromises the goal of getting ownership in the hands of people committed to quality over profits. This point lead Gilbert Cranberg, Randall Bezanson, and John Soloski, the authors of a major study of the state of journalism, to conclude that one of the most serious problems with media quality is this profit-maximizing orientation that dominates in publicly traded media companies and, *even more so*, in public conglomerates where media entities are only a limited portion of the corporation's businesses.[37] On the other hand, it is hard to find any predictable societal benefits from such nonmedia corporate ownership (unless, maybe, as a source of capital for media expansion).

My proposal 3 combines these two complaints. An ideal media merger policy could have the following two elements: (1) Media entities can be sold only to individuals or entities that, after the sale, will own no more media properties (measured by revenue) than the seller previously owned, and (2) any for-profit commercial entity that purchases a media entity must, after the purchase, be primarily in the media business – that is, receive the majority of its revenue from its media business. (I put aside important issues involving identification of the owner, that is, attributing ownership to an ultimate holder – the company that owns the company that now owns the media entity – and the portion of equity ownership that counts as "ownership." These technical issues are treated routinely by FCC rules in the media area and by other rules for antitrust, tax, and other legal purposes.) The first requirement guarantees that the sale does not increase concentration but allows any merger that would decrease it. The second assures that ownership is in the hands of a firm for which the media business is primary.

An assessment of this proposal must consider how often media mergers that would be prohibited by this rule actually produce benefits for the communications order and for the public. Clearly, some would. Still, my admittedly unscientific observations see such benefits often promised but seldom produced. Structural and theoretical reasons explain what I generally see happening: more common is a reduction of the commitment to journalism or creativity, lay-offs of journalists and other personnel, and sometimes some new packaging of old products. These actions can increase operating profits (although often less than merger planners expect), but the crucial issue of how often real benefits occur warrants discussion and examination of available evidence. If a rule as stringent as the one proposed here will predictably prevent valuable innovations, an alternative might be to allow waivers, as described in Proposal 2, when the applying purchaser can show clearly and concretely why allowing the purchase would benefit the public. The burden of demonstration, however, should be great. Purchasers always have facially plausible but usually factually misconceived claims about the public benefits of a merger.

Observe that this proposal does not in any real sense restrict a flesh-and-blood person (legally, corporate entities are often treated as "persons" for many purposes) from personally engaging in communications through the media. (Real persons should be the concern where the issue is fundamental rights to freedom; freedom of corporate or governmental entities should be evaluated instrumentally in terms of how these legal constructs serve human values, including human freedom.) A single person actually engaged in communicating her own words can hardly offer more words than a single media entity can publish or broadcast, an entity that she can try to make as successful, as "loud," as possible. Of course, a single person might direct others to formulate and distribute communications taking the general line that she proposes or favors. Directing others, however, consists not in her own freedom but in a power over others – power to control their communications. This power can be had either because of her position (e.g., others choose to make her an editor) or because of her wealth (e.g., she owns a media entity or uses personal funds to pay others to communicate as she chooses). A governmental purpose to silence her communications or to prevent audiences from hearing them should be impermissible. But structural rules inevitably affect and should purposefully affect the distribution of and power provided by wealth. Rules designed to empower the communicative opportunities of some people, despite limiting other's communicative opportunities – inevitably, any structural choice increases some and decreases other people's power over communications – do not generally violate anyone's expressive freedom. If this proposal were adopted, any individual could (if wealthy enough) own a media entity or (if appealing enough) be hired to direct a media entity. Beyond those opportunities, this individual, like others with money, can use her wealth (if any) to purchase ads in those media entities that will take them, to hire public relations firms to spread her message, or to pay others to leaflet or otherwise spread the message. Formally, the rules do not restrict her personal speech freedom (as opposed to her entrepreneurial freedom, which law necessarily structures). She has the same formal right (but personal wealth may grant a greater practical capacity) to communicate as do all others, for example, the typical person who is not an owner of a mass media entity.

4. Editorial Independence

Often, preventing mergers will not be politically possible, sometimes may not even be desirable. Whether this fact represents political reality or policy sense, its reality must be acknowledged. The question then becomes: are demands for *ownership* dispersal the only policy that those committed to the values described in chapter 1 can put on the table? The answer is no. Policies other than restricting mergers can serve the same aims even if not as well as prohibiting offending mergers. The Newspaper Preservation Act provides a model in requiring JOAs to maintain complete editorial independence of the newspapers even as they are permitted to consolidate their business operations. Economic reasons explain why the NPA has often not worked as effectively as hoped. Once one of the two papers becomes dominant in circulation, both companies in the combined operation often would benefit by eliminating the cost of operating the weaker paper, closing it, and then dividing between them the subsequent monopoly profits of the surviving paper. This division could take the form of one paper paying the other the capitalized present value of a portion of the surviving paper's future monopoly profits to agree to dissolve the JOA and close. (Whether this agreement to dissolve the JOA itself ever violates the antitrust laws is currently an open question.[38])

Unlike the case of two competing local dailies, closure of a purchased media entity in most merger contexts will not serve profitability or any other goal of the purchasing firm. The JOA approach may work better in these cases. Congress could adopt a requirement that *any media purchase, or at least any that would not meet the criteria of Proposal 3, be allowed only if structured to guarantee editorial independence of the purchased entity.* To be effective, the law would need additional provisions. For example, it should protect journalistic employees from dismissal except for cause and, grant to these employees power to veto dismissal of the editor (or other top management) at least as long as the entity continued to produce any operating profits and power to veto any selection of a new top editorial chief.

In its general aim, this proposal is not entirely unprecedented. As a consideration in approving a proposed merger, Britain considers whether the buyer guarantees editorial independence, and extension of the use of this criterion has been recommended.[39] Though not tied to mergers, the Norwegian Press Association Code of Ethics provides that the editor, not the publisher, has sole power to choose content, and this has been embodied in an "Editorial Statute."[40] Likewise, important economic subsidies to media entities in the Netherlands and Norway are conditioned on journalists having complete editorial independence.[41] And of course, as noted, the United States uses this criterion in the Newspaper Preservation Act as a condition for granting an exception to a legal prohibition on a merger.

Of course, these requirements leave a new owner less free to pursue some goals, economic or otherwise, than if an unrestricted purchase were allowed. Consequently, these requirements predictably reduce the amount a purchaser would be willing to pay. Still, allowing mergers but preserving independent editorial voices – something traditionally promised but less often provided in most chain purchases of local newspapers – can produce benefits and legitimate efficiencies for both society and the buying firm. This proposal is a less stringent restriction than barring these mergers completely. Editorial independence, however, would not maintain all the benefits of separate ownership. One key reason to oppose concentration is an empirical prediction that the *economic* choices of the smaller, nonmerged firm will favor better journalistic efforts. Merely maintaining editorial independence may not achieve this aim, Nevertheless, an effective mandated decentralization of editorial power would greatly reduce the Berlusconi fear, the danger of abuse of inordinate media power. Conflicts of interest would likewise be reduced – although not eliminated, since even those in charge of the editorially independent unit could benefit economically when other portions of the merged firm prosper. Thus, this less radical proposal could reasonably serve many but not all of the goals of preventing concentration of media power.

5. Require Journalists' Approval for Merger

Permitted mergers or ownership changes could be conditioned on approval by the journalistic, creative, and editorial employees (or a larger category) of a media entity. In 1971, the executive committee of the International Federation of Journalists adopted a five-point resolution that asserted the desirability of such a veto right for editorial employees.[42] Or, more narrowly, this approval could be required for mergers that do not meet the criteria for mergers listed in the third proposal above.

This veto power would have a number of predictable consequences. Journalists' personal and professional commitments would usually incline them to oppose mergeres that they believe would degrade the entities' journalistic or creative roles. To this extent, the rule encourages only sales that improve, or at least do not degrade, the media order. The employees' veto would also allow them to extract a share of the gain from any sale. Typically, employees would balance this financial benefit against a desire to approve only sales that contributed to the quality (and stability and remuneration) of their professional performance.[43] The higher their hold-out price (which should amount at least to the value they place on their view of any expected decline in the entities' professional quality), the more the undesirable mergers would be scuttled. In contrast, though they may still seek some of the monetary gain from a sale, they would have no professional (or economic) incentive to prevent quality-serving mergers. Also, if the approval requirement applied only when the buyer or merger partner did not meet the criteria of the third proposal, the owner would have an incentive to avoid the veto possibility by selling only in ways that decreased concentration.

Even if financial gain were the employees' only concern, the veto power would have an arguably desirable distributive effect without causing damage to the communications order. The objection would be made that this rule "takes" from owners and "gives" to employees a potentially valuable right generally connected with ownership. As a matter of constitutional law, this objection is a nonstarter. The Supreme Court has recognized that equally appropriate is the view that without this rule the sale involves the owner "taking" the benefits generated by the journalists and editors – and that the legislature has the rule to decide which base-line to use.[44] Possibly the most appropriate reply was made by Harry J. Grant, part owner and initiator of an employee ownership plan for the *Milwaukee Journal*: "It is the right of men and women whose lives go into building a newspaper to have a share in the ownership."[45] In practice, this employee veto right seems no different, except for being more egalitarian, than the "golden parachutes" that corporate executives regularly negotiate under the shadow of corporate mergers. Of course, these distributive arguments for employee rights might point broadly to the desirability of incorporating the rule into standard corporate merger law. The arguments are, however, more urgent in the media context. The proposal's ultimate basis is not merely fairness to employees but rather a policy judgment that the veto power could contribute to the quality of the media order by favorably influencing the identity of owners within that order.

6. Tax and Subsidy Policies Encouraging Dispersal and Discouraging Concentration

Widely varying sorts of direct and indirect subsidies for the media have been ubiquitous in the United States and elsewhere.[46] In this country, possibly the most obvious subsidy has been the developmentally crucial postal subsidies that began with the origins of the country. These huge postal subsidies continued the colonial practice, which Ben Franklin and William Hunter, as deputy postmasters for the colonies, had formalized in 1758 – and without them, the American press may not have been successful in helping keep the early nation together.[47] Some nineteenth-century senators even argued that the First Amendment *required* postal subsidies for newspapers. In 1832, the Senate failed by one vote, 23–22, to abolish all postage charges for newspapers. Although all political parties seemed to agree that postal rates should exist and should severely disfavor advertising content, early debates about the extent and form of the postal subsidies constantly reflected major partisan, content-based considerations. Subsidized flat distance rates benefited the Federalist's "national" city papers, while subsidized but zoned or "in county" rates benefited the original Republican Party's weekly "country" or village papers. At least since 1845, Congress actually provided that these papers receive free postage either within thirty miles of their place of publication or in their county of origin, a privilege not abolished until 1962.

The partisanship of views about rate policy was illustrated when no supporter of Andrew Jackson was among the twenty-two senators who voted to end all postal charges for newspapers. Still, national distribution of newspapers' "current intelligence" strongly benefited from these postal subsidies. In the nineteenth century, postage rates for letters (mostly sent by businessmen to each other) was six to *eighty* times – depending on distance and year – the postage rates for newspapers, and these letters produced the profit that allowed the newspaper subsidies. This represented a huge transfer from one set of speakers to another, especially valuable category. Still, leaders such as George Washington and James Madison argued that the postal charges for newspapers were too high.

Subsidies take many additional forms, some overt, either as targeted or general direct subsidy payments, and others, prior to reflection, much more inconspicuous. Daniel Hallin and Paulo Mancini suggest that a major correlate with the present level of press readership in various European countries is the degree of mass literacy in that country over a century earlier.[48] Clearly, free public education is a major subsidy of the press. Many other non-obvious subsidies greatly influence press content – consider press conferences, press releases, government-provided press facilities, and inexpensive access to government files. A study of sixteen Western democracies found that all, including the United States, provided the press with at least a moderate level of subsidies.[49] The Nordic countries especially, but also other European countries, have long used subsidies explicitly to keep competing newspapers alive, believing that partisan press competition is vital to the quality of democracy. Wise use of direct subsidies can make major contributions to the communications order by helping to correct for media markets' egalitarian and efficiency failures. Revenue for print media subsidies in Europe often comes from taxes on advertising, especially advertising in broadcasting.[50] Most European countries also exempt the press from their otherwise high value-added tax (VAT).

In this country, an almost reflexive reaction is to predict that government subsidies will undermine media independence. I suspect that the strength of this assumption contributes to a tendency not to reflect on, maybe not even to notice, valuable indirect subsidies that are ubiquitous here as well as elsewhere in the world. Indirect subsidies provided the press, such as government press releases and now video news releases or VNRs, press passes, and convenient access to governmental officials or press "officers," are a major cause of government or establishment dominance of media reporting.[51] Nevertheless, in countries that provide direct cash, targeted subsidies – for example, for the weaker or secondary papers in a locale – the evidence for the common prediction does not exist in the way American observers expect, at least if the country otherwise is committed to press independence that is protected by both popular opinion and an independent judiciary. Hallin and Mancini observe that the "media were more deferential to political elites in the 1950s, before these subsidy systems were put in place, than in the 1970s."[52] They find that "critical professionalism" gained strength in journalism precisely when subsidies were at their highest.

Tax and subsidy policies can specifically favor press competition, diversity, and media ownership dispersal. These efforts have made a real difference in some countries. Several possibilities will be noted here. First, state and local governments commonly provide economic incentives for businesses to locate or stay within the state or local community. Sometimes tax-free bonds provide support; sometimes governments forgive property taxes for extended periods; frequently they promise and provide new infrastructure support. Of course, a local newspaper, broadcaster, or cable system has no choice but to stay. Still, the "community benefits" rationale is applicable. Keeping in mind the need to protect against partisan abuse or manipulation, a state could adopt nondiscretionary rules providing tax benefits that favor prescribed categories of purchasers or creators of local media entities. For example, these benefits could be offered to favor in-state[53] purchasers or creators of media that also meet the criteria of the third proposal above. Or Congress could reduce capital gains tax rates for sales to these favored categories of owners.

Other tax subsidies are also appropriate. Democratic theory supports not merely dispersal but an ownership distribution that allows people to experience some media entities as in some sense "theirs" – an experience likely served when ownership is by members of the group with which they identify. One aspect of the FCC's 2003 ownership rules that the Third Circuit rejected as unjustified was the FCC's elimination of its last remaining policy favoring minority licensees.[54] Although often abused, prior FCC rules essentially provided economic benefits for sales of broadcast licenses to entities with a substantial racial minority ownership interest. Justice William Brennan's last decision for the Court upheld a program supporting minority ownership of broadcast licenses.[55] Though the current status of that ruling is at best questionable,[56] democratic theory clearly suggests the merits of considering tax benefits or actual subsidies to support ownership diversity. In the print context, it has long been recognized that a major cause of sales of family-owned newspapers, almost always to a media conglomerate, has been estate taxes. Policy long ago provided a limited response, but greater estate tax exemptions could favor continuance of the remaining family media enterprises.[57]

Subsidies have also effectively supported competition and dispersed ownership. Government advertising has at times been a significant source of income, especially for small newspapers. Norway uses government advertising overtly to support multiple papers – requiring all nationally relevant government advertising to be placed equally in all 156 Norwegian papers and locally relevant ads equally in all the local papers.[58] In the late nineteenth century, New York similarly promoted media pluralism and partisanship by requiring that county legal notices be published in two local papers of different political affiliations. In New York and Ohio, local government printing contracts were divided in each county between a Republican and a Democratic paper.[59] But possibly the greatest use of subsidies to maintain competing newspapers has occurred in modern Europe. The most forceful attempt to correct for market forces that tend toward local newspaper monopolies has been for the government to provide operating funds to financially weaker papers, identified by varying rules that typically require the recipient not to be the dominant paper in the locale and not to have an audience penetration above a certain level.

7. SPECIAL RESPONSIBILITIES IMPOSED ON LARGE MEDIA FIRMS

Fears of concentrated media power might be reduced if the law required large media entities to provide fair access for alternative views and voices.[60] Earlier I offered a principled rejection of the notion that a particular media entity should be forbidden from gaining audience share. The reason, however, was that no audience member should be deprived of access, not that there is no reason to be concerned about the size and power of individual media entities. Admittedly, this country has seldom viewed the growth of a media entity as an automatic basis for imposing increased obligations. On the other hand, a cable system's must-carry obligations increase as its channel carriage capacity increases, and courts have not entertained the claim that this "penalizes" being big. As this carriage point illustrates, media entities that have something like bottleneck control over a particular communication form have sometimes been required, at least in their carriage activities, to provide access opportunities for outsiders. Bottleneck control provided a reason for Congress to require, and the Court to uphold, the must-carry rules.[61] And despite the D.C. Circuit's failure to comprehend the logic of the requirement, Congress sensibly imposed requirements that a significant portion of a cable system's channels be programmed by nonaffiliated companies.

In Europe, size has been a focus of systematic policy making and, occasionally, constitutional consideration. Sweden provides special newspaper subsidies for secondary papers; papers lose the subsidy if they obtain a certain level of market penetration. British commentators have proposed special obligations on broadcasters above a certain market share.[62] The German Federal Constitutional Court has indicated that the Basic Law requires state regulation that prevents enterprises from gaining any monopoly over opinion – including, in broadcasting, pluralistic content requirements and, in both print and broadcasting, restrictions on concentration.[63]

Special obligations might be imposed on papers with market penetration levels above a certain level – possibly at a level set to include virtually all cities' dominant daily but virtually no secondary papers. For example, these dominant papers could be required to take at competitive rates advertisements presenting positions on matters of public concern. In discussions of mandating that papers allow access for alternative views, I often hear complaints about imposing such an obligation on smaller, partisan papers. *Mohammed Speaks* should not have to carry the Klan's racist diatribe, *Gay Pride Weekly* should not have to carry a Christian Fundamentalist promotion of conversion therapy, and the *Catholic Observer* should not have to carry "pro-choice" manifestos. By imposing the requirement only on dominant papers, the rule preserves these smaller papers' right to continue unabated in exclusively presenting their partisan viewpoints. The rule reflects claims of complex democracy that different media should play different democratic roles. The rule understands the dominant media, to which the requirement applies, to contribute to republican inclusive discourse, while the exempted media to be significant for liberal pluralist discourses.

The democratic role of the requirement, as well as the difference that dominance makes, is quite similar to another distinction in rights recognized in constitutional law. Many voluntary associations have a constitutional right to exclusionary membership policies.[64] Nevertheless, political parties, despite clearly having many freedom of association rights, are required to offer "access." Presumably in part because of their power in the public sphere – compare bottleneck control – the Court has found that the Constitution itself forbids at least dominant political parties or political associations[65] from engaging in racial exclusion.[66]

Imposing access requirements hardly eliminates the concern with concentrated media power in the public sphere. Still, it might alleviate the concern to some degree. Moreover, the requirement does not run counter to the principle of *Miami Herald v. Tornillo*,[67] at least once *Turner* interpreted that decision to be based on the right to reply being an unconstitutional content-based penalty on the newspaper's original criticism of an electoral candidate.[68] Requiring nondiscriminatory access to advertising space for views on matters of public importance does not penalize the newspaper for anything it previously said but, instead, turns only on its circulation level. Of course, this newspaper carriage requirement is only one possible response to market dominance. The point here is merely that responses to concentration might include imposition of special responsibilities on media above a particular level of dominance.

The seven policies considered above all respond to the goal of maintaining or increasing media ownership dispersal or, in the case of the fourth and seventh proposals, aim to reduce and "redistribute" some of the communicative power of large media firms. The first proposal concerning expanded application of antitrust principles is surely the least controversial, although it requires a more activist antitrust stance and an orientation to antitrust different from what exists at present. Even expanded antitrust enforcement is, however, overtly inadequate for the purposes identified in chapter 1. The second proposal concerning required approval of mergers, with some presumption against approval and permitted waiver of limits, presents real dangers. Still, it is not so alien to either the American or other democratic communications systems. It may well make other policy criteria for when mergers should be permitted more flexible and hence more desirable (and, maybe, more acceptable). The third proposal, to bar or presumptively bar all *mergers* that increase existing levels of concentration or ownership by nonmedia corporations, is arguably ideal. I would push strongly for its adoption. Unfortunately, existing political realities make this result very unlikely in the near term. Possibly, the proposal could serve as a standard (a regulative ideal) against which to measure other reforms. The fourth proposal, aimed at maintaining independent voices despite mergers, like its inspiration – the Newspaper Preservation Act – could contribute to the aims of diversity and independent voices that partly justify dispersing media ownership. The fifth proposal, giving employees veto power over mergers, in addition to its equally desirable economic distributive effect, could further the aims of placing decision-making power in the hands of people most dedicated to quality performance of the journalistic task, slowing the rush to concentration, and favoring mergers that actually do improve quality. Like the fourth proposal, it increases the power of media professionals and, if enacted, could make a real contribution. The sixth proposal, the use of subsidies and tax provisions, can contribute beneficially to media policy generally. Some European countries have used it specifically to maintain diversity and pluralism for example, by providing support for launching media enterprises and support for non-dominant papers. Various versions of this approach are conceivable, but I suspect they will only make a limited contribution to the specific goal of preventing media concentration. The final proposal, to impose special responsibilities on dominant media, could relieve some of the problem of concentrated power that society otherwise decides it cannot or does not want to prohibit.

Postscript: Policy Opportunism

The three primary concerns discussed in chapter 1 overlap in recommending ownership dispersal. Each, however, rested on a somewhat different goal or value relating to an ideal communications order. No matter how dispersed media ownership is, this dispersal will not fully achieve any of these three goals – it only contributes to their realization. This fact means that fully serving these goals requires additional policy measures. The policy measures advocated above also are not, to say the least, likely to be fully adopted. These facts suggest considering whether alternative policies can advance the three goals outlined. Alternatives would probably contribute differently to each of the three values. Possibly the best way to explore the wisdom of additional policies is separately to examine responses to each value. Cursory initial remarks about that project can serve as a conclusion to this book.

A More Democratic Distribution of Communicative Power

This goal is inclusionary: everyone should be able to experience some significant media as in some sense "theirs" and not experience their media interests as marginalized. It also is to some extent participatory. The goal aims at more and more fairly distributed opportunities to participate in the public sphere. As chapter 1 emphasized, these aims do not mean or require an absolutely egalitarian distribution. A strict egalitarian ambition is inconsistent with the appropriate existence of opinion leaders and with the very idea of "mass" media. Moreover, as chapters 1 and 4 observed, the republican goal of societal-wide discourses may be best interpreted as served by some dominant, inclusive, "core" media to which all can turn. To some extent these competing democratic concerns can be seen in the contrast between proposals 3's recommended severe restrictions on mergers and the earlier rejection of the possibility of limiting a single entity's audience. Proposal 3 directly serves the aim of maximum reasonable ownership dispersal, thereby contributing to the distributive aim. Contrarily, rejection of ceilings on an entity's reach allows for the development of media that serve an inclusive, common discourse. Nevertheless, three points suggest either the inadequacy of dispersal policies for serving the distributive, inclusionary, and participatory concerns or additional, more complex ways of serving these goals.

First, fair inclusion is hardly possible if virtually all the dominant mass media are in the control of a narrow group within society – the standard objection to wealthy white males (with prominent and less prominent exceptions). Even if ownership dispersal guarantees many owners, it does not guarantee that they will not still come from this narrow band. Although this book has specifically focused on concentration, the inclusive and participatory goal calls attention to a broader objective – not just dispersal but dispersal to people identified with different groups. Given the inexactness and fluidity of necessarily socially constructed group identities, no precise formulation of this objective can be given. But certainly the objective calls at least for policies designed to assure greater ethnic and racial representation in the distribution of ownership than exists today. With non-caucasian minorities predicted by the Census Bureau to constitute half of the country's population by 2050,[1] FCC Commissioner Michael Copps is surely right to characterize as shocking and embarrassing the 14 percent drop in minority *owners* (which is different from the number of minority-owned *stations*; minority ownership also is becoming more concentrated among a few minority owners) between 1996 and the time of the FCC adoption of new rules in 2003.[2] Looking at the years from 1993 to 1997/1998 reinforces the point. FCC data show that the total percentage of broadcast stations with minority ownership expanded almost imperceptibly from 2.83 percent to 2.93 percent, while the percentage owned by African Americans dropped from 2.1 percent to 1.7 percent.[3] Given the overwhelming whiteness of broadcast ownership, even if the policy was only marginally effective, the FCC surely acted appropriately in offering tax credits for sales and licensing preferences to favor locating more ownership in minority hands. Going in exactly the wrong direction, the current intensely antiregulatory FCC attempted to eliminate the last remaining such policy in its 2003 ownership proceeding, a step that the Third Circuit found unjustified.[4] Any subsidy system could appropriately favor greater group inclusion.

Second, in addition to public media such as public broadcasting, the communications order, the public sphere, consists of some balance between commodified, commercial mass media and more distributed, voluntaristic, noncommodified communications practices. No particular balance between these two is "natural." Yochai Benkler has led the discussion showing how structural choices inevitably influence the tilt of this balance. Structural choices necessarily favor certain types of communicators over others. Democratic distributive and participatory aims suggest favoring not only small media firms over the large, but also noncommercial media and, foremost, the individual speaker over the commercial firm. Observing that the classic image of the *agora* is of a communications commons, Benkler shows that the choice to propertize communicative content (e.g., copyright) and to propertize resources needed for delivery of communications (e.g., the broadcast spectrum), unless otherwise necessary for effective communication, normally has the reverse of the favored biases.[5] Copyright, for example, provides a communicator with a potential benefit – she potentially can get an economic return by selling portions of her rights to others. Copyright also can impose a cost on this communicator. She may need another's permission which sometimes is impossible to obtain and in other cases comes at a price, when she inevitably relies on past intellectual products in her own communication. For those not operating within the market, copyright operates *only* as a cost.[6] For those operating within the market, in contrast, copyright provides both costs and benefits. The costs are *least*, however, for those who own a significant stock of copyrighted material from which they can borrow without a need to pay. Specifically, copyright imposes a smaller cost on the media giants than on smaller media entities and individuals. And copyright is also likely to provide greater benefits to these media giants because of efficiencies, mostly economies of scale, in managing these rights. In other words, the democratic distributional and participatory aims support a structural presumption for resisting property "enclosures" of the intellectual commons – and a preference for only "weak" copyright protection.

Benkler has pushed this point further.[7] In broadcasting, something like property rights in spectrum was long viewed as necessary for effective broadcast communication.[8] (Although denominated licenses, given the FCC's willingness to allow their routine sale, the main significance of licensure as a form probably relates to political debates about regulatory practice. As a rhetorical matter, denominating "airwaves" as owned by the public and usage based on a license makes regulation seem more appropriate, while the aim of those advocating property rights in spectrum is to attack regulation. However, the example of land use regulation suggests that if otherwise permissible – for example, under the First Amendment – the permissibility of legal regulation is probably unaffected by whether the rights are labeled licenses or actual "ownership.") This technological necessity has changed.[9] Newer technology now allows "smart" radio receivers to distinguish between signals much the way the human ear does in the noisy restaurant or, possibly more analogously, the way software allows users' computers to distinguish between packets of information on the Internet. Unlicensed broadcasting can occur without creating the "chaos," the tragedy of the commons problem, that originally appeared to require licenses or other property-like grants to make the spectrum usable.

The democratic goal of empowering all desirous communicators, Benkler argues, would be advanced by universal dispersal of the right to use these airwaves. Now, everyone who wants to broadcast can do so without creating uninterpretable babble. By reducing the cost of communicating and by reducing the power of property owners to control and limit others' broadcast communications, an unlicensed wireless communications order creates a more democratic public sphere. Thus, here too, the democratic goal can be advanced by making more rather than less of the spectrum into an unowned, unlicensed "commons" – like highways, available for use by anyone, subject to various rules of the road. Certainly, nothing in Benkler's argument suggests abandoning the commercial mass media or structural rules necessary for it to exist. But he does expose the fallacy of any assumption that existing outcomes, which reflect "freedom" within the existing marketplace, show that people "prefer" the existing mix of commodified media and noncommodified communications. Rather, this (or any other) mix simply reflects individual choices within a particular legal structure. This structure ultimately reflects policy choices, which in turn result from either conscious judgments or unthinking default to whatever background rules exist. Democratic *values*, on which Benkler largely relies, imply that these choices should systematically favor a more participatory, more broadly distributed, and less commodified mix than exists at present. Democratic *commitments* require that these structural choices be subject to democratic decision making.

Third, one caveat to the dispersal goal is the additional democratic need for an inclusive common discourse that might require a dominant media on which all could reasonably rely. Both the aim of dispersal and the aim of a common discourse are democratic aims. Both seek inclusion

193

of all – differing in that one wants all to have their own media and the other wants all to be represented within a common media. Allowing commercial media entities to grow internally responds to this second democratic need for a common discourse but is predictably inadequate for at least two reasons. First, there is no guarantee and can be no effective legal requirement that this commercial media will actually be inclusive. Devices such as the Fairness Doctrine attempted to make broadcast media more inclusive but were an incredibly heavy-handed and probably counterproductive device, which was a central reason for the court of appeals to affirm the FCC's abandonment of the doctrine.[10] The seventh proposal's suggestion of opening advertising space in dominant media to alternative views may be less dysfunctional but will surely be inadequate to serve this aim. Second, not only is there no guarantee, but there are also substantial structural reasons to predict inadequacy. The inclusionary result is likely to be greatly distorted by advertising and partially undermined by profit-maximizing practices. Both observations were long central to the defense of a robust public broadcasting system in most European countries.[11] In the context of a democratic *common* discourse, the inclusionary aim is arguably best provided by a nonprofit public media with a remit to provide inclusionary as well as quality programming.

The more general point? The democratic *distributive* and the related participatory and inclusionary goals should not operate as an absolute policy but as a presumption. Trade-offs make sense. Other considerations, including additional democratic (e.g., "republican") considerations related to communications, can sometimes override this distributive presumption. Still, this presumption always provides a reason to favor dispersal of private media ownership. But even achieving maximum feasible dispersal is inevitably insufficient to achieve the aim of everyone having a nonmarginal mass media entity that she can view as "hers." Therefore, this distributive value should operate in all areas of structural media policy, not simply in relation to ownership.

RISK REDUCTION: AVOIDING DEMAGOGIC POWER AND PROMOTING THE WATCHDOG ROLE

In multiple ways, ownership dispersal protects democracy. It largely eliminates the basis for an individual's demagogic abuse of extraordinary power within the public sphere. It creates more decision makers who can choose whether and how they will be watchdogs. It reduces conflicts of interest that undermine this watchdog role and, more broadly, undermine the integrity of the mass media's fourth-estate contributions to a democratic society. Ownership dispersal – or structural attenuation of ownership's relation to control by mandating editorial independence (the fourth proposal) or by guaranteeing access rights (the seventh proposal) – directly reduces the danger of concentrated demagogic power. Its contribution to the second two safeguards is, however, more indirect and incomplete. Additional ways to serve these two safeguards should be considered.

One approach aims to reduce the media's gatekeeping power. Policy could enhance the capacity of nonprofessionals to provide content that contests the views of demagogic power and is relevant to watchdog performance while avoiding the media's own conflicts of interest. Proposed access requirements and the Fairness Doctrine both attempted to modify the media's gatekeeper power. Both, however, generate serious objections and provide at best limited help. Access requirements risk blunting partisan advocacy that both liberal pluralists and complex democrats see as important in a democracy. This problem explains limiting access to "dominant" entities within any media realm (the seventh proposal). Equally troubling, access requirements in themselves typically neither supply the resources needed for quality content creation nor perform the valuable editing roles properly provided by media entities. Their scope in space or time, at least as applied to major "edited" media such as television or newspapers, are inevitably marginal as compared with the entity's own editorial choices. These problems and objections do not mean that selective use of access requirements should be avoided – only that a policy maker should be cautious because of their downside and conscious of their limited contributions.

The need for care in designing any access rules is illustrated by the Fairness Doctrine. It was an explicit legal requirement that broadcasters cover important issues of public importance (a "coverage" requirement) and present all sides of the issue (a "balance" requirement). Though it is currently defunct, repeated proposals for its revival have been made. Nevertheless, the Fairness Doctrine has three main problems that largely undermine its value. First, it is hardly ideologically neutral. Its mandated balance, like an Aristotlean golden mean, is inconsistent with a major tradition of a hard-hitting, partisan, advocacy press and with a possible normative view that politics is and should be about struggle and peaceful conflict. Its inspiration represents more a republican democratic ideal than any vision of the media valued by a liberal pluralist conception of democracy. Though agreeing on the value of balance in some media, a complex democrat should also conclude that often balance should not displace more partisan journalistic forms. The policy question of whether balance or partisanship requires additional legal support is a contested normative as well as a difficult empirical issue. Still, market pressures favoring objective journalism suggest partisanship is more likely to be undernourished.

Second are problems with implementation. The Fairness Doctrine's *coverage* requirement was always virtually unenforceable. Given the world's kaleidoscope of events and issues, neither government officials nor courts will have objective or otherwise legally usable criteria with which to second-guess an editor as to which stories to cover. On the other hand, the *balance* requirement could easily deter broadcasting stories that generate fairness obligations. The FCC eventually found that this predictable deterrence occurred frequently, and relied heavily on this finding when it eliminated the Fairness Doctrine.[12]

The doctrine is also easily manipulable. Discretion is immense in deciding whether an issue is controversial, which alternative views create adequate balance, and whether a broadcaster's programming has provided it. The first difficulty is simply identifying what issue(s) a program raises. At a time when pension reform was under intense debate in Congress, NBC broadcast a Peabody award–winning program, "Pensions: The Broken Promise," that documented specific failures of the pension system. After a challenge by those who thought the show was one-sided, NBC lawyers convinced the D.C. Circuit that the program showed only that there was a problem, and, unlike the question of what, if anything, to do, the existence of a problem was not controversial.[13] This finding eliminated any need for balance! The inherent openness of the requirement to such manipulative characterizations of programs led the FCC usually to defer to broadcasters' judgments about what issue a program raised and whether the station had adequately presented the other side or sides. In 1973 and 1974, the FCC found only nineteen violations in 4,280 formal fairness complaints filed – and fourteen of these related to personal attacks or political editorials where the balance criteria are much more objective.[14]

The third problem is worse than being manipulable and unenforceable. Even attempts at honest application predictably favor the status quo. Any broadcast opposing government policy or dominant opinion is almost by definition controversial. Fairness logically mandates a renewed, responsive presentation of government or dominant views. In contrast, dominant views seldom seem controversial – particularly to people, like most FCC commissioners, who are usually close to the dominant coalition. At a time when major portions of government at long last had become concerned with smoking,[15] the FCC found that cigarette commercials raised a controversial issue that required presentation of the antismoking view.[16] Environmentalist and other countercultural groups then argued that advertising for gas-guzzling cars and snowmobiles – in fact, advertising for consumer products in general – represents one-sided support for the controversial values of a consumer-oriented, materialist world. In response, the FCC stopped applying the Fairness Doctrine to product advertising.[17] This response fits with the inclination not to require counters to the dominant government or corporate orthodoxy. During the Vietnam War, a massive antiwar movement included constant demonstrations at recruitment offices and burning draft cards. Did military recruitment ads raise an important controversial, issue? No! In the eyes of the FCC, as approved by the courts, the war might be controversial, but the country's need for troops, when at war, is not.[18] In effect, the balance requirement provides minimal help in getting dissident content broadcast but assures that if it is, it be answered with the establishment line. It is hard to imagine a more centrist requirement.

Other ways to reduce a concentrated mass media's gate-keeper power include promotion of the Internet and the "volunteer" or peer-to-peer communications that motivates much of Yochai Benkler's work. As he has shown, their development is heavily dependent on structural policy choices.[19] Great effort to change in the directions he proposes should occur. Still, hopes that these developments provide effortless and painless cures that justify abandoning efforts to achieve greatly needed structural change are misguided for three reasons. First is reach: chapter 3 showed that, and explained why, Internet audience attention tends to be incredibly concentrated and largely colonized by major corporate interests. Second is resources: a major value of mass media lies in their ability to apply considerable financial resources to the tasks of (hopefully quality) investigations, writing, and editing. Volunteer peer-to-peer or online blog publishing may eventually provide all this in a meaningful way without itself being dependent on heavy borrowing from the mass media, but it seems that we are far from there. Third is the present moment – even if the capacity for online activities to drastically reduce traditional concentrated media's gatekeeper role exists, today the commercial mass media (including their online versions or Web sites) still dominate the public sphere. As long as that is true, policy that responds to the power of this media is essential.

Probably the best way to respond to the problems described in this book concerning democratic safeguards, as well as distribution of media power and ill effects of an exclusive focus on the bottom line, is some version of a proposal presented by James Curran.[20] He envisions the media as potentially comprised of five sectors – a civic, professional, social market, private enterprise, and core. Each sector essentially has a different remit or democratic assignment. Ideally, each would have a different organization of control and different type of financial base. A strong public broadcasting system could be the primary institution of the core media, performing essentially the republican goal of being an inclusive and broadly informed discourse. The social market and civic sectors, in somewhat different ways, serve the liberal pluralist functions. Although all sectors would contribute to the watchdog role, Curran suggests that the professional sector would specialize in this role. As for a demagogic concentration of power, the different media sectors help to counter the danger. An individual demagogic figure, even if dominant within one sector, could be countered by the robust quality of the other sectors. Conflicts of interest – as well as other censorious structural pressures – may be reducible but in the end are unavoidable within any given structure. The force of any particular conflict will, however, vary depending on the sector. Having a different organizational and financial structure for each sector diminishes the extent of this problem with conflicts of interest. The same is true about the adverse effects of a single-minded bottom-line focus. Some sectors are not primarily market-based and are not operated primarily to produce profits.

Although the specifics of Curran's sectoral analysis are not essential, his basic policy prescription is. He recognizes that there is no magic bullet, no single media policy, that will be adequate for a democratic communications order. Strength lies in *structural* diversity. An ideal media realm will be pluralist in the types of media entities that it supports. Policy should encourage their operation on the basis of different principles. It will also try to prevent market corruption of media content.[21] Most importantly, policy should provide support, often varying kinds of financial support, for sectors not adequately nourished by the market.

Reducing Consequences of Market Failures in Content Production and Provision

Ownership dispersal structurally increases the likelihood that professional journalistic and creative commitments will hold more sway, and profit maximization less sway, over media practice, thereby potentially alleviating two ubiquitous market failures. The hopes are, first, for a greater emphasis on serving less profitable – usually smaller or poorer – audiences and, second, for a greater emphasis on content with positive rather than negative externalities, including content serving the watchdog function. Ownership dispersal, however, only indirectly and contingently serves these hopes by getting ownership into the hands of people likely to be responsive. Both obvious and less obvious alternative (or additional) ways of serving these aims exist.

Policy could more directly pursue the goal of getting media entities into the hands of those less structurally inclined to maximize profits or more inclined to emphasize the favored types of content. A careful study found that public stock ownership consistently exacerbated the bottom-line focus, with its socially deleterious effects.[22] Public ownership apparently increases shareholder or institutional investor pressures to produce consistently higher profits. A response advocated by Frank Blethen, publisher of the family-owned *Seattle Times*, is to "prohibit publicly traded stock ownership for daily newspapers, television stations, and broadcast houses."[23] He denied that his proposal was "outrageously radical" by observing that the United States put this prohibition into the Japanese constitution and further observed that the Japanese press, which achieves one of the highest circulation rates in the world, is content with far smaller profit margins than are the norm in the United States. Predictably, evidence seems to find both commitments to quality and less emphasis on profit in foundation-owned or nonprofit media entities.[24] These types of media entities exist in the United States, but media-specific tax and corporate legal policies might increase their number. The same points could be made about ownership by workers or journalists.[25]

The other obvious response involves subsidies. Subsidies could go to media projects not pursued by profit-oriented media. Subsidies for quality production – for example, grants for private investigative journalism or documentary film making projects – combined with decentralized grant making (to add structural pluralism and contextual sensitivity) could supplement content created with only a bottom-line focus. Combining financial support for such projects and public ownership of some significant media entities (with a structural design to insulate the entities from becoming a mouthpiece of or subservient to the governmental regime in power) could make a substantial contribution to having independent media not bound by a profit-maximizing logic. Strengthening rather than scuttling the public broadcast system may be the most feasible and important political struggle on the horizon. Requirements that cable systems carry and, importantly, provide equipment and technical and financial support for access and other PEG (public, educational, and government) channels is essentially a subsidy arrangement. Similarly, I once proposed that all broadcasters, rather than each being required to provide at least a minimum number of hours to children's "educational" television, instead be required to allocate a minimum percentage of their revenue to a local fund for such programming and to set up in each locale an independent unpaid board composed of community members (for example, of representatives from teacher and parent-teacher associations and local governments as well as a broadcast representative) to control the use of the revenue. The local board could evaluate and purchase content and pay for broadcast time either on each station or on a local station that specialized in children's programming. Variations on this proposal could apply in other areas. Some countries have diverted a portion of broadcasting's advertising revenue to newspapers. Proposals are common to divert a portion of commercial advertising revenue to support public broadcasting.[26] Consideration should be given to other proposals to divert some revenue from profit-maximizing media entities to media or media projects not so focused. More generally, these responses to a democratically dysfunctional profit-maximization focus reflect the basic logic of James Curran's pluralistic multisector proposal.[27]

POLICY SUMMARY

Stringent limits on media mergers may be the single most meaningful legitimate way to respond to the objections to media concentration and the goal of ownership dispersal. Nevertheless, *mere* ownership dispersal is inevitably an insufficient means of providing for a democratic distribution of media power and for curing market failures produced by relentless pursuit of profit. It is also only one means. Proposals 5, 6, and 7 in the preceding chapter and the additional responses noted in this chapter suggest the wisdom of and need for a multipronged approach to media policy. Here, as in a previous book, I find appealing the logic of James Curran's five-sector approach.

More generally, this policy discussion embodies three messages. First, systematic consideration of the media order is misguided to the extent that critics focus only on journalists' and editors' personal failure to produce the quality content that the critic, often rightly, thinks society needs. Self-improvement, higher standards, and greater dedication are desirable. Media critics should take media entities, editors, and journalists to task for distortion, inaccuracy, trivia, and noncoverage. Better performance is possible and the public should demand it. Still, media professionals are, I believe, mostly incredibly dedicated and mostly do good work. The *central* problems are not professional incompetence or performance failures but instead involve structure. Thus, the first message: think structurally.

Second, in many circles today, including in discussions that fuel a misguided effort of turning the media over ever more to market regulation – the self-identified "deregulatory" movement – the emphasis is almost entirely on (economic) efficiency as seen through the lens of existing preferences and existing distributions of income. Better economic analyses show how the market systematically fails to produce even this market efficiency. This better economic analysis recognizes that economics is not theoretically committed to ignoring all values except individual consumption. Nevertheless, most free market economists and their policy and publicist followers consider little else. Better economic analyses would not be so blind.[28] This leads to the second message: policy thinking should not center on the economistic conception of efficiency. The emphasis needs to be on the systematic relation of media structure to a plurality of values, especially various noncommodified distributive and process values that are central to a democratic order.

Third, the array of desirable policy interventions discussed above, even in relation to simply the three primary concerns on which chapter 1 asserted the media concentration debate should center, suggests the final message: media activists should be opportunistic. Even as scholars should be broad-based in describing ideals, activists should focus on those desirable changes that can possibly be achieved at a given time or on which a movement for reform can be grounded, while simultaneously remaining aware of justifications and needs for broader, additional changes.

I share the sense of many keen observers in this country and around the world that American democracy is in trouble. America's strikingly inegalitarian domestic policy is surely unjust; policy choices systematically favoring private consumptive over public use of resources are incredibly unwise; and much of our foreign policy is not only immoral and illegal but entirely counterproductive from the perspective of any rational conception of domestic self-interest. Whether these policies reflect, as the democratic faith demands, views dominant within the public sphere is unclear. However, if that public sphere is itself uninformed or misinformed, if it is not robust in its debate of values and policies, any democratic faith is short-changed.

I suspect that those who do not agree with these assessments, even if they accept some technical arguments and empirical observations about the media made in this book, will not feel much urgency about the topic (and are unlikely to have read the book). For those who do agree with my pessimistic assessment of our current state but retain their democratic faith, concern with the communications order should be of upmost importance and considerable urgency. Proposals made in this chapter – and others made elsewhere – are gutsy. For now, they may have little chance politically. And, unfortunately, they also will not be near adequate even for the limited task of providing a needed communications order. Still, implementing some version of these proposals would be a step in the right direction. But these proposals have *no* chance of adoption until both media professionals and engaged citizens, who need to be on the same side, realize that the mass media will continue to fail us without change to the *structure* that induces these failures.

Notes

Preface

1. C. Edwin Baker, "Press Rights and Government Power to Structure the Press," *University of Miami Law Review* 34 (1980): 819.
2. "The Law and Policy of Media Ownership in the United States," in Uwe Blaurock, *Medienkonzentration und Angebotsvielfalt zwishchen Kartell-Rundfunkrecht* (Nomos Verglagsgesellschaft: Baden-Baden, 2002), 9–70.
3. "Media Concentration: Giving Up on Democracy," *Florida Law Review* 54 (2002): 839. I should note that the present book also contains material published in C. Edwin Baker, "Media Structure, Ownership Policy, and the First Amendment," *Southern California Law Review* 78 (2005): 733.

Introduction

1. See Report and Order and Notice of Proposed Rulemaking, 18 F.C.C.R. 13,620 (2003).
2. Statement of Commissioner Jonathan S. Adelstein, dissenting, 18 F.C.C.R. 13,974, 13,977 (July 2, 2003).
3. William Safire, "The Great Media Gulp," *New York Times* (May 22, 2003): A33.
4. William Safire, "Big Media's Silence," *New York Times* (June 26, 2003): A33; William Safire, "Localism's Last Stand," *New York Times* (July 17, 2003): A27.
5. Pub. L. No. 108–199, §629, 118 Stat. 3, 99 (2004) (adopting statutory directive to lower the FCC's new national television ownership cap of 45% to 39%).
6. *Prometheus Radio Project v. FCC*, 373 F.3d 372 (3rd Cir. 2004).
7. A. J. Liebling, *The Wayward Pressman* (Garden City, N.Y.: Doubleday, 1947), 265. In slightly different words – "freedom of the press is guaranteed only to those who own one" – the same remark is quoted from later sources. E.g., A. J. Liebling, *The Press* (New York: Pantheon, 1981), 32.
8. See, e.g., Peter J. Humphreys, *Mass Media and Media Policy in Western Europe* (New York: Manchester U. Press, 1996), 66–110; Daniel C. Hallin and Paolo Mancini, *Comparing Media Systems: Three Models of Media and Politics* (New York: Cambridge U. Press, 2004).
9. Richard B. Kielbowicz, *News in the Mail: The Press, Post Office, and Public Information, 1700–1860s* (Westport, Conn.: Greenwood Press, 1989).

10. Gerald J. Baldasty and Jeffrey Rutenbeck, "Money, Politics and Newspapers: The Business Environment of Press Partisanship in the Late 19th Century," *Journalism History* 15 (1988): 60, 63–65. Norway's similar requirement that the government place identical advertisements in all newspapers or, for locally relevant ads, all newspapers of that area, illustrates one of many modern European efforts to promote competition and diversity. Anthony Smith, *Subsidies and the Press in Europe* (London: PEP, 1977), 51.

11. *Associated Press v. United States*, 326 U.S. 1. 20 (1945).

12. House Debate, 81st Cong., 1st Sess., Aug. 15, 1949 (quoted in Maurice E. Stucke and Allen P. Grunes, "Antitrust and the Marketplace of Ideas," *Antitrust Law Journal* 69 (2001): 249, 260.

13. Pub. L. No. 91–353, §2, 84 Stat. 466 (1970) (codified at 15 U.S.C. §§1801–1804 (2000)).

14. See Commission on Freedom of the Press, *A Free and Responsible Press: A General Report on Mass Communication* (Chicago: University of Chicago Press, 1947), 1, 5, 17, 37–44, 83–86. Although similarly emphatic about the dangers of media concentration, commission member Zachariah Chafee was skeptical of use of law to restrict it, suggesting that the antitrust laws could do little and noting dangers of their abuse. See Zechariah Chafee, Jr., *Government and Mass Communications, A Report from the Commission on Freedom of the Press* (Chicago: University of Chicago Press, 1947), 2: 537–677, especially at 674–77.

15. Cf. Chafee, supra note 14, at 617 ("It is obvious, then, that bigness in the press is here to stay, whether we like it or not.").

16. C. Edwin Baker, *Advertising and a Democratic Press* (Princeton: Princeton U. Press, 1994), 16, 146 n. 34; Walt Brasch, "The Media Monolith: Synergizing America," *Counterpunch* (Feb. 9, 2002), at http://www.counterpunch.org/braschmedia.html. In addition, as of 2003, another twelve cities had newspapers with Joint Operating Agreements (JOA), that is, two or more papers that operate commercially as one business but are required to be editorially independent. *2004 Facts about Newspapers*, at http://www.naa.org/info/facts04/joa.html (accessed Jan. 14, 2005).

17. See, e.g., the discussion in Fred S. Siebert, Theodore Peterson, and Wilbur Schramm, *Four Theories of the Press* (Urbana: University of Illinois Press, 1956), chap. 3 (elaborating a "social responsibility theory of the press"); John C. Nerone, ed., *Last Rights* (Urbana: University of Illinois Press, 1995), 77–124.

18. Mark Crispin Miller, "The National Entertainment State," *Nation* (June 3, 1996): 22, 23–26.

19. Ben H. Bagdikian, *The Media Monopoly* (Boston: Beacon Press, 1983), xviii, 4ff.

20. Ben H. Bagdikian, *The New Media Monopoly* (Boston: Beacon Press, 2004), 3.

21. See Humphreys, supra note 8, at 94. The partisan aspects should not be overstated. Apparently in Britain, for example, a consensus between the right and left has existed in opposing media concentration. Eric Barendt, "Control of Media Concentrations: Regulation in the United Kingdom," in Uwe Blaurock, *Medienkonzentration und Angebotsvielfalt zwischen Kartell-Rundfunkrecht* (Nomos Verglagsgesellschaft: Baden-Baden, 2002), 71, 72, 79; Damian Tambini, "Through with Ownership Rules? Media Pluralism in the Transition to Digital," in Damian Tambini, with Liz Forgan, Clare Hall, and Stefan Verhulst, eds., *Communication Revolution and Reform* (London: IPPR, 2001), 21, 22.

22. Robert W. McChesney is possibly the best-known progressive currently emphasizing the concern. See his *Rich Media, Poor Democracy* (New York: New Press, 2000); Edward S. Herman and Robert W. McChesney, *The Global Media: The New Missionaries of Corporate Capitalism* (London: Cassell, 1997). Slightly more centrist is Bagdikian, *The New Media Monopoly*, supra note 20. A partial dissent might describe the central problem of a democratic media as not the specifics of ownership but the market forces that are the main determinant of media content. See, e.g., Robert Britt Horwitz, *Communication and Democratic Reform in South Africa* (New York: Cambridge U. Press, 2001); Robert Britt Horwitz, "Media Concentration and the Diversity Question," *The Information Society* 21 (2005): 181 (although emphasizing that ownership is not irrelevant, he suggests that ownership "curbs are likely to be of limited efficacy" by themselves). Horwitz emphasized, as I do in chapter 5, the need for a "mixed media system." Objection to the distorting effects of market-based commercialism was, for example, the basis of the European commitment to public broadcasting. Most European courts find a public monopoly over broadcasting to be consistent with broadcasting freedom, and some countries view the existence and adequate support of public broadcasting, at least in some contexts, to be constitutionally required. Eric Barendt, *Broadcasting Law: A Comparative Study* (New York: Oxford U. Press, 1993), 57–59, 69–70, 74. Obviously, the same critic can object to both concentrated private ownership and market forces.

CHAPTER 1. DEMOCRACY AT THE CROSSROADS: WHY OWNERSHIP MATTERS

1. Potter Stewart, "Or of the Press," *Hastings Law Journal* 26 (1975): 631, 634. Stewart relied on Thomas Carlyle's attribution to Burke.
2. Id. See also William J. Brennan, Jr., "Address," *Rutgers Law Review* 32 (1979): 173.
3. See C. Edwin Baker, *Media, Markets, and Democracy* (New York: Cambridge U. Press, 2002), pt. II.
4. Joseph A. Schumpeter, *Capitalism, Socialism, and Democracy* (1942; rpt., New York: Harper & Row, 1976). In the formulation above, there is still a normative element in the notion of what counts as better results but, still, democracy is valued solely as a means to this independently specified end.
5. *Reynolds v. Sims*, 377 U.S. 533 (1964).
6. The classic conception of "public opinion" is opinion expressed in public in the context of informed public discussion or debate that often generates reflection. As such, public opinion contrasts to the "private opinion" or aggregated individual opinion – expressed privately and often with no thoughtful consideration – measured by modern opinion polls. However, this contrast only scratches the surface of the concept. Both the classical and modern notions of public opinion are relevant to arguments about media ownership, but I will not undertake the task of sorting between them; however, the importance of both opinion's publicness and its informed quality should be kept in mind. An excellent introduction to the issues can be found in Theodore L. Glasser and Charles T. Salmon, *Public Opinion and the Communication of Consent* (New York: Guilford Press, 1995). See also Robert M. Entman and Susan Herbst, "Reframing Public Opinion as We Have Known It," in

W. Lance Bennett and Robert M. Entman, eds., *Mediated Politics: Communication in the Future of Democracy* (New York: Cambridge U. Press, 2001).

7. This terminology is taken from Jürgen Habermas, *Between Facts and Norms* (Cambridge, Mass.: MIT Press, 1996).

8. Rules Relating to Multiple Ownership, First Order and Report, 22 F.C.C.2d 306, 311 (1970).

9. Federal Communications Commission, Policy Statement on Comparative Broadcast Hearings, 1 F.C.C.2d. 393, 394 (1965).

10. *FCC v. National Citizens Committee for Broadcasting*, 436 U.S. 775, 795 (1978) (quoting *Associated Press v. United States*, 326 U.S. 1, 20 (1945)).

11. See John Rawls, *A Theory of Justice* (Cambridge, Mass.: Harvard U. Press, 1971), 85.

12. I more fully describe and evaluate four influential theories of democracy, which I model as elite, republican, liberal pluralist, and complex democracy, in Baker, supra note 3, 129–53.

13. Elihu Katz, "And Deliver Us from Segmentation," *Annals of the American Academy of Political & Social Sciences* 546 (1996): 22.

14. James Curran, "Crisis of Public Communication: A Reappraisal," in Tamar Liebes and James Curran eds., *Media, Ritual and Identity* (London: Routledge, 1998), 175.

15. See also Lee Bollinger, "Freedom of the Press and Public Access: Toward a Theory of Partial Regulation of the Mass Media," *Michigan Law Review* 75 (1976): 1.

16. C. Edwin Baker, *Human Liberty and Freedom of Speech* (New York: Oxford U. Press, 1989), 37–46.

17. Steven H. Shiffrin, *Dissent, Injustice, and the Meanings of America* (Princeton: Princeton U. Press, 1999).

18. *Metro Broadcasting v. FCC*, 397 U.S. 547 (1990).

19. *Prometheus Radio Project v. FCC*, 373 F.3d 372, 386 (3rd Cir. 2004) (two million communicating to FCC).

20. Pew Research Center, "Strong Opposition to Media Cross-Ownership Emerges" (July 13, 2003). The Pew Research Center reported that the portion of the public that had heard of the controversy increased from 26% in February 2003, before the FCC ruling, to 48% in July 2003, after the decision.

21. Id.

22. James Fallows, "The Age of Murdoch," *The Atlantic Monthly* 82 (Sept. 2003): 95.

23. *FCC v. National Citizens Committee for Broadcasting*, 436 U.S. 775 (1978); *United States v. Storer Broadcasting Co.*, 351 U.S. 192 (1956). See also *Associated Press v. United States*, 326 U.S. 1, 20 (1945).

24. *Time Warner Entertainment Co. v. FCC*, 240 F.3d 1126, 1133–36 (D.C. Cir. 2001) (invalidating FCC rule restricting single company from owning cable systems controlling more than 30% of the national audience but opining that a rule preventing a single company from controlling more than a 60% share, thereby guaranteeing at least two cable companies in the country, might be justified); *Fox Television Stations v. FCC*, 280 F.3d 1027, 1040–45 (D.C. Cir. 2002) (invalidating the FCC's national TV station ownership rule); Christopher Yoo, "Architectural Censorship and the FCC," *Southern California Law Review* 78 (2005): 669.

25. Starting in 1940, the FCC began placing numerical limits, initially ranging from three to seven per service type (AM, FM, and television) until settling on a 7-7-7 rule in 1954, with the power to impose these limitations being upheld by the Supreme

Court in *United States v. Storer Broadcasting Co.*, 351 U.S. 192 (1956). Beginning in 1984, a new deregulatory FCC began reducing limits – with a 12–12–12 limit and national audience reach cap of 25%, although it clearly would have reduced restrictions further but bowed to pressure from several congressional committees. This history is superbly outlined in Henry Geller, "Ownership Regulatory Policies in the U.S. Telecom Sector," *Cardozo Arts & Entertainment Law Journal* 13 (1995): 727. The Telecommunications Act of 1996 continued this relaxation, leading to Clear Channel's current ownership totals.

26. Fed. Communications Commission, Report on Chain Broadcasting 65 (1941), upheld against constitutional challenge, *National Broadcasting Corporation v. United States*, 319 U.S. 190 (1943). The rules have since been eliminated for radio and relaxed in relation to television. See, e.g., Review of Rules and Policies Concerning Network Broadcasting by Television Stations: Elimination or Modification of Section 73.658(c) of the Commission's Rules, Report and Order, 4 F.C.C.R. 2755 (1989).

27. *FCC v. National Citizens Committee for Broadcasting*, 436 U.S. 775, 780 (1978).

28. In March 2005, Forbes reported that Wal-Mart is the country's largest corporation measured by revenue, Citigroup the largest by assets and by Forbes's overall criteria, and Exxon-Mobil is the largest by market capitalization and by profits. In contrast, Time Warner, the largest media corporation, ranks 51st overall among global companies. Scott DeCarlo, "The Forbes Global 2000" (March 31, 2005), at http://www.forbes.com/2005/03/30/05f2000land.html.

29. The suggestion that "the medium is the message" catches the fact that different formats change the impact or message despite an attempt to communicate the same content.

30. I say "purportedly" because the claims of content variation are bedeviled by intrinsic methodological measurement problems that cannot be solved in a value-neutral way.

31. The most common version of this discussion goes under the label of the "Steiner effect," referring to a classic article showing that, under specific circumstances, a monopolist is likely to provide more of certain types of content diversity in order to avoid competing with itself. Peter O. Steiner, "Program Patterns and Preferences, and the Workability of Competition in Radio Broadcasting," *Quarterly Journal of Economics* 66 (1952): 194.

32. Amendment of Rules Relating to Multiple Ownership of Standard, FM, and Television Stations, Second Report and Order, 59 F.C.C.2d 1046, 1079–80 (1975) (emphasis added).

33. Of course, mere dispersal does not eliminate the risk in relation to specific policy issues when the interests of diverse owners correspond. For a study of how this power operates, see J. H. Snider, *Speak Softly and Carry a Big Stick: How Local TV Broadcasters Exert Political Power* (New York: iUniverse, 2005).

34. C. Edwin Baker, "Campaign Expenditures and Free Speech," *Harvard Civil Rights–Civil Liberties Law Review* 33 (1998): 1.

35. Many cities have tried to limit demonstrations of the size of those that helped to bring down Soviet-era Eastern European governments. See Timothy Williams, "Keeping Great Crowds Off the Great Lawn," *New York Times* (April 27, 2005): B1 (describing a proposal to limit gatherings in Central Park to 50,000). A variety of other procedures typically imposed by local American governments would have made illegal many of the demonstrations that have been central to the collapse of regimes and the

democratization of governments. See C. Edwin Baker, "Unreasoned Reasonableness: Mandatory Parade Permits and Time, Place, and Manner Regulations," *Northwestern Law Review* 78 (1983): 937 (arguing that these limits should be held to violate the First Amendment); Baker, supra note 16, 125–93. Constitutional law in this area might change, however, to become more protective. See *Watchtower Bible and Tract Society v. Stratton*, 536 U.S. 150 (2002) (invalidating permit requirement, in part for many of the reasons advanced in the article cited above).

36. Paul Ginsborg, *Silvio Berlusconi: Television, Power and Patrimony* (London: Verso, 2004); Elisabeth Povoledo, "Berlusconi Resigns as Italian Premier, but May Not Actually Leave," *New York Times* (April 21, 2005); "Silvio Berlusconi," Wikipedia entry, at http://en.wikipedia.org/wiki/Silvio_Berlusconi (accessed Jan. 16, 2005).

37. C. Edwin Baker, *Advertising and a Democratic Press* (Princeton: Princeton U. Press, 1994), 9–43. More recently, I have argued that whether more partisan, pluralist media or more "republican," inclusive media are most needed is an empirical matter not subject to abstract solution. Still, I noted reasons to expect that the market will most underserve the first need. Baker, supra note 3, at 143–53, 202, 213.

38. Commission on Freedom of the Press (Hutchins Commission), *A Free and Responsible Press* (Chicago: University of Chicago Press, 1947). See Fred S. Siebert, Theodore Peterson, and Wilbur Schramm, *Four Theories of the Press* (Urbana: U. of Illinois Press, 1956).

39. See Edward S. Herman and Robert W. McChesney, *The Global Media: The New Missionaries of Global Capitalism* (Washington, D.C.: Cassell, 1997).

40. Contrary to received wisdom, considerable evidence suggests that "the 'yellow press' was not a significant factor in leading the country to war," and according to Schudson, the contrary view reflects post–World War I revisionist history. Michael Schudson, *The Power of News* (Cambridge: Harvard U. Press, 1995), 231 n. 53.

41. See James Fallows, "The Age of Murdoch," *Atlantic Monthly* (Sept. 2003).

42. Daniel C. Hallin and Paolo Mancini, *Comparing Media Systems: Three Models of Media and Politics* (New York: Cambridge U. Press, 2004), 155.

43. 512 U.S. 622 (1994).

44. Rather than request carriage, the TV station could refuse permission to the cable system unless the cable system paid. The station's choice presumably reflected its evaluation of the power situation – whether the fact of carriage more valuable to the station or to the cable system.

45. Turner II, 520 U.S. 180 (1997).

46. E.g., *Time Warner Entertainment Co. v. FCC*, 240 F.3d 1126 (D.C. Cir. 2001), discussed in chapter 4.

47. In the Matter of 2002 Biennial Regulatory Review – Review of the Commission's Broadcast Ownership Rules, Report and Order and Notice of Proposed Rulemaking (adopted June 2, 2003, released July 2, 2003), FCC 03–127.

48. C. Edwin Baker, *Ownership of Newspapers: The View from Positivist Social Science* (monograph, Shorenstein Barone Center of JFK School of Government, Harvard University, 1994), available at http://www.law.upenn.edu/cf/faculty/ebaker/workingpapers/Ownership%20of%20Newspapers.pdf.

49. I do not mean that economic analyses cannot recognize this value but only that their typical commodity focus frequently prevents them from doing so. Cf. Baker, supra note 3, with Yoo, supra note 24.

50. I say "purportedly" objective because choice of criteria represents an ideologically loaded notion of the significance of various features that can mislead analysis.

51. There were exceptions. For example, some studies sought to find the impact of chain ownership on resources devoted to editorial content, a concern to which I return in discussing the third objection to ownership concentration.

52. I elaborate these and other problems with quantitative positivist social science studies of the impact of ownership forms in Baker, supra note 48, at 15–20.

53. These and other remarks here reflect my study, supra note 48.

54. Simeon Djankov, Carelee McLiesch, Tatiana Nenova, and Andrei Shleifer, "Who Owns the Media?" *Journal of Law & Economics* 46 (2003): 341. Though this article was riddled with other methodological errors, its failure to consider the most plausible hypothesis in relation to autocracy made its results insignificant. Possibly the reason that they held autocracy constant was an undefended belief that all governments are bad, but the badness is directly proportional to its level of autocracy. My preliminary investigation using roughly their data categories finds support for the more complex hypothesis noted above, which predicts beneficial results of government ownership or intervention only in the context of democracies. For a more astute investigation of national context that could be relevant for various predictions, see Hallin and Mancini, supra note 42.

55. I discuss a number of examples in Baker, supra note 48.

56. Id. (discussing illustrations of this type of misreading).

57. Rules Relating to Multiple Ownership, First Order and Report, 22 F.C.C.2d 306, 311 (1970).

58. Dan Gillmore, *We the Media: Grassroots Journalism by the People, for the People* (Sebastopol, Calif.: O'Reilly Press, 2004).

59. David L. Protess et al., *The Journalism of Outrage: Investigative Reporting and Agenda Building in America* (New York: Guilford Press, 1991).

60. James Curran, "Mass Media and Democracy Revisited," in James Curran and Michael Gurevitch, eds., *Mass Media and Society*, 2nd ed. (London: Arnold, 1996), 81, 88–89.

61. The economics of this section is elaborated in detail in Baker, supra note 3, part I.

62. Michael Walzer, *Spheres of Justice* (New York: Basic Books, 1983).

63. The classic text is Edward H. Chamberlin, *The Theory of Monopolistic Competition: A Reorientation of the Theory of Value*, 8th ed. (Cambridge: Harvard U. Press, 1962). Similar insights can be based on other traditional economic analyses when done carefully – as long as the analyst does not automatically equate increased profitability with increased efficiency in serving public welfare.

64. There are other problematic features of competition in products of this sort, including nonproduction of media content whose value would be greater than its cost and the problem of market competition in some circumstances worsening the situation, causing a net loss in consumer welfare. These features are discussed in Baker, supra note 3.

65. Jonathan Levy, Marcelino Ford-Livene, and Anne Levine, "Broadcast Television: Survivor in a Sea of Competition," 37 *OPP Working Paper Series*, p. 34, table 16 (Office of Plans and Policy, Federal Communications Commission, Sept. 2002). Given that purchases of stations produce a heavy debt expense that is paid in the form of interest, cash flow may be the more relevant criterion of profitability, and it is even higher, often adding 10 to 20 or more percentage points to the profitability

percentage. See id. at 33. The higher average profit margin for independent stations in 2000 seems to be a historical anomaly – between 1975 and 1995 it was significantly lower than for affiliates – but there has more recently been a substantial decline in the number of independents, many joining a new network, so it may have been only the most profitable that remained independent, explaining the results reported in the text. Id. at 29 and 34, Table 16.

66. Id.

67. Id. at 33, Table 14.

68. Id. Again the largest markets have the best numbers – cash flow equaling 55.6% of net revenue.

69. Id. at 34, Table 16.

70. Id. at 31, 33–34, Tables 14 and 15.

71. George Williams and Scott Roberts, "Radio Industry Review 2002," 13–16, 21 (Media Bureau Staff Research Paper, Federal Communications Commission, Sept. 2002).

72. Gilbert Cranberg, Randall Bezanson, and John Soloski, *Taking Stock: Journalism and the Publicly Traded Newspaper Company* (Ames: Iowa State U. Press, 2001), 34, 37.

73. Katharine Q. Seelye, "Newsday Employees Vote to Accept New Contract," *New York Times* (Jan. 9, 2006): B3 (Newspaper statements of this sort are always a little suspect. The meaning of what is called "profit margin" is not specified, and reporters are sometimes loose on the specifics – it might improperly refer, for example, to operating profits or to EBITDA, which would reflect a decline from Cranberg's report for 1998, although still a hefty margin.) I used the "U.S. Institutional Database," copyrighted in 2006 by Core Data, in the Lexis-Nexis Data Base, to examined twelve companies – the thirteen publicly traded examined by Cranberg for 1998 except for three – Gray Comm, Central Newspapers (since purchased by Gannett), and Tribune Corporation (since purchased by Media General) – to which I added McClatchy and Knight Ridder. The data base seemed to use two inconsistent measures of EBITDA, though I used what it described as "EBITBA margin." For the ten on which I and Cranberg overlapped, the EBITDA margin had gone up for only two – the Journal Register and the Washington Post. I found the overall average EBITDA for the twelve examined was 22.1, very high but down from the 27% that Cranberg reported. A report in 2005 said that newspapers made 23 cents for every dollar of revenue they took in the year before. Paul Farhi, "A Bright Future for Newspapers," *American Journalism Review* 54 (June/July 2005).

74. See, e.g., Ruy A. Teixeira, *Why Americans Don't Vote* (New York: Greenwood, 1987), 88. Although correlations hardly indicate the causal direction (it is likely to work both ways), in a self-report of frequent, infrequent, and nonreaders of newspapers, 75% of the frequent readers reported voting in the 1984 election, as compared with 55% of nonreaders, and the frequent readers were also more likely to discuss current events and to be involved in their communities. Leo Bogart, *Press and Pulic*, 2nd ed. (Hillsdale, N.J.: Lawrence Erlbaum Associates, 1989), 85. A careful study found newspaper readership very strongly related to community political involvement, while TV viewing had no statistical relationship, though in some contexts with a negative slant. Leo W. Jeffres, David Atkin, and Kimberly A. Neuendorf, "A Model Linking Community Activity and Communication with Political Attitudes and Involvement in Neighborhoods," *Political Communication* 19 (2002): 387. See also Patricia Moy, Marcos Torres, Keiko Tanaka, and Michael R. McCluskey, "Knowledge or

Trust: Investigating Linkages between Media Reliance and Participation," *Communication Research* 32 (2005): 59 (finding in study of media reliance and political participation relating to the Seattle WTO meeting, that "media reliance – particularly on newspapers – increases the likelihood of political participation" and that "only newspaper reliance showed a consistently positive relationship to either knowledge of and trust in the WTO," though the effect of these two later variables operated in opposite directions on participation).

75. William B. Blankenberg, "Newspaper Ownership and Control of Circulation," *Journalism Quarterly* 59 (1982): 390, 398.

76. *Miami Herald Publishing Co. v. Tornillo*, 418 U.S. 241, 256 (1974).

77. Cranberg et al., supra note 72.

78. Some empirical evidence finds that chain editors are more likely than nonchain editors to report that "profits" drive their organization. David Pearce Demers, "Corporate Structure and Emphasis on Profits and Product Quality at U.S. Daily Newspapers," *Journalism Quarterly* 68 (1991): 15, 23; David Pearce Demers and Daniel Wackman, "Effect of Chain Ownership on Newspaper Management Goals," *Newspaper Research Journal* 9 (1988): 59, 63–64.

79. John C. Busterna, "How Managerial Ownership Affects Profit Maximization in Newspaper Firms," *Journalism Quarterly* 66 (1989): 302, 305–6. The study involved 37 weeklies or small dailies, with the result supported $p < .01$.

80. Blankenberg found empirical evidence relating to profits that he interpreted to support this view. Blankenberg, supra note 75; William Blankenberg and Gary W. Ozanich, "The Effects of Public Ownership on the Financial Performance of Newspaper Corporations," *Journalism Quarterly* 70 (1993): 68. To the extent that, as compared with the editor, the publisher is more likely to focus on financial success and that the roles are more likely to be combined in the case of family or individual ownership, it may be that this latter category will experience pressure to identify with both financial success (though not necessarily maximization) and quality.

81. Doug Underwood, *When MBAs Rule the Newsroom* (New York: Columbia U. Press, 1993).

82. C. K McClatchy, "How Newspapers Are Owned – And Does It Matter?" *Press Enterprise Lecture Series* 23 (1988): 7–8.

83. Conversation with author, fall 1992, Cambridge, Mass. See also Bill Kovach, "Big Deals, with Journalism Thrown In," *New York Times* (Aug. 3, 1995): A25.

84. Katherine Q. Seelye, "Dow Jones Goes Out of Newsroom in Selecting Its Chief Executive," *New York Times* (Jan. 4, 2006): C1 (naming Richard Zannino and "bypassing" Karen Elliot House, the *Journal*'s current "high profile" publisher and a former Pulitzer Prize-winning journalist).

85. Project for Excellence in Journalism (PEJ), "Does Ownership Matter in Local Television News" (April 29, 2003), available at http://www.journalism.org/resources/research/reports/ownership/best.asp. In measuring quality, the PEJ study took the advice of 14 respected local TV news professionals, and isolated as basic factors (1) cover the whole community, (2) be significant and informative, (3) demonstrate enterprise and courage, (4) be fair, balanced, and accurate, (5) be authoritative, and (6) be highly local – and then used social science experts to convert these into measurable criteria. The methodology is summarized as appendix A of the study, available at http://www.journalism.org/resources/research/reports/ownership/quality.asp.

See also James T. Hamilton, *All the News That's Fit to Sell: How the Market Transforms Information into News* (Princeton: Princeton U. Press, 2004), 143 (finding that "stations owned by a company with more than one broadcast station are less likely to provide hard news").

86. For a collection of sources, see Stephen Lacy and Alan Blanchard, "The Impact of Public Ownership, Profits, and Competition on Number of Newsroom Employees and Starting Salaries in Mid-sized Daily Newspapers," *Journalism and Mass Communication Quarterly* 80 (2003): 949, 955, 967n44.

87. Id.

88. Peter DiCola, "Employment and Wage Effects of Radio Consolidation," in Philip Napoli, *Media Diversity and Localism: Meaning and Metrics* (Mahwah, N.J.: Lawrence Erlbaum, 2006). Interestingly, DiCola found consolidation also correlates with reduced wages of those employed, while the Lacy and Blanchard study found some increase in wages at the publicly owned papers.

89. The primary complaint of Cranberg et al. related to public ownership creating misguided structural pressures to maximize profits, although they also noted that large corporate ownership (even if not public) might generate many of the same problems. Cranberg et al., supra note 72, at 106. Their primary recommendations, however, seem to accept that public corporate ownership will continue to dominate. Thus, they suggest changes in compensation structure (i.e., editors' and executives' pay should be tied not to profits but to quality), different structures of board of directors, and related changes that could lead to less focus on short-term profitability and more on creating quality journalism. Id. at 142–46. Although all their proposals are structurally well-thought-out, the authors do not explain the motivation for a public company to adopt them voluntarily. On my reading, whether the authors would propose legally mandating the changes was left unclear.

90. Policy Statement on Comparative Broadcast Hearings, 1 F.C.C. 2d 393, 395 (1965).

91. Cranberg et al., supra note 72, at 96, 149–50. See also Carl Sessions Stepp, "Journalism without Profit Margins," *American Journalism Review* (Oct. 5, 2004); Christopher Jencks, "Should News Be Sold for Profit," in D. Lazere, ed., *American Media and Mass Culture: Left Perspectives* (Berkeley: University of California Press, 1987), 564–67.

92. Anthee Carassava, "Shipping Magnate Bids for Greek Media Group," *New York Times* (Jan. 18, 2005): C10. Greece passed in January 2005 a "media transparency law" that would have prevented 1% owners of media companies from participating in public sector contracts. In April 2005, the European Commission told Greece that the law violated EU law and threatened to freeze funds for Greek public works projects, leading eventually to Greece's withdrawal of the law. The complete story is told in Stylianos Papathanassopoulos, *Television in the 21st Century* (Athens: Kastaniotis Editions, 2005) (in Greek). The story dramatically illustrates sensible, democratically needed legal reforms aimed at both preventing corruption of government and preserving the integrity of the media being sacrificed to supposed free trade principles. Chapter 5 discusses the merits of more generally barring mergers of media and nonmedia companies.

93. Baker, supra note 37, ch. 2.

94. Hearings Pursuant to H. R. Res. 802, Before the House Committee on the Judiciary, 93rd Cong., 2d Sess., bk. VIII, 321–23 (1974).

95. "Pleasantville's Velvet Trap," *Publisher's Weekly* (June 17, 1968): 49, discussed in Ben H. Bagdikian, *The Media Monopoly*, 5th ed. (Boston: Beacon Press, 1997), 163.

96. Martin A. Lee and Norman Solomon, *Unreliable Sources: A Guide to Detecting Bias in News Media* (New York: Carrol Publishing Group, 1990), 75.

97. See Neil Weinstock Netanel, "Market Hierarchy and Copyright in Our System of Freedom of Expression," *Vanderbilt Law Review* 53 (2000): 1879, 1923–24.

98. Lawrence K. Grossman, "CBS, 60 Minutes and the Unseen Interview," *Columbia Journalism Review* 39 (Jan. 1996).

99. Id. Editorial, "Self-Censorship at CBS," *New York Times* (Nov. 12, 1995): Sec. 4, p. 14.

100. Edward Helmore, "Tobacco Can Be Harmful to Journalism's Health," *The Independent (London)* (Nov. 20, 1995): 16; Editorial, "Second Thoughts at '60 Minutes,'" *St. Louis Post-Dispatch* (Nov. 23, 1995): 18. See also Bill Carter, "'60 Minutes Ordered to Pull Interview in Tobacco Report," *New York Times* (Nov. 9, 1995): A1; Marvin Kitman, "The Marvin Kitman Show: A CBS Smoke Screen," *Newsday (New York)* (Nov. 19, 2005): 22; Walter Goodman, "Covering Tobacco: A Cautionary Tale," *New York Times* (April 2, 1996): C16.

101. Ben H. Bagdikian, "Newspaper Mergers," *Columbia Journalism Review* (March/April 1997): 19–20, discussed in Bagdikian, supra note 95, at 162–63.

102. Leo Bogart, *Commercial Culture* (New York: Oxford U. Press, 1995), 53–54 (citing Richard Clurman, *The End of Time: The Seduction and Conquest of a Media Empire* (New York: Simon and Schuster, 1992), 309).

103. Andre Schiffrin, *The Business of Books: How International Conglomerates Took Over Publishing and Changed the Way We Read* (New York: Verso, 2001), 132.

104. Id. For example, Schiffrin also referred to a decision not to publish a book by Chris Patten that was critical of China at a time when Murdoch's media enterprises were seeking entry into the China market. Id. at 133. See generally, Fallows, supra note 41.

105. See Baker, supra note 37.

106. Jeff Leeds, "Clear Channel to Spin Off Its Entertainment Division," *New York Times* (April 30, 2005): C2.

107. Hamilton, supra note 85, at 145. As I read him, Hamilton means by "news program" not a single episode but the program over time, e.g., a specific ABC affiliate's six o'clock news over the month is one program, while that affiliate's eleven o'clock news is another.

108. Id. at 148.

109. See Peter DiCola and Kristen Thomson, "Radio Deregulation: Has It Served Citizens and Musicians?" (Future of Music Coaltion, 2002), at http://www.futureofmusic. org/images/FMCradiostudy.pdf. But see Andrew Sweeting, "Music Variety, Station Listenership and Station Ownership in the Radio Industry" (working paper no. 49, Aug. 9, 2004), at http://www.csio.econ.northwestern.edu/papers/2004/csio-wp-0049.pdf.

110. Theodore L. Glasser, David S. Allen, and S. Elizabeth Banks, "The Influence of Chain Ownership on News Play," *Jounalism Quarterly* 66 (1989): 607. See also Roya Akhavan-Majib, Anita Rife, and Sheila Gopinath, "Chain Ownership and Editorial Independence," *Journalism Quarterly* 68 (1991) 59; Ronald G. Hicks and James

S. Featherston, "Duplication of Newspaper Content in Contrasting Ownership Situations," *Journalism Quarterly* 55 (1978): 549.

111. In the Matter of 2002 Biennial Regulatory Review, supra note 47.

112. Cf. Yoo, supra note 24.

113. Stephen Lacy, Mary Alice Shaver, and Charles St. Cyr, "The Effects of Public Ownership and Newspaper Competition on the Financial Performance of Newspaper Corporations: A Replication and Extension," *Journalism and Mass Communications Quarterly* 73 (1996): 332, 338–39; Lacy and Blanchard, supra note 86, at 959, 961.

114. Robert M. Entman and Steven S. Wildman, "Reconciling Economic and Non-Economic Perspectives on Media Policy: Transcending the 'Marketplace of Ideas,'" *Journal of Communications* 42 (Winter 1992): 5, 6, 14. Though it goes to the same end as proposed to Entman and Wildman, I have argued that any adequate economics *must*, to be true to its logic of evaluating economic performance's relation to value production, include these externalities and noncommodifiable values within its analysis. See Baker, supra note 3.

115. *Prometheus Radio Project v. FCC*, 373 F.3d 372 (3rd Cir. 2004).

116. See, e.g., 2002 Biennial Regulatory Review – Review of the Commission's Broadcast Ownership Rules and Other Rules Adopted Pursuant to Section 202 of the Telecommunications Act of 1996, Report and Order and Notice of Proposed Rulemaking, 18 F.C.C.R. 13620 (2003), paras. 343–45, 358, discussing Thomas C. Spavins, Loretta Denison, Jane Frenette, & Scott Roberts, "The Measurement of Local Television News and Public Affairs Programs" (Sept. 2002) (MOWG Study No. 7).

117. Spavins et al., supra note 116. Note that, my objection is not to the study, which I find technically flawless, but to its interpretation and use by the majority of the FCC as noted above.

118. Id.

119. See, e.g., Steven Kull, Clay Ramsey, and Evan Lewis, "Misperceptions, the Media, and the Iraq War," *Political Science Quarterly* 118 (2003): 569. The classic study showing people actually getting information about the world much more from newspapers than from television, discrediting the notion of television being the public's main source of news, is John P. Robinson and Mark R. Levy, *The Main Source: Learning from Television News* (Beverly Hills: Sage, 1986). See also Bogart, supra note 74, at 242–48.

120. See, e.g., Jeffres et al., supra note 74; Moy et al., supra note 74.

121. See, e.g., Eric Klinenberg, "Convergence: News Production in a Digital Age," *Annals of the American Academy of Political & Social Sciences* 597 (2005): 48.

122. Baker, supra note 3, at 44–71.

123. Formally, if the merged company produces a profitable new synergistic Product A that generates an increased surplus a (producer surplus plus consumer surplus) over the surplus of the company's products that it replaces, but puts out of business Products B, C, and D, which formally produced surpluses of b, c, and d, the social welfare question is whether $a > b + c + d$. Neither Producer A's market success nor abstract theory gives reason to predict that it would. The text above describes situations where this is unlikely.

124. See C. Edwin Baker, "The Ideology of the Economic Analysis of Law," *Philosophy & Public Affairs* 5 (1975): 3.

125. Snider, supra note 3; J. H. Snider and Benjamin I. Page, "Covert Bias," *Does Media Ownership Affect Media Stands? The Case of the Telecommunications Act of 1996*, at http://newamerica.net/Download_Docs/pdfs/Pub_File_1237_1.pdf.

126. For example, several executives of small or family-owned media companies have been among the leaders of those opposing media concentration. See, e.g., Jim Goodmon, Testimony before U.S. Senate on Commerce, Science & Transportation, at http://commerce.senate.gov/hearings/testimony.cfm?id=758& wit_id=2050 (Goodmon is president and CEO, Capital Broadcasting Co.); "Editorial: Maintain Current FCC Media Policy," *The Herald-Sun (Durham, N.C.)* (May 29, 2003): A8; Frank Blethan, "The Case for Independent and Family Ownership of Newspapers and Other News and Journalistic Enterprises," *News in the Public Interest: A Free and Subsidized Press – The Breaux Symposium 2004* 106,110 (Baton Rouge: Louisiana State University, n.d.) (Blethan is publisher of the *Seattle Times*).

127. See supra, page 35.

128. Amy Harmon, "Shake-up at AOL: The Former Executive," *New York Times* (July 19, 2002): C1; David D. Kirkpatrick, "Man in Middle of AOL Deal Is Now in Center of a Storm," *New York Times* (July 27, 2002): A1. Of course, another possibility is that mergers made long-term sense but investors and corporate directors have simply been unwilling to await that result.

129. See Richard M. Clurman, *To the End of Time* (New York: Touchstone, 1993), 348–56.

130. Pat Gish and Tom Gish, "We Still Scream: The Perils and Pleasures of Running a Small-Town Newspaper," in William Serrin, ed., *The Business of Journalism* (New York: New Press, 2000), 3–25.

131. Donald McDonald, "The Media's Conflict of Interests," *Center Magazine* (1976): 15, 24.

132. Robert C. Cottrell, *Izzy: A Biography of I. F. Stone* (New Brunswick, N.J.: Rutgers U. Press, 1992).

133. The claim is that if percentages are the same, a higher number of owners deciding in favor of exposés will increase the number of meaningful exposés. This would not follow if the smaller number of committed, courageous leaders within the concentrated context could assure that each of their subunits chooses a strong investigative stance. Thus, my claim implicitly assumes that cautious conglomerate heads will be more effective at inducing avoidance among subordinates (e.g., editors of entities owned by the conglomerate) than their courageous counterparts will be at the opposite. In other words, I suspect that the "safer" response will be more likely in multilevel organizations given that, due to increasing the potential decision makers that must sign off on "risky" decisions, caution is the more likely default rule.

134. Cranberg et al., supra note 72, at 104 (public ownership of papers encouraged more risk aversion as well as more overwhelming focus on financial performance).

Chapter 2. Not a Real Problem:
Many Owners, Many Sources

1. Ben H. Bagdikian, *The Media Monopoly* (Boston: Beacon Press, 1983), xvi, see also 4–28.

2. Id. at xvi, xix, 20.

3. Ben H. Bagdikian, *The New Media Monopoly* (Boston: Beacon Press, 2004), 3 (emphasis added). Though he is not entirely clear, "most" appears here (and in the earlier book) to mean more than 50% of the business – i.e., revenue – in each of these industries.

4. Benjamin M. Compaine and Douglas Gomery, *Who Owns the Media?: Competition and Concentration in the Mass Media Industry*, 3rd ed. (Mahwah, N.J.: Lawrence Erlbaum Associates, 2000). Compaine has been an author since the first edition. Gomery, representing a view explicitly in opposition to Compaine's, first participated in the third edition and is the primary author of about half the chapters. Except where noted, my references will be to chapters for which Compaine was responsible.

5. For a summary of Compaine's published work in this area, see his home Web page, http://www1.primushost.com/~bcompain. I testified opposite Compaine before the U.S. Senate Commerce Committee, Sept. 28, 2004, and debated him on Chicago Public Radio's *Odyssey*, June 18, 2003.

6. Compaine, supra note 4, at 560.

7. Id. at 560 (my calculation from Compaine's table).

8. Id. at 481.

9. Id. at 558. This was based on data showing the fourteen largest of the country's 2,500 book publishers accounting for 75% to 80% of the book publishing revenue. In contrast, his co-author, Douglas Gomery, though agreeing that book publishing "is not as concentrated as other mass media industries," id. at 80, described it as a "loose and open oligopoly," id. at 136, dominated by "10 oligopolists," with two, Bertelsmann AG and Peason PLC, standing out as the giants. Id. at 84. At the time Bertelsmann bought Random House, Mark Crispen Miller complained that United States book publishing was dominated by "seven corporations, most of them foreign." Mark Crispen Miller, "And Then There Were Seven," *New York Times* (March 26, 1998): A27. While disagreeing on the implications and with the views of "Miller and his ilk" and painting a quite rosy view, Pia Nordlinger reported that the big seven owned by "major media conglomerates" "account for 87 percent of trade books sold – about 22 percent of total U.S. book sales." Pia Nordlinger, "Keeping the Books," *The Weekly Standard* (May 4, 1998): Books & Arts sec., 37, which immediately raises the question of whether, in speaking of dominance, the focus should be within categories, e.g., trade books, children's books, or textbooks, or all together.

10. Id. at 574.

11. Benjamin M. Compaine, "The Myths of Encroaching Global Media Ownership," *Open Democracy*," Nov. 6, 2001, at http://www.opendemocracy.net/document store/Doc807–5.pdf.

12. Compaine, supra note 4, at 560–61.

13. Id. at 560, 562. Even if one goes beyond the largest firms, according to Compaine, the largest 50 received 81.8% of the revenue in 1997 and 78.7% in 1986.

14. I have not compiled the industry data, so my subjective impression may be wrong. In a new study, Compaine asserts that concentration has continued to decline since 2000, though as for national industry-wide concentration, he provides neither data nor cites to any study for the claim. This is regrettable because he does, in my view, correct some errors in the book discussed here and – also in my view – introduce new ones. Benjamin M. Compaine, *The Media Monopoly Myth: How New Competition Is*

Expanding Our Sources of Information and Entertainment (2005). I have decided not to try to review his newest arguments here.

15. Compaine, supra note 4, at 578. Other leading observers are equally skeptical about claims of concentration. See, e.g., Eli M. Noam, "Media Concentration in the United States: Industry Trends and Regulatory Responses," at http://www.vii.org/papers/medconc.htm.

16. Compaine, supra note 4, at 579 (quoting Philip Meyer, "Clinton-Crazy? No, Net Floods Us with News," *USA Today*, Oct. 4, 1998, News Section, Opinion Column).

17. 2002 Biennial Regulatory Review – Review of the Commission's Broadcast Ownership Rules and Other Rules Adopted Pursuant to Section 202 of the Telecommunications Act of 1996, Report and Order and Notice of Proposed Rulemaking, 18 F.C.C.R. 13620 (2003).

18. *Prometheus Radio Project v. FCC,* 373 F.3d 372 (3rd Cir. 2004).

19. See Compaine, supra note 4, at 547.

20. Id.

21. See Maurice E. Stucke and Allen P. Grunes, "Antitrust and the Marketplace of Ideas," *Antitrust Law Journal* 69 (2001): 249.

22. Compaine and Gomery, supra note 4, at 555 (emphasis added).

23. To the extent the economist emphasizes that price discrimination cures the inefficiency, she indicates lack of concern with the wealth transfer point.

24. U.S. Dept. of Justice & the Federal Trade Comm'n, "Horizontal Merger Guidelines 0.1" (1992, rev. 1997). http://www.usdoj.gov/atr/public/guidelines/horiz_book/hmg1.html.

25. See Compaine, supra note 4, at 573. See also his remarks quoted in this and the next paragraph of the text.

26. See id. at 559–61.

27. Id. at 577.

28. Id. at 574.

29. See text accompanying notes 12 and 13.

30. Compaine, supra note 4, at 561, 562.

31. See, e.g., id. at 560–61.

32. Id. at 542.

33. Bruce Owen, *Economics and Freedom of Expression: Media Structure and the First Amendment* (1975). See also Damian Tambini, "Through with Ownership Rules? Media Pluralism in the Transition to Digital," in Damian Tambini, with Liz Forgan, Clare Hall, and Stefan Verhulst, *Communication Revolution and Reform* (London: IPPR, 2001), 22 ("Where a company controls both networks and content there is a threat not only to competition but to plurality if that company seeks to deny competitors' content access to its networks").

34. 47 U.S.C. §533(b) (1984).

35. This view did not fare well in the courts, which apparently could not understand this logic to be rational and subjected these restrictions to First Amendment attack. *Chesapeake & Potomac Telephone Co. v. United States,* 42 F.3d 181 (4th Cir. 1994), vacated, 516 U.S. 415 (1996); *U.S. West, Inc. v. United States,* 48 F.3d 1092 (9th Cir. 1994), vacated, 516 U.S. 1155 (1996). Nor did it prevail in a deregulatory Congress under the 1996 Telecommunications Act. See generally C. Edwin Baker,

"Merging Phone and Cable," *Hastings Communications & Entertainment Law Journal* 17 (1994): 97.

36. *Turner Broadcasting System v. FCC*, 520 U.S. 189 (1997). Although the Court reports no disagreement on the "initial premise [that] . . . cable operators . . . are entitled to the protection of the . . . First Amendment," *Turner I*, 512 U.S. 622, 636, rate regulation also seems to pose no serious constitutional problems (see *Time Warner Entertainment Co. v. FCC*, 56 F.3d 151, 186 n.13 (D.C. Cir. 1995)), although rate regulation would be quite questionable as applied to newspapers.

37. 47 U.S.C. §312(a)(7) & §315(a) & (b) (2000); *CBS v. FCC*, 453 U.S. 367 (1981).

38. *CBS v. Democratic National Committee*, 412 U.S. 94, 131, 170–204 (1973).

39. *Denver Area Education Telecommunications Consortium v. FCC*, 518 U.S. 727 (1996).

40. Review of Prime Time Access Rule, Section 73.658(k) of the Commission's Rules, 11 F.C.C.R. 546, at 1–4 (1995) (repealing prime time access rule); Evaluation of the Syndication and Financial Interest Rules, 8 F.C.C.R. 3282, at 1 (1983) (repealing fin/syn rules); see also *Schurz Communications v. FCC*, 982 F.2d 1043 (7th Cir. 1992) (rejecting the logic of fin/syn rules).

41. Most antitrust actions against, and most government refusals to approve, media mergers relate to preventing undue power in the advertising market.

42. See H. Peter Nesvold, "Note, Communication Breakdown: Developing an Antitrust Model for Multimedia Mergers and Acquisitions," *Fordham Intellectual Property, Media & Entertainment Law Journal* 6 (1996): 781, 823 n. 262, 856 n. 452.

43. *Id.* at 823–29. See also *United States v. Times Mirror Co.*, 274 F. Supp. 606, 617 (C.D. Cal. 1967).

44. See, e.g., *United States v. CBS*, 63 Fed. Reg. 18,036 (Department of Justice April 13, 1998); Sarah Elizabeth Leeper, "The Game of Radiopoly: An Antitrust Perspective of Consolidation in the Radio Industry," *Federal Communication Law Journal* 52 (2000): 473, 482–83.

45. Cf. Mark W. Stuhlfaut, "Economic Concentration in Agricultural Magazine Publishing: 1993–2002," *Journal of Media Economics* 18(1) (2005): 21–33. On difficulties of identifying product markets in the media context, see Howard A. Shelanski, "Antitrust Laws as Mass Media Regulation: Can Merger Standards Protect the Public Interest?" *California Law Review* 94 (2006): 371.

46. See, e.g., Rudolph J. R. Peritz, *Competition Policy in America: History, Rhetoric, Law* (2000); see also Eleanor M. Fox and Andrew A. Sullivan, "Antitrust – Retrospective and Prospective: Where Are We Coming From? Where Are We Going?" *New York University Law Review* 68 (1987): 936; Eleanor M. Fox, "The Battle for the Soul of Antitrust," *California Law Review* 75 (1987): 917, 1214; Louis B. Schwartz, "'Justice' and Other Non-economic Goals of Antitrust," *University of Pennsylvania Law Review* 127 (1979): 1076; Louis B. Schwartz, "Institutional Size and Individual Liberty: Authoritarian Aspects of Bigness," *Northwestern University Law Review* 55 (1960): 4, 19–14, 22–24 (objecting to ill effects of size with special concern for concentration of media power); Andrew A. Sullivan, "Economics and the More Humanistic Disciplines: What Are the Sources of Wisdom of Antitrust?" *University of Pennsylvania Law Review* 125 (1979): 1214.

47. *Standard Oil Co. v. United States*, 221 U.S. 1, 83 (1911) (Harlan, concurring in part and dissenting in part).

48. *United States v. Aluminum Co. of America*, 148 F.2d 416, 428 (2d Cir. 1945).
49. Robert Pitofsky, "The Political Content of Antitrust," *University of Pennsylvania Law Review* 127 (1979): 1051, 1051.
50. *Associated Press v. United States*, 326 U.S. 1, 27–28 (1945) (Frankfurter, concurring). See generally Stucke and Grunes, supra note 21.
51. Neil W. Averitt and Robert H. Lande, "Consumer Sovereignty: A Unified Theory of Antitrust and Consumer Protection Law," *Antitrust Law Journal* 65 (1997): 713, 752.
52. Id. at 752.
53. Id. at 715, 752–53.
54. 326 U.S. 1, 20 (1945).
55. Stucke and Grunes, supra note 21.
56. C. Edwin Baker, "Media Structure, Ownership Policy, and the First Amendment," *Southern California Law Review* 78 (2005): 733, 748–49.
57. James T. Hamilton, *All the News That's Fit to Sell: How the Market Transforms Information into News* (Princeton: Princeton U. Press, 2004).
58. See C. Edwin Baker, *Advertising and a Democratic Press* (Princeton: Princeton U. Press, 1994) (describing and observing how advertising intensifies the trend toward one-newspaper towns in the United States).
59. The classic cite for this point is Peter O. Steiner, "Program Patterns and Preferences, and Workability of Competition in Radio Broadcasting," *Quarterly Journal of Economics* 66 (1952): 194. Steiner's point has been elaborated in slightly different forms by other scholars, many of whom are summarized in Bruce M. Owen and Steven S. Wildman, *Video Economics* (Cambridge: Harvard U. Press, 1992).
60. Amendment of Rules Relating to Multiple Ownership of Standard, FM, and Television Stations, Second Report and Order, 59 F.C.C. 2d 1046, 1079–80 (1975) (emphasis added) (also quoted in chapter 1).
61. This merely recasts in a different light the Steiner effect mentioned in the previous note.
62. Statistical studies provide evidence that newspaper competition increases the number of journalists employed by an individual paper. Stephen Lacy and Alan Blanchard, "The Impact of Public Ownership, Profits, and Competition on Number of Newsroom Employees and Starting Salaries in Mid-sized Daily Newspapers," *Journalism and Mass Communication Quarterly* 80 (2003): 949, 959.
63. Averitt and Lande, supra note 51, at 753 n. 154; Stucke and Grunes, supra note 21, at 297, 302.
64. In Rawlsian terms, this represents a pure process approach, while many of the social scientist investigations of ownership's effect on diversity adopt a perfect or imperfect process approach. John Rawls, *A Theory of Justice* (Cambridge, Mass.: Harvard U. Press, 1971), 85.
65. Federal Communications Commission, Policy Statement on Comparative Broadcast Hearings, 1 F.C.C.2d. 393, 394 (1965).
66. Id.
67. 326 U.S. 1 (1945).
68. Id. at 20 (emphasis added).
69. Based on my Lexis search.

70. Patricia Aufderheide, *Communication Policy and the Public Interest: The Telecommunications Act of 1996* (New York: Guilford Press, 1999); J. H. Snider, *Speak Softly and Carry a Big Stick: How Local TV Broadcasters Exert Political Power* (New York: iUniverse, 2005).

71. C. Edwin Baker, *Media, Markets, and Democracy* (New York: Cambridge U. Press, 2002), pt. I.

72. In the Matter of 2002 Biennial Regulatory Review – Review of the Commission's Broadcast Ownership Rules, Report and Order and Notice of Proposed Rulemaking (adopted June 2, 2003, released July 2, 2003), FCC 03–127 (hereinafter 2003 Order). See also Action: Final Rule, 47 C.F.R. pt. 73, Broadcast Ownership Rules, Cross-Ownership of Broadcast Stations and Newspapers, Multiple Ownership of Radio Broadcast Stations in Local Markets, and Definition of Radio Markets, Part II, 68 Fed. Reg. 46,286 (August 5, 2003). The text of the new rules can be found in 2003 Order, supra, Appendix H.

73. 373 F.3d 372 (3d Cir. 2004).

74. Id. at 402–12.

75. See, e.g., Philip M. Napoli and Nancy Gillis, "Reassessing Communications Research's Potential Contribution to Communications Policy: The Case of Media Ownership and the Diversity Index" (n.d.); Mark Cooper, "When Law and Social Science Go Hand in Glove" (2004) (presented at Telecommunications Policy Research Conference, Oct. 3, 2004), 21.

76. 2003 Order, supra note 72, para. 391.

77. §202(c)(2), 47 U.S.C. §303 (2004).

78. 2003 Order, supra note 72, para. 391.

79. See *Prometheus Radio Project v. FCC*, 373 F.3d at 412 (finding that the lack of public notice of the FCC's consideration of the DI was "not without prejudice" and that, on remand, the FCC should give public notice of any new attempt to devise such a metric).

80. This empirical focus may be an unfortunate aspect of *Turner Broadcasting System v. FCC*, 512 U.S. 622, 684 (1994). Until then, the Court expected only a reasonable explanation for a structural regulation of the media.

81. The HHI was explained supra, text between notes 24 and 25.

82. See, e.g., Robert W. McChesney, *The Problem of the Media: U.S. Communication Politics in the Twenty-first Century* (New York: Monthly Review Press, 2004); Edward S. Herman and Robert W. McChesney, *The Global Media* (London: Cassell, 1997).

83. Using a generally more realistic assessment of survey respondent reports on how they use the media to learn about local matters, Mark Cooper of the Consumer Unions calculated their proportionate importance for local news of various media types. (He also criticized the FCC's decision to include these different media in the same analysis given differences in the ways the different media are used by members of the public.) Cooper's results – with the comparable FCC's calculations presented in parentheses – were television broadcasters 35% (33.8%), daily papers 45% (20.2%), weekly papers 12% (8.6%), radio 6% (24.9%), and Internet 3% (12.5%). Cooper found that the FCC grossly overstated the importance for local news of radio- and Internet-originated content (neither he nor the FCC credited the Internet for access to news provided by the local paper). Cooper, supra note 75, at 21. (I do not completely

follow Cooper's methodology, and he seems to get different percentages in different presentations within the paper, but his data appeared better than the FCC's.)

84. The report used Kansas City as one of its key illustrations. See 2003 Order, supra note 72, para. 473, 475–76. Interestingly, at another point in the report, Kansas City is listed as having only one daily newspaper. See id., para. 98.

85. SRDS *Circulation 2005*, at 408, 543 (Standard Rate and Data Service).

86. See 2003 Order, supra note 72, Appendix C.

87. Thomas C. Spavins, Loretta Denison, Jane Frenette, and Scott Roberts, "The Measurement of Local Television News and Public Affairs Programs" (Sept. 2002) (MOWG Study No. 7).

88. Loy A. Singleton and Steven C. Rockwell, "Silent Voices: Analyzing the FCC's Media Voices Criteria Limiting Local Radio-Television Cross-Ownership," *Communications Law & Policy* 8 (2003): 385, 398.

89. *Prometheus Radio Project v. FCC*, 373 F.3d at 406–8.

90. Id.

91. 2003 Order, supra note 72, Appendix C; *Prometheus Radio Project v. FCC*, 373 F.3d at 408.

92. Technically, this is not quite the case because of the way the DI attributes different significance to different media categories. In practice, however, I doubt that there would ever be a DI higher than the HHI calculated over the same entities. Of course, the fact that the HHI evaluation would normally not include all the different media means that its scores will be even more systematically higher than any DI score.

93. Bruce M. Owen, "Confusing Success with Access: 'Correctly' Measuring Media and Online Concentration" (Discussion Draft for "Media Concentration and the Internet," Columbia Institute for Tele-Information (CITI), April 15, 2004), at http://ssrn.com/abstract=545302. Various versions are available online, and a slightly revised version, published by the Progress and Freedom Foundation (release 12.11, July 2005), is at http://www.pff.org/issues-pubs/pops/pop12.11owen.pdf.

94. Id. at 9 (citing John Milton, *Areogpagitica* (1644), John W. Hales, ed. (New York: Oxford U. Press, 1961)).

95. Id. at 10, 18.

96. Id. at 18.

97. Id. at 20, 21. In fact, though sharing much of the view embodied in the DI, one of Owen's criticisms is that when the same owner controlled two outlets, the DI counted that owner as having more power, creating a slightly higher DI. Id. at 23. Owen's claim is that if the *New York Times* also owned the New York City affiliate of ABC, it would merely be "one" voice, in principle no different from the Dutchess County Community College television station or, I assume, anyone's unread blog.

98. Compaine, supra note 4, at 576 (emphasis added).

99. Id. at 577.

100. See, e.g., C. Edwin Baker, *Freedom of Speech and Human Liberty* (New York: Oxford U. Press, 1989), chaps. 1–3; Stanley Ingber, "The Marketplace of Ideas: A Legitimatizing Myth," *Duke Law Journal* 1984 (1984): 1.

101. Steven H. Shiffrin, *Dissent, Injustice, and the Meaning of America* (Princeton: Princeton U. Press, 1999).

102. Owen, supra note 93, at 12 (emphasis added), quoting John Dimmick, "Diversity and Diversification," *Journal of Media Economics* 17 (2004): 2.
103. Baker, supra note 71, pt. 1.

Chapter 3. Not a Real Problem: The Market or the Internet Will Provide

1. For a superb critique, see Herbert Gintis, "Consumer Behavior and the Concept of Sovereignty: Explanations of Social Decay," *American Economic Review; Papers, Proceedings and Supplement* 62 (1972): 267.
2. These market failures were discussed briefly in chapter 1 and more fully in C. Edwin Baker, *Media, Markets, and Democracy* (New York: Cambridge U. Press, 2002), pt. I.
3. The two often diverge. Profit maximization is served, for example, by externalizing costs of pollution or undermining labor's capacity to demand higher wages. Normally, neither practice increases "efficiency." Rather, they may decrease welfare while increasing profits and affecting wealth distributions, usually in an inegalitarian direction.
4. See Max Weber, *Economy and Society*, Guenther Roth and Claus Wittich, eds. (Berkeley: U. of California Press, 1978).
5. See, e.g., two Jurgen Habermas, *The Theory of Communicative Action: Lifeworld and System: A Critique of Functionalist Reason*, vol. 2, Thomas McCarthy, trans. (Boston: Beacon Press, 1987).
6. This market determination thesis was one of several, alternative reasons for not identifying commercial speech – that is, speech of profit-oriented entities – with individual freedom and hence for arguing that commercial speech should be subject to governmental regulation. See C. Edwin Baker, *Human Liberty and Freedom of Speech* (New York: Oxford U. Press, 1989), chap. 9, 194–224; C. Edwin Baker, "Paternalism, Politics, and Citizen Freedom: The Commercial Speech Quandary in *Nike*," *Case Western Law Review* 54 (2004): 1161; C. Edwin Baker, "Commercial Speech: A Problem in the Theory of Freedom," *Iowa Law Review* 62 (1976): 1. Cf. *First National Bank of Boston v. Bellotti*, 435 U.S. 765, 804–5 (1978) (White, dissenting) ("corporate expression . . . is not fungible with communications emanating from individuals. . . . [W]hat some have considered to be the principal function of the First Amendment, the use of communication as a means of self-expression, self-realization, and self-fulfillment, is not at all furthered by corporate speech"). White's views subsequently were adopted by a majority of the Court in *Austin v. Michigan Chamber of Commerce*, 494 U.S. 652 (1990).
7. The classic text is Edward H. Chamberlin, *The Theory of Monopolistic Competition: A Re-orientation of the Theory of Value*, 8th ed. (Cambridge, Mass.: Harvard U. Press, 1962). See the discussion in chapter 1 of this book.
8. There is continual bemoaning of the loss of newspaper readership, which is a continuing and recently increasing trend. This worry should be tempered by two considerations. First, some or all of the loss is not real as to readership; rather, the readers are merely shifting to online versions. When online readership is taken into account, it is not clear that there has been any loss of readership in recent years. The Newspaper Association of America reports that 77% of those over 18 in the

top 50 markets read a newspaper at least once a week, totaling over 115 million readers (readership is different from circulation both because of multiple readers of the same paper and online readership). Circulation has gone down from 62.3 million in 1990, which was close to its high and several million higher than in the 1960s, to 54.6 million in 2004 (Newspaper Audience Database (fall 2005 release), at www.naa.org/nadbase). Online readership, however, had risen from zero to 47 million unique visitors during September 2005, who visited on average over seven times per person (http://www.naa.org/utilartpage.cfm?TID=NR&AID=7284). More to the point here, newspapers know roughly how to keep print circulation as well as readers: they gain readers when they devote more resources to quality content, keep copy prices low, and maintain marketing budgets. The problem is that the money they raise or save by raising prices and cutting expenditures is more than the money they lose by losing customers. Moreover, because the cost of paper, ink, and delivery for most newspapers is less than the paper receives directly from the purchaser, who is made valuable only due to being able to sell readers to advertisers, some papers intentionally cut circulation to people not valued by their advertisers – cutting, for instance, circulation outside their own metropolitan area or in poor, minority areas. This process increases as papers become increasingly bottom line–oriented, often due to chain or conglomerate ownership. That is, loss of circulation is largely a result of conscious choices by papers to lose them. Blankenburg calls this process "censorship" because of how it disfavors civic knowledge and the consequent civic participation by the people to whom the paper chooses not to supply the news. William B. Blankenburg, "Newspaper Ownership and Control of Circulation to Increase Profits," *Journalism Quarterly* 59 (1982): 390.

9. André Schiffrin, *The Business of Books: How International Conglomerates Took Over Publishing and Changed the Way We Read* (New York: Verso, 2001), 91, 95, 108.

10. Id. at 91.

11. Douglas Gomery concludes, "In terms of the exploitation of concentrated ownership, book publishing and sales have generated less problems than other mass media," and in his terms, "book publishing must be judged as a loose and open oligopoly." Benjamin M. Compaine and Douglas Gomery, *Who Owns the Media?: Competition and Concentration in the Mass Media Industry* (Mahwah, N.J.: Lawrence Erlbaum Associates, 2000), 135, 136. He reports U.S. government data as listing 2,503 book publishing companies in the United States in 1992 – although most were exceedingly small – and suggests that even this number is low because of the government's restrictive definition of publisher. Id. at 63–64.

12. Schiffrin, supra note 9, at 91, 95, 108.

13. Id. at 108.

14. Data and reports here vary. Mark Crispin Miller asserts that seven companies dominated book publishing as of 1998, while Gomery concludes that a dozen companies publish about half the books sold in the country. Compaine and Gomery, supra note 11, at 62, 135. Concentration is also apparently greater within particular book categories.

15. Schiffrin, supra note 9, at 91.

16. Id. at 118–19.

17. Id. at 130–33, 136.

18. See C. Edwin Baker, *Advertising and a Democratic Press* (Princeton: Princeton U. Press, 1994), 7–44. Profitable competitive local daily papers are much more likely if there is greater, audience-valued product differentiation. That condition is more likely if: (1) there is partisan sponsorship of papers, (2) the public is very politically engaged and, consequently, more strongly desires a more partisan paper, (3) other factors make the market much more fundamentally divided (such as into different language groups), or, the point emphasized in the text, (4) advertising plays a less significant role in the newspaper's financial success.

19. Average operating margins in daily newspapers in 1997 were 19.5%, an extraordinarily high rate that should encourage new competitors except under conditions supporting "natural" monopolies or when particular "legal monopolies," such as patents in the drug industry, protect such profits. Gilbert Cranberg, Randall Bezanson, and John Soloski, *Taking Stock: Journalism and the Publicly Traded Newspaper Company* (Ames: Iowa State U. Press, 2001), 18. See also Ben H. Bagdikian, *The Media Monopoly*, 5th ed. (Boston: Beacon Press, 1997), 13; Comments of Consumers Union et al., App. A (statement of Ben Bagdikian), In the Matter of Cross-Ownership of Broadcast Stations and Newspapers: Newspaper/Radio Cross-Ownership Waiver Policy, MM Docket Nos. 01–235, 96–197 (filed Dec. 3, 2001).

20. Blankenberg, supra note 8.

21. Historically, operating margins in the daily newspaper industry have been a relatively high 10% to 15%, but more recently papers owned by the publicly traded companies range from 20% to 30% or higher. Cranberg et al., supra note 19, at 10; see also id. at 111 (describing rates moving from historic norms of 8% to 10% to increasingly higher rates, now 30% or higher, and attributing the change to replacement of owners with pride and involvement in the community to stock owners interested only in profits). Stephen Lacy and Alan Blanchard, "The Impact of Public Ownership, Profits, and Competition on Number of Newsroom Employees and Starting Salaries in Mid-sized Daily Newspapers," *Journalism and Mass Communication Quarterly* 80 (2003): 949.

22. Of course, profit maximization might be required after the potential income stream was capitalized in the winning bid to purchase an existing monopoly paper. Cf. Todd Bonder, "A 'Better' Marketplace Approach to Broadcast Regulation," *Federal Communications Law Journal* 36 (1984): 27, 29, 68 (noting and approving the possibility of this effect in an ideally structured broadcast arena).

23. Compaine and Gomery, supra note 11, at 574. See also Eugene Volokh, "Cheap Speech and What It Will Do," *Yale Law Journal* 104 (1995): 1805, critiqued in C. Edwin Baker, "New Media Technologies, the First Amendment, and Public Policies," *Communications Review* 1 (1996): 315.

24. Compaine and Gomery, supra note 11, at 579 (quoting Philip Meyer, "Clinton-Crazy? No, Net Floods Us with News," *USA Today* (Oct. 4, 1998), at Opinion Column, News Section).

25. Id. at 541, 575.

26. Bruce Owen, "Confusing Success with Access: 'Correctly' Measuring Concentration of Ownership and Control in Mass Media and Online Services," Working Paper 283 (Stanford: Stanford Institute for Economic Policy Research, May 2004), at 21. See also a slightly revised version of this paper published by the Progress and Freedom Foundation (release 12.11, July 2005), at http://www.pff.org/issues-pubs/pops/pop12.11owen.pdf.

27. Id. at 23–24.
28. Eli Noam, "Media Concentration in the United States: Industry Trends and Regulatory Responses," at http://www.vii.org/papers/medconc.htm. On the same day (Aug. 24, 2001) that I first read Noam's paper, I also read an online column by Norman Solomon, "Denial and the Ravaging of Cyberspace," where Solomon asserted, "Websites operated by just four corporations account for 50.4 percent of the time that U.S. users of the Web are now spending online" (Norman Solomon, "Denial and the Ravaging of Cyberspace", Media Beat, Aug. 23, 2001, at http://www.fair.org/mediabeat/010823.html).
29. The Internet apparently played a role in the demonstrations that recently brought down the old regime in the Ukraine. See Timothy Garton and Timothy Synder, "The Orange Revolution," New York Review of Books (April 28, 2005): 28, 29. Possibly one of the most hopeful signs on the world political stage is the role played by popularly supported, nonviolent street demonstrations in bringing down authoritarian, corrupt, or simply out of touch administrations in Eastern Europe, Latin America, Turkey, and the Philippines as well as the unwillingness or inability of the old regime to use (sufficient) violence to suppress these demonstrations. See, e.g., C. J. Chivers, "How Spies in Ukraine Changed the Nation's Path," New York Times (Jan. 17, 2005): A1. Interestingly, despite the First Amendment, these demonstrations, many of them "peaceable assemblies," would be illegal under current American law. For a contrary interpretation of the First Amendment that would mostly recognize the legality of these demonstrations, see C. Edwin Baker, Human Liberty and Freedom of Speech (New York: Oxford U. Press, 1989), 125–93.
30. Seth Schiesel, "The President under Fire: The Internet," New York Times (Jan. 26, 1998): A14; Frank Rich, "The Strange Legacy of Matt Drudge," New York Times (Dec. 4, 1999): A17.
31. The strangest aspect of this event is that issues surrounding some documents used in the 60 Minutes program eclipsed discussion about whether the program's claims about Bush were true. Much of the condemnation of the program was itself very questionable. Corey Pein, "Blog-gate," at http://www.alternet.org/mediaculture/20923.
32. Compaine and Gomery, supra note 11, at 575.
33. Carol Sanger, "Girls and the Getaway: Cars, Culture, and the Predicament of Gendered Space," University of Pennsylvania Law Review 144 (1995): 705, 729.
34. Yochai Benkler, The Wealth of Networks: How Social Production Transforms Markets and Freedom (New Haven: Yale U. Press, 2006); Yochai Benkler, "Coase's Penguin, or Linux and the Nature of the Firm," Yale Law Journal 112 (2002): 369.
35. In one model, a maverick South Korean journalist, Oh Yeon Ho, edits about 200 news items a day from "tens of thousands" of volunteer reporters who make up to $30 for a story, items subsequently rated by readers. This online journalism has created a paper that has been a major success, and reportedly helped elect reformer Roh Moo-hyun as president. Arthur Johnson, "You Be the Reporter: Tired of Media Concentration? Take a Lesson from South Korea," This Magazine 38 (Nov. 2004): 310.
36. Benkler discusses some of these issues, especially of credentialization, in "Coase's Penguin." Wikipedia, after a scandal involving a false story about a former journalist, John Seigenthaler, tightened up its structure by prohibiting anonymous contributions or edits. Wikipedia received recognition from a Nature report that found it almost as accurate in its science reporting as the Encyclopedia

Britannica – although both have a significant number of errors per article. Dan Mitchell, "Insider Editing at Wikipedia," *New York Times* (Dec. 24, 2004): C5; George Johnson, "The Nitpicking of the Masses vs. the Authority of Experts," *New York Times* (Jan. 3, 2006): F2.

37. I have argued, however, that product differentiation historically muted this spiral effect but that increased advertising intensified the incentive to reach a larger audience, reducing the value of differentiation, thereby changing the equilibrium point for daily newspapers from multiple differentiated papers to local monopoly papers. Baker, supra note 18.

38. Lincoln Dahlberg, "The Corporate Colonization of Online Attention and the Marginalization of Critical Communication?" *Journal of Communication Inquiry* 29 (April 2005): 160, 163, 168.

39. James T. Hamilton, *All the News That's Fit to Sell: How the Market Transforms Information into News* (Princeton: Princeton U. Press, 2004), 190.

40. Data from U.S.C. Annenberg School Center for the Digital Future, *Digital Future Report* (Sept. 2004), as reported in Project for Excellence in Journalism, "Online – Public Attitudes," *The State of the News Media 2005*, at http://www.stateofthemedia. org/2005 (accessed April 13, 2005) (hereafter PEJ Report).

41. Steven S. Wildman and Stephen E. Siwek, *International Trade in Films and Television Programs* (Cambridge, Mass.: Ballinger, 1988). See also Baker, supra note 2, at pt. III.

42. Lee Rainie, Pew Internet & American Life Project, "The State of Blogging" (Jan. 2005), at http://www.pewinternet.org/PPF/r/144/report_display.asp (accessed April 13, 2005).

43. Tom Zeller, Jr., "When the Blogger Blogs, Does the Employer Intervene?" *New York Times* (April 18, 2005): C1.

44. Http://www.blogpulse.com/index.html (accessed Oct. 18, 2005).

45. Http://www.sifry.com/alerts/archives/000343.html (accessed Jan. 11, 2006).

46. Http://www.technorati.com/press/graphics.html (accessed Jan. 11, 2006).

47. Http://www.sifry.com/alerts/archives/000343.html (accessed Jan. 11, 2006).

48. Again, estimates vary. A study by comScore reports that "50 million U.S. Internet users visited blogs sites in the first quarter of 2005, [which] is roughly 30% of all US Internet users" and one-sixth of the U.S. population. ComScore Networks, *Behavior of the Blogoshere* (Aug. 2005), at 2, available at http://www.comscore.com/ blogreport/comScore Blog Report.pdf.

49. Rainie, supra note 42.

50. Blogads, "Reader Survey for blog advertising" (May 21, 2004), at http:// blogads.com/survey/blog_reader_survey.html (accessed April 13, 2005).

51. The four for which "twice daily or more" was the answer were: Talkingpointsmemo, Instapundit, Daily Kos, and Atrios; the one for which "rarely" was the most common answer was DrudgeReport, though that answer was only slightly greater than "twice daily or more." Another way to look at the data, though, emphasizes how much most of these blogs were read – over half were read at least once a day by 10% of these heavy blog readers. Id.

52. Data from http://www.truthlaidbear.com/TrafficRanking.php (accessed April 13 and Oct. 14, 2005, and Jan. 25, 2006). Unless otherwise noted, the text refers to data found in the January 2006 visit.

53. Cf. *Hudgens v. NLRB*, 424 U.S. 507 (1979) (overruling an earlier decision and holding that there is no First Amendment right to engage in picketing at a privately owned shopping center), with *Pruneyard Shopping Center v. Robins*, 447 U.S. 4 (1980) (holding that California's recognition of this right under its own constitution did not violate the U.S. Constitution).

54. The data for this sentence and the rest of the paragraph come from The Truth Laid Bear, http://truthlaidbear.com/TrafficRanking.php (accessed June 7, 2006); Carl Bialik, "Measuring the Impact of Blogs Requires More Than Counting," Wall Street Journal Online (May 26, 2005) (noting that TTLB covers 23,000 blogs); David Sifry, "State of the Blogosphere, April 2006, Part 1: On Blogosphere Growth," available at http://www.sifry.com/alerts/archives/000432.html; Newspaper Association of America, Newspaper Audience Database, Spring 2006 Release, available at http://www.naa.org/nadbase/2006_NADbase_Report.pdf (accessed June 8, 2006).

55. Newspaper Audience Database, supra note 54 at 4. During 2005, the unique audience for newspaper Web sites increased by over 20%. See "Spring 2006 Nielsen/NetRatings Web site data," available at id. It could also be noted that using the data of comScore, discussed and doubted below, the top newspaper sites have more unique visitors than the top blog sites, but the concentration of unique visitors is much greater over the top twenty blogs as compared with the top twenty newspapers. See chart above and comScore Networks, supra note 48, at 6.

56. Id.

57. Http://www.technorati.com/pop/blogs (accessed Jan. 9, 2006).

58. Http://www.truthlaidbear.com/TrafficRanking.php (accessed April and October 2005, and January 2006). It is also the case that TTLB's ratings, which are done daily, are quite variable for even some of the most visited sites.

59. Other reasons to doubt the data exist. Blogad's survey of 17,000 heavy blog readers found four blogs that were read daily more often than the Drudge Report. Specifically, the precentage of these readers who reported one or more visits to Atrios was 56%, to Talking Points Memo was 50%, to Daily Kos 48%, to Instapundit was 47%, and to Drudge Report was 39%. But comScore found that of these four, Daily Kos had roughly 1/15 and Talking Points Memo roughly 1/28 the visits as Drudge Report, and two of these sites, Instapundit and Atrios, were not among comScore's top twenty visited sites (supra note 50).

60. "Online – Audience," PEJ Report, supra note 40.

61. Dan Gillmore, *We the Media: Grassroots Journalism by the People, for the People* (Sebastopol, Calif.: O'Reilly Media, 2004).

62. Dahlberg, supra note 38, at 16–68; Johnson, supra note 35. Consider also the development of Indymedia, discussed infra note 92.

63. "Online – Audience," PEJ Report, supra note 40.

64. Julia Angwin and Joseph T. Hallinan, "Newspaper Circulation Continues Decline, Forcing Tough Decisions," *Wall Street Journal* (May 2, 2005); Newspaper Audience Database, supra note 54, at 4.

65. "Online – Audience," PEJ Report, supra note 40.

66. "Online – Ownership," PEJ Report, supra note 40.

67. Though the study is not explicit, these four may represent browsers presetting them as the home page.

68. "Online – Content Analysis," PEJ Report, supra note 46. Though the PEJ data seem correct until roughly January 2004, according to reports by the Online News Association, relying on Nielsen/NetRatings, since then the distance between the fourth site, AOL, and the third has consistently widened. By March 2006, the first three sites had from 29 to 24 million unique visitors during the month, while AOL had slightly less than 16 million, more comparable to the *New York Times*'s 13 million. Data available at http://www.cyberjournalist.net/top_news_sites(accessed June 9, 2006).

69. Dahlberg, supra note 38, at 164.

70. Hamilton, supra note 39, at 197. I found this still true as of 2005 by examining data in sources, supra note 6 from table and note 55.

71. Other online communication suppliers are even more concentrated. In January 2005, Nielsen data indicated that Google supplied directly 47.1% of all searches by American Internet users, while the top three search engines (including Yahoo! and MSN) provided 81%. This understates the concentration, however, since outsourcing actually results in Google and Yahoo! providing most of the searches for several sites, so that on a search provider basis these three conduct 89% of the searches. Danny Sullivan, "Nielsen NetRatings Search Engine Ratings" (March 22, 2005), at http://searchenginewatch.com/reports/article.php/2156451.

72. Google has planned to digitize all the copyrighted works of a number of university libraries and then allow people to search for terms used in the books, but not to make the digital copy available, presumably forcing people to then borrow (e.g., from libraries) or purchase the actual book. The Open Content Alliance has designed a similar Open Library project, founded in part by Yahoo! and with major corporate and nonprofit supporters including Microsoft, Hewlett-Packard, and the Smithsonian. Some book publishers and authors, however, have challenged the project, claiming that this copying in order to make the books searchable violates copyright law. Neil Netanel, *Copyright's Paradox: Property in Expression/Freedom of Expression* (New York: Oxford U. Press, forthcoming). Kevin Kelly, "Scan This Book!" *New York Times* (May 14, 2006), sec. 6, p. 43; Edward Wyatt, "Googling Literature: The Debate Goes Public," *New York Times* (Nov. 19, 2005): B7. See also Ann Bartow, "Electrifying Copyright Norms and Making Cyberspace More like a Book," *Villanova Law Review* 48 (2003): 13.

73. Yochai Benkler, "Free as the Air to Common Use: First Amendment Constraints on Enclosure of the Public Domain," *New York University Law Review* 74 (1999): 354; Benkler, "Coase's Penguin," supra note 34.

74. Fortunately, this book has been written. See Benkler, *The Wealth of Networks*, supra note 34.

75. "Online – Content Analysis," PEJ Report, supra note 40.

76. "Online – News Investment," PEJ Report, supra note 40.

77. "Online – Economics," PEJ Report, supra note 40.

78. Id.

79. "Online – Intro," PEJ Report, supra note 40.

80. Baker, supra note 26.

81. BverfGE 73, 118, 180f., translated as *Fourth Broadcasting Case* (1986), in *Decisions of the Bundesverfassungsgericht – Federal Constitutional Court – Federal Republic of Germany, Vol. 2/Part 1: Freedom of Speech 1958–1995* (Baden-Baden: Nomos Verlagsgesellschaft, 1998), 313, 339–40.

82. Katharine Q. Seelye, "Jobs Are Cut as Ads and Readers Move Online," *New York Times* (Oct. 10, 2005): C1.
83. Katy Bachman, "TNS/CMR: Ad Spending Grew 9.8% in '04," *Adweek Online* (March 8, 2005).
84. P. V. Sahad, "The Rise of Online Advertising," *Business Today* (Oct. 9, 2005).
85. Id.
86. Saul Hansell, "Profit Rises Sevenfold at Google," *New York Times* (Oct. 21, 2005): C1. Not all of this revenue, however, relates to Google's search function. A significant portion of Google's revenue comes from placing ads for advertisers on content sites, including blogs. In this respect, Google's "Adsense" program supports content – although the social benefit is not unequivocal. Ads on sites that discuss certain topics – sex or computer hardware – apparently provide more revenue (for the site and for Google), with the result that there is an incentive for content sites to discuss these topics, intensifying the way advertising distorts content choices in traditional mass media. Bob Tedeschi, "Google's Shadow Payroll Is Not Such a Secret Anymore," *New York Times* (Jan. 16, 2006): C7; Baker, supra note 18.
87. "Indymedia is a collective of independent media organizations and hundreds of journalists offering grassroots, non-corporate coverage. Indymedia is a democratic media outlet for the creation of radical, accurate, and passionate tellings of truth." Http://www.indymedia.org/en/index.shtml (accessed June 10, 2006); Jeffrey S. Juris, "The New Digital Media and Activist Networking within Anti-corporate Globalization Movements," *Annals of the American Academy of Political and Social Sciences* 597 (2005): 189; Sara Platon and Mark Deuze, "Indymedia Journalism: A Radical Way of Making, Selecting and Sharing News," *Journalism* 4 (2003): 336; Gal Beckerman, Edging Away from Anarchy," *Columbia Journalism Review* (Sept./Oct. 2003), at 28; John Tarleton, "Protesters Develop Their Own Global Internet News Service," *Nieman Reports* (Winter 2000): 54.
88. See Timothy Curry and Lynn Shibut, "The Cost of the Saving and Loan Crisis: Truth and Consequences," *FDIC Banking Review* 13 (Dec. 2002): 26. Other estimates of the cost have been common, with $500 billion often cited. See, e.g., John Allen Paulos, "The S & L Bailout in Perspective," *New York Times* (June 28, 1990): A25.
89. Essentially the same observation is often applied in debates about the impact of television news on the public sphere. Do economic advantages of presenting video dramatization, which produce larger audiences, cause broadcasters to replace serious but more complex and less advantageously pictured content with these dramatizations to our collective detriment? And does the appeal and ease of viewing these dramatizations lead to audience neglect of media that would, with adequate resources for investigative journalism, produce more socially important news content? Nevertheless, claims that broadcasting's accessibility and appeal, as opposed to other market processes and advertising, have been the central cause of the purported decline in newspapers may be substantially overblown. See Baker, supra note 18. Moreover, the two media may largely serve different informational and social functions. If so, often newspapers and TV news may not substitute in people's consumption practices as much as the above argument implies.
90. Gillmore, supra note 66.
91. Somewhat arbitrary enforcement of prohibitions on racist or "hate" speech is probably the major exception. Official secrets acts, which are among the limitations on

the press based on real or purported national security concerns, exist within most democracies and can involve troublesome restrictions on democratic discourse, especially when they in effect restrict informed debate. Libel laws may chill (i.e., suppress) some critical exposés. Moreover, the proper line between public discourse and other activities is often unclear and contested, as illustrated by arguments about privacy, copyright, and commercial speech. Still, the dominant democratic concern today is probably focused less on what can be said legally than on the distribution of effective capacity to speak and obtain an audience.

92. Zeller, supra note 43; "These Bloggers Lost Their Jobs," *Detroit Free Press* (Aug. 8, 2005).

CHAPTER 4. THE FIRST AMENDMENT GUARANTEE OF A FREE PRESS:
AN OBJECTION TO REGULATION?

1. *Associated Press v. United States*, 326 U.S. 1, 20 (1945) (emphasis added).
2. As a matter of intellectual and legal history, it is curious the extent to which courts and commentators have portrayed broadcast cases as a secondary, deviant tradition and view print media as the dominant tradition. See Marvin Ammori, "Another Worthy Tradition: How the Free Speech Curriculum Ignores Electronic Media and Distorts Free Speech Doctrine," *Missouri Law Review* 70 (2005): 59. See also C. Edwin Baker, "Turner Broadcasting: Content-Based Regulation of Persons and Presses," *Supreme Court Review* (1994): 57 (arguing that precedent is consistent with finding the same principles allowing structural regulation at work in both the print and broadcast media).
3. *Red Lion Broadcasting Co. v. FCC*, 395 U.S. 367, 389 (1969). Although the Court cited *Joseph Burstyn v. Wilson*, 343 U.S. 495, 503 (1952), to explain that differences in media justify differences in the First Amendment standards applied to them, *Joseph Burstyn* emphasized at the point cited that "the basic principles of freedom of speech and the press, like the First Amendment's command, do not vary." This constancy explains reliance on a newspaper case for the basic principle applied in broadcast cases; presumably the point should also apply vice versa.
4. 376 U.S. 254 (1964).
5. Id. at 270.
6. When France eased its legislative restriction on newspaper mergers, "the Conseil held [it] . . . unconstitutional as infringing pluralism and the interests of readers," and Germany has indicated it might follow a similar approach. Similarly, once commercial broadcasting was permitted, constitutional courts in France, Germany, and Italy found competition laws that favor a multiplicity of voices (not, apparently, merely economic efficiency goals) are constitutionally required, although Berlusconi was able to get around this ruling. Eric Barendt, *Freedom of Speech*, 2nd ed. (New York: Oxford U. Press, 2005), 433, 447.
7. A similar view was often invoked in earlier periods but gained little traction in the courts, as the *Associated Press* and *Red Lion* cases illustrate. Robert Entman has noted the way that the First Amendment is regularly invoked as a premise that limits government power to intervene and foreshortens needed policy thought. Robert M.

Entman, "Putting the First Amendment in Its Place: Enhancing American Democracy through the Press," *University of Chicago Legal Forum* 1993 (1993): 61.

8. *Time Warner Entertainment v. FCC*, 240 F.3d 1126 (2001).
9. 47 C.F.R. §76.503 (2005).
10. 47 C.F.R. §76.504 (2005).
11. 240 F.3d at 1128.
12. Id. at 1129.
13. In legal terms, the court indicated that the rules pass "intermediate scrutiny," which requires that a rule "advances important governmental interests" and does "not burden substantially more speech than necessary to further those interests." A careful reading suggests that the court did not reach the First Amendment claim in respect to the 30% audience-reach ownership rule because the court first found that the FCC had acted beyond its statutory authority. Still, the court's manner of evaluating the FCC's argument was heavily colored by the court's view of First Amendment requirements.
14. 2002 Biennial Regulatory Review – Review of the Commission's Broadcast Ownership Rules and Other Rules Adopted Pursuant to Section 202 of the Telecommunications Act of 1996, Report and Order and Notice of Proposed Rulemaking, 18 F.C.C.R. 13,620 (2003) (hereinafter 2003 Biennial Review Order), para. 13.
15. Id.
16. Id. at para. 16 (emphasis added).
17. Id. at paras. 327, 452.
18. Id. at para. 441.
19. Benjamin M. Compaine and Douglas Gomery, *Who Owns the Media?: Competition and Concentration in the Mass Media Industry*, 3rd ed. (Mahwah, N.J.: Lawrence Erlbaum Associates, 2000), 556.
20. Id. at 557.
21. *Prometheus Radio Project v. FCC*, 373 F.3d 372 (3d Cir. 2004).
22. Christopher Yoo, "Architectural Censorship and the FCC," *Southern California Law Review* 78 (2005): 669, 731.
23. Id. at 674–75.
24. See, e.g., *Associated Press v. National Labor Relations Board*, 301 U.S. 103 (1937).
25. Such a right was apparently rejected in *Branzburg v. Hayes*, 408 U.S. 665 (1972), but many lower federal courts read the four dissenting Justices plus Justice Powell's concurrence to justify recognizing a limited reporters' privilege, as have most state courts on the basis of legislation, state constitutions, common law, or their interpretation of *Branzburg*. The Supreme Court recently declined to revisit the issue. See *Cooper v. United States*, 125 S. Ct. 2977 (2005) (denying petition for writ of certiorari in case concerning reporters' privilege).
26. 240 F. 3d at 1128.
27. Yoo, supra note 22, at 674, 685, 701, see also 713, 731.
28. Id. at 726.
29. See, e.g., id. at 730.
30. *Richmond Newspapers v. Virginia*, 418 U.S. 555, 585 (1980) (Brennan joined by Marshall, concurring); *New York Times v. United States*, 403 U.S. 713, 719–20 (1971) (Black joined by Douglas, concurring).

31. This might be an overstatement. Advances in technology have raised questions of whether the scientists or organizations discovering a particular gene line or the person from whom the gene or DNA material was taken should own this "intellectual property." See James Boyle, *Shamans, Software, and Spleens: Law and the Construction of the Information Society* (Cambridge, Mass.: Harvard U. Press, 1996). Quite obviously, debates over abortion could be conceived as raising the question of whether a woman owns her own body and can expel unwanted intruders. Likewise, the law that gave a husband veto power over a woman's choice to abort was an explicit attempt to structure her body legally – but was rejected by the Court as unconstitutional in *Planned Parenthood v. Danforth*, 428 U.S. 52 (1976). This case illustrates that debates in these areas take place on a ground of presumptive recognition of the integrity of the person in a way that would be almost incoherent to apply in the corporate regulatory context.

32. Note that "explicitly" is key. I argue below that various judicial decisions make little sense absent a reading of the First Amendment roughly of the sort Justice Stewart offered.

33. Potter Stewart, "Or of the Press," *Hastings Law Journal* 26 (1975): 631; William J. Brennan, Jr., "Address," *Rutgers Law Review* 32 (1979): 173.

34. Id. See also C. Edwin Baker, *Human Liberty and Freedom of Speech* (New York: Oxford U. Press, 1989), chap. 10.

35. *Associated Press v. United States*, 326 U.S. 1, 20 (1945).

36. Id.

37. 395 U.S. at 389.

38. See 17 U.S.C. §107 (2005).

39. See *Independent News Service v. Associated Press*, 248 U.S. 215 (1918) (Brandeis, dissenting).

40. See C. Edwin Baker, "First Amendment Limits on Copyright," *Vanderbilt Law Review* 55 (2002): 891.

41. *West Virginia State Board of Education v. Barnette*, 319 U.S. 624 (1943).

42. Id. See also *Wooley v. Maynard*, 430 U.S. 705 (1977).

43. *Turner Broadcasting System, Inc. v. FCC* (*Turner II*), 520 U.S. 180 (1997); *Turner Broadcasting System, Inc. v. FCC* (*Turner I*), 512 U.S. 622 (1994); *Columbia Broadcasting System, Inc. v. FCC*, 453 U.S. 367 (1981); *Red Lion Broadcasting Co. v. FCC*, 395 U.S. 367 (1969). Consider also requirements with respect to children's broadcasting. Broadcasters are also required to carry PEG (public access, educational, and governmental) channels even if they contain indecent material that the broadcaster wishes not to carry. See *Denver Area Educational Telecommunications Consortium, Inc. v. FCC*, 518 U.S. 727 (1996).

44. See discussion of *Branzburg*, supra note 25.

45. 418 U.S. 241 (1974).

46. Id. at 258

47. See Daniel C. Hallin and Paolo Mancini, *Comparing Media Systems: Three Models of Media and Politics* (New York: Cambridge U. Press, 2004), 40 n. 4, 175; Peter J. Humphreys, *Mass Media and Media Policy in Western Europe* (Manchester: Manchester U. Press, 1996), 108–9.

48. *Hausch v. Donrey of Nevada*, 833 F. Supp. 822 (D. Nev. 1993). The law in this area is unsettled. Cf. *Nelson v. McClatchy Newspapers*, 936 P.2d 1123 (Wash. 1997) (state

protection of editorial news employee's right to engage in political activity violates the First Amendment).

49. I argue below that some media entities must be able to be strongly partisan, but it is not clear that this is a universal requirement of democracy-serving media entities.

50. 418 U.S. at 256.

51. 418 U.S. at 257.

52. Id. (quoting 376 U.S. at 279).

53. Cable Protection and Competition Act of 1992 §§4–5, Pub. L. No. 102–385, 106 Stat. 1460 (codified in relevant part at 47 U.S.C. §§534–35 (Supp. IV 1988)).

54. 512 U.S. 622 (1994).

55. Id. at 653.

56. Id. at 653–54, 656. This penalty interpretation also justifies Justice Brennan and Justice Rehnquist's joint concurrence in *Miami Herald V. Tornillo*, where they said that the case did not speak to the issue of whether a newspaper could be required to publish a retraction for a libelous statement. 418 U.S. at 258–59 (Brennan and Rehnquist, concurring). Deterrence of false speech – knowingly false speech is generally unprotected – hardly involves the same concern with censorship as does a penalty on fully protected speech. If protection of accidentally false speech in *New York Times v. Sullivan* is premised on the inevitability of mistakes during the newspaper's search for truth, the paper could be essentially estopped from complaining about being required to print the truth once found on the issue it had chosen to raise.

57. In *Turner I*, the Court sent the case back for fact finding to see whether the "must carry" rules were adequately justified before eventually upholding them in *Turner II*, 520 U.S. 180 (1997).

58. *Lewis Publishing Co. v. Morgan*, 229 U.S. 288 (1913).

59. *Miami Herald*, 418 U.S. at 258.

60. See, e.g, *New York Times v. Sullivan*, 376 U.S. 254 (1964); *Brandenburg v. Ohio*, 395 U.S. 444 (1969); *Tinker v. Des Moines Independent School District*, 393 U.S. 503 (1969); *Cohen v. California*, 403 U.S. 15 (1971); *Chicago Police Department v. Mosley*, 408 U.S. 92 (1972); *Grayned v. Rockford*, 408 U.S. 104 (1972); and other cases protecting civil rights and antiwar demonstrators.

61. 436 U.S. 775 (1978).

62. Pub. L. No. 91–353, 84 Stat. 466 (1970).

63. H.R. Rep. No. 1193, 91st Cong., 2d Sess. (1979), quoted in *Committee for an Independent P-I v. Hearst Corp.*, 704 F. 2d 467, 481 (9th Cir. 1983).

64. *Committee for an Independent P-I. v. Hearst Corp.*, 704 F.2d 467 (9th Cir. 1983). The court's reasoning on some other points was less than persuasive.

65. *Landmark Communications v. Virginia*, 435 U.S. 829 (1978); *Florida Star v. B.J.F.*, 491 U.S. 524 (1989); *Nebraska Press Association v. Stuart*, 427 U.S. 539 (1976). None of the Justices who refused the government's request for an injunction against publication questioned the government's right to try to keep the Pentagon Papers secret. *New York Times v. United States (Pentagon Papers Case)*, 403 U.S. 713 (1971).

66. Possibly the most important issue for "purpose theory" is the relation of "motive" or "intent" of lawmakers (or law appliers) to the "purpose" of laws or practices. The latter seems a much more interpretative, social, meaning-based inquiry that knowledge of authorial psychology can inform but not determine. Consider: can you offer a plausible answer to the question: What is the purpose of that chair or a

podium? What about knowing the intent of a chair? Most people find the first but not the second question coherent. See C. Edwin Baker, "Injustice and the Normative Nature of Meaning," *Maryland Law Review* 60 (2001): 578. It is the first that should ultimately be the concern in constitutional law. Possibly the most important issue for "effects theory" is how to curb its application, a task that is partially achieved by a scrutiny analysis that changes its force depending on context. This method of limiting the doctrine's force is sometimes challenged on the ground that laws with similar effects sometimes are and sometimes are not clearly problematic, leading to speculation that varying the scrutiny is really a disguised method of identifying where bad purposes lurk.

67. The leading case is *Washington v. Davis*, 426 U.S. 229 (1976). I have defended the merits of a properly understood "purpose" analysis in both equal protection and other contexts. C. Edwin Baker, "Outcome Equality or Equality of Respect: The Substantive Content of Equal Protection," *University of Pennsylvania Law Review* 131 (1983): 933; C. Edwin Baker, "Harm, Liberty, and Free Speech," *Southern California Law Review* 70 (1997): 979. In contrast, many liberals, sometimes adopting a "victim's" perspective in place of a disparagingly labeled "perpetrator's" perspective, argue that the huge effect of laws or practices on people's lives – people who are the presumed beneficiaries of the constitutional rights – justifies "effects" being the constitutional focus. E.g., Alan Freeman, "Legitimizing Racial Discrimination through Antidiscrimination Law: A Critical Review of Supreme Court Doctrine," *Minnesota Law Review* 62 (1978): 1049.

68. The textual claim is standard doctrine. It turns out that content discrimination is often upheld if the contextually prohibited content categories interfere with a proper use of government resources. It is also upheld if the discriminatory law or practice can be seen as *promoting* particular content (sometimes even particular viewpoints; see, e.g., *Arkansas Educational Television Commission v. Forbes*, 523 U.S. 666 (1998) (approving viewpoint-discriminatory practices of "governmental journalists")) in a particular context if that promotion is appropriate for the project or institution involved. Obviously, often a controversial interpretative issue is whether the law or practice should be seen as suppressing or as promoting content, an issue that typically turns on an interpretation of the background normative baseline.

69. These laws often negatively effect some speech content or viewpoints much more than others. Susan Williams once argued that this differential effect could justify treating these as content-based speech restrictions. Susan Williams, "Content Discrimination and the First Amendment," *University of Pennsylvania Law Review* 139 (1991): 201. If the objection to content-based laws comes from an "effects" analysis, for example, the effect of distorting some idealized "marketplace of ideas," her point has great force – but not so if the objection is to bad purpose. The Court's unwillingness to follow her suggestion, therefore, further illustrates its implicit view that bad purpose is the basis for the objection of content-suppressing laws.

70. *United States v. O'Brien*, 391 U.S. 367, 377 (1968).

71. Charles Lawrence, "The Id, the Ego, and Equal Protection: Reckoning with Unconscious Racism," *Stanford Law Review* 39 (1987): 317.

72. Steve Shiffrin reasonably argues that courts should place a thumb on the balance in favor of speech – thereby avoiding a utilitarian reductionism – but this obviously provides a court with no guidance for determining the importance of the state's

nonspeech interests. See Steve H. Shiffrin, *The First Amendment, Democracy, and Romance* (Cambridge, Mass.: Harvard U. Press, 1990).

73. Though made by many other commentators, these objections were raised with particular elegance by Justice Felix Frankfurter in his concurrence in *Dennis v. United States*, 341 U.S. 494, 517 (1951). An alternative to Frankfurter's preference for leaving judgments about restricting speech to Congress is to see the appropriate inquiry as different from the balancing analysis he outlined.

74. See Yoo, supra note 22.

75. *Patterson v. Colorado*, 205 U.S. 454, 462 (1907).

76. Sir William Blackstone, *Commentaries on the Laws of England*, vol. 4. (1769), 151–52. On the correctness of this historical view, cf. Leonard W. Levy, *The Emergence of a Free Press* (New York: Oxford U. Press, 1985), with David A. Anderson, "The Origins of the Press Clause," *U.C.L.A. Law Review* 39 (1983): 455. Though Levy argues that the original conception of freedom of the press was basically to prohibit only prior restraints, he emphatically rejects, just as the framers probably rejected (see Jefferson Powell, "The Original Understanding of the Original Intent," *Harvard Law Review* 99 (1985): 865), the view that the framers' intent should control current interpretations of constitutional provisions. See Leonard Williams Levy, *Original Intent and the Framers Constitution* (New York: Macmillian, 1988).

77. *New York Times v. United States (Pentagon Papers Case)*, 403 U.S. 713 (1971).

78. The view that injunctions should not be viewed as especially problematic has been powerfully presented; see, e.g., John Jeffries, "Rethinking Prior Restraints," *Yale Law Journal* 92 (1983): 409. Persuasive reasons for the traditional view are presented in Vince Blasi, "Toward a Theory of Prior Restraint: The Central Linkage," *Minnesota Law Review* 66 (1981): 11.

79. Yoo, supra note 22, at 701, 713. In other passages, Yoo says that the regulations reduce the quantity, quality, and diversity of "programming." Id. at 674, 678, 685, 700, 713, 731.

80. I could not find an explicit identification of a purpose of the First Amendment in Yoo's argument. Still, I assume the attribution stated above as a logically implied premise. An alternative reading, however, would be that Yoo merely believes that promoting quantity, quality, and diversity are the aims of *the legislation*, and its failure to achieve its aims justifies striking it down. I did not see him presenting this alternative. Moreover, this alternative still requires an explanation of how the regulation even presumptively presented a constitutional problem such that its being inept creates a constitutional rather than merely a policy problem. It also contradicts the primary rhetorical move of his article: the constant claim that the effect constitutes "censorship." Of course, this is merely a *rhetorical* move. Whether the *effect* of reducing the quantity or diversity of speech (or even a purpose contextually to reduce speech but with no purpose to suppress particular content – for example, in a quiet area around the Vietnam Memorial or during a moment of silence called for by a public school teacher) constitutes constitutionally problematic *censorship* requires much more demonstration, which I suspect could not be forthcoming.

81. *Cohen v. Cowles Media*, 501 U.S. 663 (1991), involved the issue of whether the press had the right to ignore its promise to a source of confidentiality when it concluded that the biggest story was about the source trying to manipulate the press and,

thereby, the public by planting misleading information in the press. Several law and economics-oriented analyses argued that making such promises legally enforceable is desirable because it would aid the press in obtaining sources and hence having more to report. Note, "Damages for a Reporter's Breach of Confidence, the Supreme Court, 1990 Term: Leading Cases," *Harvard Law Review* 105 (1991): 277; Joseph H. Kaufman, "Beyond *Cohen v. Cowles Media Co.*: Confidentiality Agreements and Efficiency with the 'Marketplace of Ideas,'" *University of Chicago Legal Forum* (1993): 255. In contrast, given that reporters will *generally* keep confidences even if the promise is not enforceable, and given that most *legitimate* sources will rely on such unenforceable promises, the main effect of making the promise enforceable may be to increase this misuse and manipulation of the press and increase information of bad quality. When the commodity is predictably bad, economists are wrong to think more is better. See Baker, supra note 2, at 119–22.

82. The critique of the marketplace of ideas metaphor should take different approaches in respect to the Speech Clause and the Press Clause. My initial First Amendment scholarship rejected this dominant metaphor for freedom of speech in favor of treating a precise conception of individual liberty as central for interpreting the Speech Clause. C. Edwin Baker, "Commercial Speech: A Problem in the Theory of Freedom," *Iowa Law Review* 62 (1976): 1; Baker, supra note 34, chaps. 1 and 2. I have been more sympathetic to this instrumental value of the marketplace in relation to the Press Clause, with the caveat that there is no "natural" marketplace. The government is necessarily responsible for the form of this marketplace and should take conscious, thoughtful responsibility for creating a structure that assures the marketplace's robustness and for making it serve a free and democratic society. More recently – the argument in this book is illustrative – I have argued that the democratic role of the press is more multifaceted and not reducible at all to proper commodity production and distribution.

83. In the legal literature, the best recent treatment of the problematics of commodification is Margaret Jane Radin, *Contested Commodities* (Cambridge, Mass.: Harvard U. Press, 1996).

84. Elihu Katz, "And Deliver Us from Segmentation," *Annuals of the American Academy of Political & Social Sciences* 546 (1996): 22. For a critique of Katz's argument, see James Curran, "Crisis of Public Communications: A Reappraisal," in Tamar Liebes and James Curran, *Media, Ritual and Identity* (London: Routledge, 1998).

85. James Curran, "Rethinking Media and Democracy," in James Curran and Michael Gurevitch, eds., *Mass Media and Society*, 3rd ed. (New York: Oxford U. Press, 2000), 120.

86. Jürgen Habermas, *Between Facts and Norms* (Cambridge: MIT Press, 1996), 166–67, 180, 283–86, 296–302; Jürgen Habermas, "Three Normative Models of Democracy," *Constellations* 1 (1994): 1.

87. C. Edwin Baker, *Media, Markets, and Democracy* (New York: Cambridge U. Press, 2002), 143–47.

88. Nancy Fraser, "Rethinking the Public Sphere," in Craig Calhoun, ed., *Habermas and the Public Sphere* (Cambridge: MIT Press, 1992), 109.

89. See, e.g., Paul Brest, "The Conscientious Legislator's Guide to Constitutional Interpretation," *Stanford Law Review* 27 (1975): 585.

90. See generally Larry Kramer, *People Themselves: Popular Constitutionalism and Judicial Review* (New York: Oxford U. Press, 2004). More specifically, in respect to the First Amendment, see Michael Kent Curtis, *Free Speech: "The People's Darling Privilege"* (Durham, N.C.: Duke U. Press, 2000); James Gray Pope, "Labor's Constitution of Freedom," *Yale Law Journal* 106 (1997): 941.

91. After arguing that the most activist vote that a judge can make is to strike down an act of Congress, a study of the Court from the time it took its (then) present form in 1994 until the personnel changed due to resignations in 2005 found that of the 64 acts of Congress that the Court either upheld or struck down during that time, the most activist Justices in those votes (i.e., voting to invalidate an act of Congress) were Thomas (the most activist), Kennedy, and Scalia – in these cases voting to invalidate in over 64.0% of the time. Justices exhibiting a middle level of activism were Rehnquist, O'Connor, and Souter, voting to invalidate 46.9%, 46.8%, and 42.2%, respectively. And the least activist were Stevens, Ginsberg, and Breyer, all voting to invalidate less than 40%, and in Breyer's case less than 30% of the time. Paul Gewirtz and Chad Golder, "So Who Are the Activists?" *New York Times* (July 6, 2005): A19.

92. Justice Stevens (and in different ways, Justices Marshall and Burger) has rejected tiered review in the equal protection analysis. See, e.g., *Craig v. Boren*, 429 U.S. 190, 211 (1976) (Stevens, concurring); *Cleburne v. Cleburne Living Center*, 473 U.S. 432, 450 (1985) (Stevens, concurring); Suzanne B. Goldberg, "Equality without Tiers," *Southern California Law Review* 78 (2004): 481; Baker, supra note 67.

93. See, e.g., *Simon and Schuster v. New York State Crime Victims Board*, 502 U.S. 105, 125–26 (1991) (Kennedy, concurring); Baker, supra note 2.

94. *Herceg v. Hustler Magazine*, 814 F.2d 1017, 1019 (5th Cir. 1987) (opinion of the court by Alvin B. Rubin).

95. 395 U.S. 444 (1969).

96. See C. Edwin Baker, "Harm, Liberty, and Free Speech," *Southern California Law Review* 70 (1997): 979 (discussing these and other examples where the Court invalidated laws that an honest application of scrutiny analysis would likely uphold).

97. *Hustler Magazine v. Falwell*, 485 U.S. 46 (1988).

98. *Brandenburg v. Ohio*, 395 U.S. at 447.

99. The impropriety of censoring particular content also explains a later case, *Denver Area Educational Telecommunications Consortium v. FCC*, 518 U.S. 727 (1996), where a slim majority struck down Congress's grant of effective authority to cable systems to restrict indecent programming on PEG channels. Over strong dissents, however, enough Justices to constitute a different majority found a similar authorization as applied to the cable system's mandatorily leased channels merely to remove a restriction on the cable system's freedom, with the result that this portion of the law was upheld.

100. *Committee for an Independent P-I v. Hearst Corp.*, 704 F.2d 467 (9th Cir. 1983).

101. Id. at 481.

102. See, e.g., Yoo, supra note 22.

103. *Associated Press v. National Labor Relations Board*, 301 U.S. 103 (1937).

104. Howard A. Shelanski, "Antitrust Law as Media Regulation: Can Merger Standards Protect the Public Interest?" *California Law Review* 94 (2006): 371, 418 (emphasis

added) (citing *Turner I*, 512 U.S. at 662 and *FCC v. National Citizens Committee for Broadcasting*, 436 U.S. 775, 800–802 (1978).

105. 436 U.S. 775 (1978).

106. See 47 C.F.R. §§73.35, 73.240, 73.636 (1976).

107. This claim involves interpreting both *Miami Herald* and *Denver Area Educational Telecommunications Consortium* as involving objections to content regulation.

108. 476 U.S. 488 (1986).

109. On remand, purportedly following the Court's directions, a lower court did find the arrangement unconstitutional. *Los Angeles v. Preferred Communication*, 13 F.3d 1327 (9th Cir. 1994).

110. In remanding because "the ordinance is challenged on colorable First Amendment grounds," the Court emphasized that the challenger's disputable factual claim was that there was "sufficient excess physical capacity and *economic demand* for cable television operators in the area which respondent sought to serve." 476 U.S. at 494, 493 (emphasis added).

111. *Turner Broadcasting System v. FCC (Turner I)*, 512 U.S. 622 (1994).

112. Cable Television Consumer Protection and Competition Act of 1992, §§4–5, Pub. L. No. 102–385, 106 Stat. 1460 (codified in relevant part at 47 U.S.C. §§534–35 (Supp. IV 1988)).

113. See *Turner Broadcasting System v. FCC (Turner II)*, 520 U.S. 180 (1997).

114. "Toothless" is how many commentators, including those critical of the Court on this point, interpret the version of intermediate scrutiny applied by the Court in the follow-up case, *Turner II*. See Yoo, supra note 22; Glen O. Robinson, "The Electronic First Amendment: An Essay for the New Age," *Duke Law Journal* 47 (1998): 899.

115. *Time Warner Entertainment Co. v. FCC*, 240 F.3d 1126 (D.C. Cir. 2001).

116. Actual approval had to await *Turner II*, 520 U.S. 180 (1997).

117. *Turner I*, 512 U.S. at 684 (O'Connor, dissenting) (emphasis added).

118. *Time Warner*, 240 F.3d at 1139, see also 1130, 1137. In fairness, the circuit court held only that the government had not justified the precise percentage of channels reserved for nonaffiliated channels, leaving open the possibility that in further proceedings the FCC could offer a justification for that or some other set-aside. The court, however, did not mention that the law challenged in *Turner* required carriage of a formulaically limited number of local broadcast stations, with the number varying with the number of channels carried by the cable system – analogous to the percentage requirement involved in *Time Warner* – and the Supreme Court did not seem to require any evidence that this was an appropriate number or percentage.

119. Actually, James Curran described how in England during the early and middle nineteenth century the workers' robust, leftist papers were not seriously undermined by the Stamp Tax because they illegally avoided paying the tax, which aided them in competition with the more mainstream media, which did pay. Some members of Parliament saw that abolishing the Stamp Act would favor the mainstream press in its competition with the more radical papers, which helped to influence Parliament to abolish the tax, relying on market competition (combined crucially with a huge advertising "subsidy" only for the mainstream papers) to kill off the radical press.

120. C. Edwin Baker, "Corrupting the Press," *New York Law Journal* 2 (Jan. 24, 2005) (arguing that for the government to pay reporters to report a view without

identifying the report as essentially an advertisement violates First Amendment protection of the institutional integrity of the press).

121. Steven H. Shiffrin, *Dissent, Injustice, and the Meaning of America* (Princeton: Princeton U. Press, 1999).

122. See, e.g., Vince Blasi, "The Checking Value in First Amendment Theory," *American Bar Foundation Research Journal* (1977): 521; Cass Sunstein, *Democracy and the Problem of Free Speech* (New York: Free Press, 1993). I have argued that despite the great merit of Blasi's and Sunstein's arguments as applied to the press, their readings lack appeal or justification in relation to the speech clause. Baker, *Turner Broadcasting*, supra note 2; Baker, *Human Liberty*, supra note 34, chaps. 2, 9–10. Cf. Robert C. Post, "Meiklejohn's Mistake: Individual Autonomy and the Reform of Public Discourse," in Robert C. Post, *Constitutional Domains* (Cambridge, Mass.: Harvard U. Press, 1995), 268–89.

123. The most commonly noted exception is the Thirteenth Amendment's prohibition on slavery or involuntary servitude, which either governmental or private actors can violate.

124. Literalists will observe that the First Amendment directs only "Congress" not to abridge the freedoms. Interestingly, turning the literal language precisely on its head, the central argument for the newspapers made in oral argument, and accepted by three of the Justices, was that enjoining publication was improper at least as long as Congress had not authorized it! *New York Times v. United States* (*Pentagon Papers Case*), 403 U.S. 713, 727–48 (1971) (concurrences by Justices Stewart, White, and Marshall).

125. See, e.g., Sunstein, supra note 122; Owen Fiss, "Free Speech and Social Structure," *Iowa Law Review* 71 (1986): 1405; Owen Fiss, "Why the State," *Harvard Law Review* 100 (1987): 781. Although drawn from the "equal protection" context, *Shelley v. Kramer*, 334 U.S. 1 (1948), is the most famous Supreme Court case suggesting this approach. There, judicial enforcement of a *privately* created covenant – which differs little in terms of the state's role from judicial recognition of the legal existence of a privately created, merged corporate entity – violated the Constitution. *New York Times v. Sullivan*, 376 U.S. 254 (1964), likewise, explicitly finds a constitutional violation in a state allowing private parties to rely on the state's tort (libel) laws.

126. I put aside the somewhat technical issue of who would have legal "standing" to initiate the suit. Possibly only a specially harmed party, whether a media consumer or competing media entity, could bring the suit.

127. See Humphreys, supra note 47, at 119.

128. See *Cable Penny Case*, BVerfGE 90, 60 (1994); *North Rhine-Westphalia Broadcasting Case*, BVerfGE 83, 238 (1991); *Third Broadcasting Case*, BVerfGE 57, 295 (1981); Humphreys, supra note 47, at 137–38. These cases are translated into English in *Decisions of the Bundesverfassungsgericht, Federal Constitutional Court, Federal Republic of Germany, Parts I & II: Freedom of Speech* (1998), vol. 2, 199–219, 493–534, 587–619.

129. See supra note 6.

130. *Columbia Broadcasting System v. Democratic National Committee*, 412 U.S. 94 (1973) (Brennan and Marshall, dissenting).

131. Id. (White, Blackmun, and Powell, concurring).

CHAPTER 5. SOLUTIONS AND RESPONSES

1. Royal Commission on the Press, *1961–1962 Report* (1962), 93–95. I critiqued Kaldor's proposal in C. Edwin Baker, *Advertising and a Democratic Press* (Princeton: Princeton U. Press, 1994), 93–95, but proposed a plan similar in many respects. My Tax Advertising–Subsidize Revenue proposal would tax advertising revenue and redistribute it to papers based on their circulation revenue. This proposal would not directly penalize increased circulation but would encourage papers to provide more audience-desired content in a manner that would predictably lead to more product differentiation and more successful, competing papers.

2. Peter J. Humphreys, *Mass Media and Media Policy in Western Europe* (New York: Manchester U. Press, 1996), 99–100.

3. As a speaker, a person would have grounds to object to a rule that blocked her from using for her speech those resources – including media entities – that the law provides her. *Buckley v. Valeo*, 424 U.S. 1 (1976), taught this lesson when the Court, while approving campaign financing, said that "the concept that government may *restrict* the speech of some elements of our society in order to enhance the relative voice of others is wholly foreign to the First Amendment." Id. at 48 (emphasis added). The Court's statement must be treated with care – arguably it is not appropriate for the limited context in which it originated; see C. Edwin Baker, "Campaign Expenditures and Free Speech," *Harvard Civil Rights–Civil Liberties Law Review* 33 (1998): 1. Still, its basic message is right: directly and purposefully restricting a person's speech in the general public sphere as a means to achieve other aims, including equalizing aims, presumptively violates the First Amendment. Regulation of ownership, however, leaves a person as free as anyone else to use her wealth to try, for example, to place ads in media in order to advance her views.

4. Humphreys, supra note 2, at 96.

5. *Buckley v. Valeo*, 424 U.S. 1, 48 (1976). The deletions relate the quotation specifically to political campaigns. For reasons I have described elsewhere, I agree with the quote generally but specifically not in the context of electoral campaigns, which are integral parts of the governmentally created elections, a government structure that ought to be designed to maximize the fairness of this governmental process. See Baker, supra note 3.

6. 476 U.S. 488 (1986).

7. In a 1958 decision, the D.C. Circuit directed the FCC to deny an application for an available broadcast license *if* those opposing the applicant could show that the new license would be detrimental to the public interest. *Carroll Broadcasting v. FCC*, 258 F.2d 440 (D.C. Cir.1958). (On remand, the FCC found that the challengers had not met this burden.) A new license might be detrimental, the court opined, if the market provided insufficient advertising revenue to allow the combination of new and incumbent licensees to provide the public with programming as good as the incumbent licensees did alone – a theory of "ruinous competition." This argument might also be used to justify a monopoly cable system under the Supreme Court's standard. Though frequently invoked, the "Carroll doctrine" never became the basis of a license denial, and, eventually, an antiregulatory FCC repudiated the doctrine, in effect rejecting the economic validity of the theory of ruinous competition. In the

Matter of Policies Regarding Detrimental Effects of Proposed New Broadcast Stations on Existing Stations, 3 F.C.C.R. 638 (1987).

8. *Red Lion*, 395 U.S. at 389 (citing *National Broadcasting Co. v. United States*, 319 U.S. 190, 227 (1943)).

9. *Genesee Radio Corp.*, 5 F.C.C. 183 (1938). This denial occurred despite the current absence of any competing applicants. This duopoly rule became embodied in FCC rules in 1941.

10. 47 U.S.C.A. §533(b), which was part of the Cable Communications Policy Act of 1984, was repealed by the Telecommunications Act of 1996. Circuit courts had found the law to violate First Amendment rights of telephone companies, e.g., *Chesapeake & Potomac Telephone Co. v. United States*, 42 F.3d 181 (4th Cir. 1994), vacated and remanded 516 U.S. 415 (1996) (to determine if moot, presumably because of the repeal). I have challenged the view that this requirement is unconstitutional. C. Edwin Baker, "Merging Phone & Cable," *Hastings Communications & Entertainment Law Journal* 17 (1994): 97.

11. Section 11(c) of the Cable Television Consumer Protection and Competition Act of 1992, Pub. L. No. 102–385, 106 Stat. 1460 ("1992 Cable Act"), amending 47 U.S.C. §533; and *Time Warner Entertainment v. FCC*, 240 F.3d 1126 (D.C. Cir. 2001).

12. *FCC v. National Citizens Committee for Broadcasting*, 436 U.S. 775 (1978).

13. 15 U.S.C. §18 (1988). Section 7 prohibits mergers "where in any line of commerce . . . in any section of the country, the effect of such acquisition may be to substantially lessen competition or tend to create a monopoly." Id. Also relevant are the Sherman Act, which refers to an "unfair method of competition," 15 U.S.C. §1 (1988), and Section 5 of the FTC Act, which applies to an "unfair method of competition," 15 U.S.C. §45 (1988). For an overview, see H. Peter Nesvold, Note, "Communication Breakdown: Developing an Antitrust Model for Multimedia Mergers and Acquisitions," *Fordham Intellectual Property, Media & Entertainment Law Journal* 6 (1996): 781.

14. Pub. L. No. 91–353, §2, 84 Stat. 466 (1970) (codified at 15 U.S.C. §§1801–1804 (2000)).

15. In agreeing to the Westinghouse purchase of Infinity Broadcasting, the Antitrust Division required the sale of stations that would have allowed Westinghouse's share of the radio advertising market in Philadelphia to rise from 28% to 45% and in Boston from 15% to 40%, indicating that sometimes a 40% share is too much. Ira Teinowitz and Michael Wilke, "Justice Department Sets 40% as Guide on Radio Mergers: Solutions Tied to Target Audience Paves Way for Westinghouse Deal for Infinity," *Advertising Age* 65 (Nov. 18, 1996).

16. The research often claims to be indeterminate, though my literature review reached two conclusions. First, overall the research showed that chain ownership had bad effects but that those effects were not all that compelling as a basis for concern. Second, effects that should be feared and also should be expected were not investigated, possibly because of inadequacies in the methodologies that the researchers were able to imagine. C. Edwin Baker, *Ownership of Newspapers: The View from Positivist Social Science* (monograph, Shorenstein Barone Center of JFK School of Government, Harvard University, 1994).

17. *Time Warner Entertainment Co. v. FCC*, 240 F.3d 1126 (D.C. Cir. 2001).

18. The court did not discuss why the normal antitrust horizontal concentration guideline's HHI standard (described in chapter 2) was not employed in evaluating monopsony power. Two buyers, one with 60% and the other with 40% of the market, would lead to an HHI of 5200, well above the 1800 generally indicating monopoly power.
19. Sarah Elizabeth Leeper, "The Game of Radiopoly: An Antitrust Perspective of Consolidation in Ratio," *Federal Communications Law Journal* 52 (2000): 473; Bryan Gruley, "U.S. Challenges Radio Stations Accord," *Wall Street Journal* (Oct. 25, 1996): B9.
20. Eric Pfanner, "German Regulators Reject Takeover of TV Broadcaster," *New York Times* (Jan. 11, 2006): C3.
21. 15 U.S.C. §18(a).
22. This assurance is not a guarantee – the government still has authority to challenge a merger after it is completed, but these challenges have apparently been rare since adoption of the Hart-Scott-Rodino Act requiring notification and opportunity for pre-merger review of most mergers of significant size. Scott A. Scher, "Closed but Not Forgotten: Government Review of Consummated Mergers under Section 7 of the Clayton Act," *Santa Clara Law Review* 45 (2004): 41.
23. H. Stephen Harris, Jr., "U.S.–China Trade: Opportunities and Challenges: An Overview of the Draft China Antimonopoly Law," *Georgia Journal of International & Comparative Law* 34 (2005): 131, 131.
24. Humphreys, supra note 2, at 95–96.
25. Id. at 94–95.
26. Id. at 100–101.
27. *News America Publishing v. FCC,* 844 F.2d 800 (D.C. Cir. 1988); Thomas B. Rosenstiel, "Media Mogul, Kennedy Do Battle," *Los Angeles Times* (Jan. 9, 1988): 2.
28. See *News America Publishing,* 844 F.2d at 807–8. Originally, the law would also have prevented granting a permanent waiver for Murdoch's ownership of both the *New York Post* and a New York television station, but that aspect of the litigation was dropped when Murdoch sold the *Post.* Subsequently, however, Murdoch repurchased the *Post* and was granted a permanent waiver, and, although the propriety of the waiver was questionable, the waiver was upheld. *Metropolitan Council of NAACP Branches v. FCC,* 46 F.3d 1154 (D.C. Cir. 1995).
29. Id.
30. James D. Squires, *Read All About It!* (New York: Times Books, 1993), 123.
31. James Fallows, "The Age of Murdoch," *Atlantic Monthly* 82 (Sept. 2003): 90.
32. See *Cox v. New Hampshire,* 312 U.S. 569 (1941) (allowing permit requirement); *Lovell v. Griffin,* 303 U.S. 444 (1938) (invalidating permit requirement that gave official discretion in granting permit). See also *Watchtower Bible v. Village of Stratton,* 536 U.S. 150 (2002) (finding even discretion-free permit impermissible); C. Edwin Baker, *Human Liberty and Freedom of Speech* (New York: Oxford U. Press, 1989), chap. 7 (objecting to constitutionality of mandatory parade ordinances).
33. *FCC v. National Citizens Committee for Broadcasting,* 436 U.S. 775, 802 n. 20 (1978).
34. *Committee for an Independent P-I v. Hearst Corp.,* 704 F.2d 467 (9th Cir. 1983).
35. Lucas A. Powe, Jr., *The Fourth Estate and the Constitution* (Berkeley: U. of California Press, 1991), 217–20 (discussing both the Seattle and Detroit JOAs).
36. The Court has recognized this point, *Andrus v. Allard,* 444 U.S. 51 (1979) (unanimously holding that prohibiting the sale, while allowing the possession, donation,

or devise, of Indian artifacts containing eagle feathers did not constitute a taking of the owners' property), although some property theorists dispute the conclusion. I considered and rejected these property theorists' *Lochner*-like arguments in C. Edwin Baker, "Property and its Relation to Constitutionally Protected Liberty," *University of Pennsylvania Law Review* 134 (1986): 741. The argument centers around the permissibility of society restricting maximum commoditization, a theme best developed by Margaret Jane Radin, *Contested Commodities* (Cambridge, Mass.: Harvard U. Press, 1996).

37. Gilbert Cranberg, Randall Bezanson, and John Soloski, *Taking Stock: Journalism and the Publicly Traded Newspaper Company* (Ames: Iowa State U. Press, 2001).

38. Cf. *Hawaii v. Gannett Pacific Corp.*, 99 F. Supp. 2d 1241 (D. Hawaii 1999) (finding that an agreement to end a JOA and close one of the papers could violate antitrust laws), with *Reilly v. Hearst Corp.*, 107 F. Supp. 2d 1192 (N.D. Cal. 2000) (finding no violation of antitrust laws in closing a failing paper that was part of a JOA agreement), discussed in Maurice E. Stucke and Allen P. Grunes, "Antitrust & the Marketplace of Ideas," *Antitrust Law Journal* 69 (2001): 249, 271–73.

39. In Britain, the Competition Commission (CC) is specifically required "to take free expression into account when deciding whether a newspaper merger may be expected to operate against the public interest," and in approving a media merger, "editorial independence from the commercial interests of the owner is one of the factors considered by the CC." Eric Barendt, "Control of Media Concentrations; Regulation in the United Kingdom," in Uwe Blaurock, *Medienkonzentration und Angebotsvielfalt zwischen Kartell-Rundfunkrecht* (Nomos Verglagsgesellschaft: Baden-Baden, 2002), 75. See also Damian Tambini, "Through with Ownership Rules? Media Pluralism in the Transition to Digital," in Damian Tambini, with Liz Forgan, Clare Hall, and Stefan Verhulst, *Communication Revolution and Reform* (London: IPPR, 2001), 40–41, 43–44 (suggesting that "the consent for further mergers . . . be conditional on a strengthening and extension of editorial and journalistic independence"). More generally, varying degrees of "internal freedom" – editorial freedom from owner control – commonly exist in Europe independent of merger regulation.

40. Hallin and Mancini, supra note 48, at 175; Humphreys, supra note 2, at 109.

41. Humphreys, supra note 2, at 107.

42. Harry L. Connor, "The Newspaperman's Quest for a Voice in Newsroom Decisionmaking: A Look at the United States and Selected European Countries" (Master's thesis, University of Delaware, 1976), 63 (citing "IFJ Urges a Staff Voice in Newspaper Operations," *The Guild Reporter* 4 (Oct. 13, 1972)).

43. A number of subrules could also be important. The buyer (or seller) could be prohibited from making deals with individual employees, thereby assuring that exercise of the approval/veto power made by the employees provided its benefits, as seen by the majority, to them all. Also, long-term employees might merit greater benefit if the result was sharing the financial gain or greater deference in terms of a commitment to professional quality. Thus, votes might be allocated by years of service rather than one person/one vote.

44. Cf. *West Coast Hotel v. Parrish*, 300 U.S. 379 (1937).

45. Quoted in Werner J. Severin, "*The Milwaukee Journal*: Employee-Owned Prizewinner," *Journalism Quarterly* 56 (1979): 783, 784.

46. I make no systematic attempt to either describe or evaluate the full variety of subsidies in developed countries with democratic traditions. Some useful places to begin are Humphreys, supra note 2, at 102–7; Everette Dennis, "A Free and Subsidized Press? – The European Experience with Newspaper Subsidies and Other Government Interventions," in *News in the Public Interest: A Free and Subsidized Press – The Breaux Symposium 2004* (Baton Rouge: Louisiana State University); Paul Murschetz, "State Support for the Daily Press in Europe: A Critical Appraisal," *European Journal of Communication* 13 (1998): 291; Robert Picard, "Levels of State Intervention in the Western Press," *Mass Communications Review* 11 (Winter/Spring 1984): 27.

47. This and the next paragraph are based on Richard B. Kielbowicz, *News in the Mail: The Press, Post Office, and Public Information 1700–1860s* (New York: Greenwood Press, 1989); Richard B. Kielbowicz, "Origins of the Second-Class Mail Category and the Business of Policymaking, 1863–1879," *Journalism Monographs* 96 (1986). The discussion here abridges a more extensive treatment in C. Edwin Baker, "Turner Broadcasting: Content-Based Regulation of Persons and Presses," *Supreme Court Review* (1994): 57, 97–99, 105–8.

48. Daniel C. Hallin and Paolo Mancini, *Comparing Media Systems: Three Models of Media and Politics* (New York: Cambridge U. Press, 2004), 63–64.

49. Picard, supra note 46, at 33.

50. Dennis identifies taxes on advertising, often advertising on broadcast media, as the most common source of money for newspaper subsidies, and he provides specific discussions of systems in France, the Netherlands, and Sweden. Dennis, supra note 46, at 125–26. Taxes on advertising, especially on commercial broadcast television (or on its revenue, which amounts to roughly the same thing) are regularly proposed as a source for subsidizing favored media, for example, noncommercial public radio and television, an approach that I heartily endorse for multiple reasons. See Lawrence K. Grossman, "Should the Government Subsidize the Press," in *News in the Public Interest: A Free and Subsidized Press – The Breaux Symposium 2004* (Baton Rouge: Louisiana State University), 135, 139; Baker, supra note 1, at 111–15.

51. See Edward S. Herman and Noam Chomsky, *Manufacturing Consent: The Politics of the Mass Media* (New York: Pantheon Press, 1988); Humphreys, supra note 2, at 51 (same problem in Germany).

52. Hallin and Mancini, supra note 48, at 163.

53. This proposal for financially favoring in-state ownership should prevail over predictable constitutional challenges for violating Article I's "negative" or "dormant" commerce clause and Article IV's "Privileges and Immunities" clause. If this were doubted, roughly the same result would be achieved by requiring that, to get the benefit, the primary owners must be involved in the day-to-day operation of the media entity. I do not pursue this discussion here.

54. *Prometheus Radio Project v. FCC*, 373 F.3d 372, 420–21, 435 (3rd Cir. 2004).

55. *Metro Broadcasting v. FCC*, 497 U.S. 547 (1990).

56. A more conservative Court has repudiated the decision's general approach to affirmative action without speaking to its specific holding in the broadcast context. *Adarand Constructors v. Pena*, 515 U.S. 200 (1995). Many commentators conclude that these preferences based on diversity grounds (as opposed to remedial grounds) are of doubtful constitutionality. Ronald J. Krotoszyski, Jr., and Richard M. Blaiklock,

"Enhancing the Spectrum: Media Power, Democracy, and the Marketplace of Ideas," *University of Illinois Law Review* (2000): 813.

57. James N. Dertouzos and Kenneth E. Thorpe, *Newspaper Groups: Economies of Scale, Tax Law, and Merger Incentives* (Santa Monica, Calif.: Rand Corporation, 1982).

58. Anthony Smith, *Subsidies and the Press in Europe* (London: PEP, 1977), 51.

59. Gerald J. Baldasty, *The Commercialization of News in the Nineteenth Century* (Madison: University of Wisconsin Press, 1992), 108, 132; Gerald J. Baldasty and Jeffrey B. Rutenbeck, "Money, Politics and Newspapers: The Business Environment of Press Partisanship in the Late 19th Century," *Journalism History* 15 (1988): 60, 63, 65.

60. The classic American work on public access is not specifically tied to the media entity's dominant status – that is, to the regulated entity's audience reach. Jerome A. Barron, *Freedom of the Press for Whom? The Right of Access to the Media* (Bloomington: Indiana U. Press, 1973); Jerome A. Barron, "Access to the Press: A New First Amendment Right," *Harvard Law Review* 80 (1967): 1641.

61. *Turner Broadcasting System, Inc. v. FCC,* 512 U.S. 622 (1994).

62. Tambini, supra note 39, at 41, 44.

63. In broadcasting, the German Constitutional Court has read the Basic Law to impose various requirements of content provision and diversity, but held that as long as these tasks are performed, as currently required, by public broadcasting, somewhat less extensive regulation of private (commercial, presumably largely advertising-supported) broadcasting is constitutionally permissible. BverfGE 73, 118, 180f., translated as *Fourth Broadcasting Case* (1986), in *Decisions of the Bundesverfassungsgericht – Federal Constitutional Court – Federal Republic of Germany, Vol. 2/Part 1: Freedom of Speech 1958–1995* (Baden-Baden: Nomos Verlagsgesellschaft, 1998), 313, 324–28, 333–37. Nevertheless, the Basic Law still requires regulation of private broadcasting to assure balanced plurality. Id. at 313. Regulation must assure "the possibility for all tendencies in opinion, including those of minorities, to secure expression." Id. The Court constantly reads "broadcasting freedom" to *require* regulation of broadcasting, including commercial broadcasting, to provide for plurality of opinion. The Court finds that legislators have a constitutional duty "to oppose concentration," id. at 325, and to prevent "the emergence of dominating power over opinion." Id. at 313, 325, 333, 335.

In the print media, after describing various requirements of its constitution (Basic Law) guaranteeing the "institution 'Free Press,'" the German Constitutional Court added in dicta the statement: "but one might also conceive of a duty on the State to ward off threats that could arise for a free press from the formation of monopolies over opinion," a statement often taken to mean that the constitution requires control of mergers in the print realm. BverfGE 20, 162, 176, translated as the *Spiegel Case* (1966), id., at 71, 77.

64. *Boy Scouts of America v. Dale,* 530 U.S. 640 (2000) (upholding the right of the Boy Scouts to discriminate against gays); *Hurley v. Irish-American Gay, Lesbian and Bisexual Group of Boston,* 515 U.S. 557 (1995). *Dale* may require interpreting *Roberts v. United States Jaycees,* 468 U.S. 609 (1984), holding that the Jaycees could not discriminate against women, and many nondiscrimination laws, as tied to the regulated associations or activities being commercial – the approach Justice O'Connor relied on in her concurrence in *Roberts.* Even if *Dale's* view of freedom of association is largely accepted, *Dale* might be wrong on other grounds, for example, a society's

right to be concerned about the upbringing of children. See Seana Valentine Shiffrin, "What Is Really Wrong with Compelled Association," *Northwestern University Law Review* 99 (2005): 839.

65. Size and circumstance apparently make a difference in the rights of political parties. See *Brown v. Socialist Workers*, 459 U.S. 87 (1982) (holding that a minor party has a First Amendment right, under the circumstances shown, to be exempted from disclosure requirements applicable to major parties).

66. *Terry v. Adams*, 345 U.S. 461 (1953). This, the last in a series of "white primary" cases coming out of Texas, was recently cited with approval in *Morse v. Republican Party of Virginia*, 517 U.S.186 (1996). I discuss the principled justification of the "white primary" cases in Baker, supra note 3.

67. 418 U.S. 241 (1974).

68. *Turner Broadcasting System, Inc. v. FCC*, 512 U.S. 622, 653–54, 656 (1994).

Postscript

1. Robert Pear, "Racial and Ethnic Minorities Gain in the Nation as a Whole," *New York Times* (Aug. 12, 2005), A16.

2. Statement of Commissioner Michael J. Copps, dissenting, "Re: 2002 Biennial Regulatory Review – Review of the Commission's Broadcast Ownership Rules and Other Rules Adopted Pursuant to Section 202 of the Telecommunications Act of 1996."

3. National Telecommunications and Information Administration, Minority Commercial Broadcast Ownership in the United States (percentages mine calculated from raw numbers), at http://www.ntia.doc.gov/opadhome/minown98/main.htm.

4. *Prometheus Radio Project v. FCC*, 373 F.3d 372 (3d Cir. 2004).

5. Yochai Benkler, "Free as the Air to Common Use: First Amendment Constraints on Enclosure of the Public Domain," *New York University Law Review* 74 (1999); Yochai Benkler, "Overcoming Agoraphobia," *Harvard Journal of Law & Technology* 11 (1998): 287.

6. This is a slight overstatement. To the extent that copyright caused something to be created that otherwise would not have been, it provides a benefit of a greater legacy of material from which even noncommercial speakers can draw. This point, although suggesting a possible empirical case for "some" copyright protection, does not affect the comparative point in the text.

There is a tiring but continually repeated argument that copyright also promotes other legitimate interests – sometimes it is said that it promotes the autonomy – of the creator by allowing her to prevent others from using her creation for communicative purposes of which she disapproves. It is certainly true that copyright would increase her power *over* other speakers. However, "autonomy" to do what one wants and "power" to make another do what one wants are very different things. A variety of desirable instrumental aims are served by one person having power over another – that is what money and markets provide. But having power to control what another person says is not a matter of autonomy but at most an instrumental value. It should be viewed as presumptively illegitimate, *at least* without the other agreeing (for instance, in a contractual or market agreement) to the limitation on her freedom to speak.

7. This paragraph loosely interprets Benkler, "Overcoming Agoraphobia," supra note 5.
8. *Red Lion Broadcasting v. FCC*, 395 U.S. 367 (1969), explained this "tragedy of the commons" argument quite clearly.
9. See also Kevin Werbach, *Radio Revolution: The Coming Age of Unlicensed Wireless* (Washington, D.C.: New America Foundation, n.d.), at http://werbach.com/docs/ RadioRevolution.pdf.
10. *Syracuse Peace Council v. FCC*, 867 F.2d 654 (D.C. Cir. 1989).
11. Humphreys, supra note 2, at 119.
12. *Syracuse Peace Council v. FCC*, 867 F. 2d 654 (D.C. Cir. 1989). Chief Judge Wald, concurring in part and dissenting in part, found this a persuasive objection to the "balance" requirement but did not see that the FCC had justified abolishing the "coverage" requirement.
13. *National Broadcasting Co. v. FCC*, 516 F. 2d 1101 (D.C. Cir. 1974), a decision eventually vacated as moot, 516 F.2d at 1180.
14. Denial of Reconsideration, 58 F.C.C.2d 691 (1976) (Commissioner Robinson, dissenting).
15. The health dangers of smoking were clear enough to informed observers in 1935 that Seldes could describe how the advertising power of the industry led newspapers to suppress the information. George Seldes, *Freedom of the Press* (Indianapolis: Bobbs-Merrill, 1935), 50–51. See also Ben H. Bagdikian, *The Media Monopoly*, 3rd ed. (Boston: Beacon Press, 1990), 168–73.
16. *Branzhaf v. FCC*, 405 F.2d 1082 (D.C Cir. 1968). Antismoking television ads turn out to be much more effective at achieving antismoking aims than commercials are at promoting smoking, but tobacco firms were forced to advertise to maintain market share even as their ads gave a basis for antismoking ads that were undermining the total cigarette market. Unsurprisingly, tobacco interests were very happy with legislation that required them (or, it might be said, allowed them without competitive disadvantage) to leave the airwaves.
17. The FCC decision not to apply the Fairness Doctrine to product advertising was affirmed in *Public Interest Research Group v. FCC*, 522 F.2d 1060 (1st Cir. 1975).
18. *Green v. FCC*, 447 F.2d 323 (D.C. Cir. 1971).
19. Yochai Benkler, *The Wealth of Networks: How Social Production Transforms Markets and Freedom* (New Haven: Yale U. Press, 2006).
20. James Curran, "Rethinking Media and Democracy," in James Curran and Michael Gurevitch, eds., *Mass Media and Society*, 3rd ed. (London: Arnold, 2000), 120–54.
21. See, e.g., Ellen P. Goodman, "Stealth Marketing and Editorial Integrity" (forthcoming).
22. Gilbert Cranberg, Randall Bezanson, and John Soloski, *Taking Stock: Journalism and the Publicly Traded Newspaper Company* (Ames: Iowa State U. Press, 2001).
23. Frank Blethan, "The Case for Independent and Family Ownership of Newspapers and Other News and Journalistic Enterprises," in *News in the Public Interest: A Free and Subsidized Press – The Breaux Symposium 2004* (Baton Rouge: Louisiana State University), 106, 110.
24. Karen Brown Dunlap, "A Study of Nonprofit Ownership of News Media," in *News in the Public Interest: A Free and Subsidized Press – The Breaux Symposium 2004* (Baton Rouge: Louisiana State University), 92. Dunlap lists the *New London (Conn.) Day*,

St. Petersburg (Fla.) Times, Manchester (N.H.) Union Leader, Anniston (Ala.) Star, and *Tupelo (Miss.) Northeast Mississippi Daily Journal* as examples.

25. Werner J. Severin, "*The Milwaukee Journal:* Employee-Owned Prizewinner," *Journalism Quarterly* 56 (1979): 783.

26. See, e.g., Lawrence K. Grossman, "Should the Government Subsidize the Press," in *News in the Public Interest: A Free and Subsidized Press – The Breaux Symposium 2004* (Baton Rouge: Louisiana State University), 135.

27. Curran, supra note 88. For a similar conclusion that Curran's approach provided an appropriate response to media concentration, see Robert Horwitz, "On Media Concentration and the Diversity Problem," *Information Society* 21 (2005): 181.

28. This is the main point of the first part of my book, *Media, Markets, and Democracy* (New York: Cambridge U. Press, 2002).

Index

Titles in the series (*continued from page iii*)

Hernan Galperin, *New Television, Old Politics: The Transition to Digital TV in the United States and Britain*

Myra Marx Ferree, William Anthony Gamson, Jürgen Gerhards, and Dieter Rucht, *Shaping Abortion Discourse: Democracy and the Public Sphere in Germany and the United States*

Richard Gunther and Anthony Mughan, eds., *Democracy and the Media: A Comparative Perspective*

Daniel C. Hallin and Paolo Mancini, *Comparing Media Systems: Three Models of Media and Politics*

Robert B. Horowitz, *Communication and Democratic Reform in South Africa*

Philip N. Howard, *New Media Campaigns and the Managed Citizen*

Pippa Norris, *Digital Divide: Civic Engagement, Information Poverty, and the Internet Worldwide*

Pippa Norris, *A Virtuous Circle: Political Communications in Postindustrial Society*

Adam F. Simon, *The Winning Message: Candidate Behavior, Campaign Discourse*

Gadi Wolfsfeld, *Media and the Path to Peace*